An EXPLOSION OF BEING

An American Family's Journey into the Psychic

By Doug and
Barbara Dillon

Old St. Augustine Publications
Altamonte Springs, Florida

New edition published by Old St. Augustine Publications
Altamonte Springs, Florida
www.oldstaugustinepublications.com

First published by Parker Publishing, an imprint of Prentice Hall in 1984

© 1984 and 2011
by Douglas and Barbara Dillon
No part of this book may be reproduced or stored in any form without specific permission of the authors.
Contact at www.dougdillon.com.

Library of Congress Control Number: 2011905855

ISBN 978-0-9833684-0-3

Dedicated to
The Memory of Walter W. Dillon

Preface to the New Edition

Parker Publishing, an imprint of Prentice Hall, originally published *An Explosion of Being* in 1984. Once the book was in print, my wife Barb and I found ourselves giving radio and television interviews across the United States as well as the being involved in bookstore appearances. As we spoke with listeners during call-in radio programs and talked to people while signing books, many of them told us how relieved they were that we had gone public with our story. "Thank you," they would say. "Some of the things you wrote about have happened to me. It is so good to talk to someone who understands."

Over time, though, the book went out of print. Barb and I stored precious copies of *An Explosion of Being* in a closet and turned our full attention back to the world of paying bills and raising our kids. I immersed myself in teaching and writing articles while Barb began a very successful career in sales.

Through all those years since 1984, however, the lessons learned during our exploration of the paranormal have remained with us as constant reminders of our connections to All That Is. Our children have been adults for a long time now, but they have maintained a beautiful openness to the unseen depths of human existence.

In 2010, though, something unexpected began to happen. Friends and associates started asking about the "paranormal book" we wrote back in the day. In response, we gave out some old loaners. Eventually, people began asking where they could get their own copies. Really? After all this time? To my amazement, I found that Amazon.com had a few used versions of the book so we were able to refer people there.

In the meantime, I was preparing to publish the first book in my young adult series titled, **The St. Augustine Trilogy**. In those books, the paranormal is a major theme. As Barb and I thought about how the trilogy debut was converging with the developing interest in our out-of-print book, we decided to also publish this new edition of *An Explosion of Being*-new edition, meaning the addition of this preface and changing some of the book's other front matter. You will find the introduction that follows and all the text thereafter exactly as we wrote it so long ago. The photo on the back cover shows us as we were in the early 1980s in order to maintain consistency with the time when our story took place.

How very much Barb and I hope you will find what you read here of interest and of value. If you want to learn more about my young adult trilogy and other writing efforts, come join me at the website below:

www.dougdillon.com

Doug Dillon
Altamonte Springs, Florida
Fall, 2011

Introduction

There are those times in most of our lives when, perhaps for just an instant, we stand back and question the very nature of physical existence. The penetrating event causing our hesitation may be a shocking realization of life's fragility, the absolute bitterness of injustice, or some strange inexplicable departure from the norms of reality as we know them. Whatever the reason for the momentary lapse of certainty about the world, it has stopped us dead in our tracks, whether anyone else recognized what was happening or not.

Usually, we recover from these occurrences by smoothing them over with forgetfulness or by applying a long held standard of belief that seems to give us some sort of answer. Even if we wanted to, it often isn't very acceptable to poke and prod these events for new or different understandings. Such activity simply makes most people uncomfortable, including ourselves, so why bother? On we move, then, with daily life as it existed before, but with a dim awareness something important may have been abandoned.

Seven years ago, our lives fit this pattern perfectly and seven years ago, a multitude of jolting, unusual incidents shocked us into a very conscious decision to pursue our questions, regardless of where they might lead. Since then, we have uncovered a wealth of information that might be called psychic, or spiritual, opening doors of perception for our family we never even knew existed.

This book is our attempt to share with you the fullness of our explorations into those unseen portions of life's essence. We don't ask for your acceptance of what you are about to read, but we do ask that you look for a part of yourself within our struggle for understanding.

Doug and Barb Dillon
Altamonte Springs, Florida
November, 1982

Table of Contents

Preface to the New Edition 5
Introduction 7
1. An Encounter with a Medium 11
2. Death, the Searing Reminder 15
3. The Search Begins 23
4. A Closer Look at Reality 34
5. Touching the Unknown 45
6. Probing with Some Age-Old Questions 65
7. Life and Afterlife as Learning Concepts 83
8. Children-Colleagues in Awareness 109
9. Death Experiences Viewed Differently 132
10. Startling Dream Events 156
11. Reflections 168
12. To the Reader from a Source with No Name 179
13. Our Purposeful Lineage with You 193
Appendix: Revitalizing Your Natural Psychic Heritage . . . 195
Bibliography 211
Index 215

1

An Encounter with a Medium

THE SPIRITUALIST COMMUNITY of Cassadaga, Florida, lies just thirty miles or so from our home. While most of the Sunshine State is notoriously flat, the hills and winding roads surrounding that tiny hamlet give it the quaint appearance of having been transplanted directly from the New England countryside. The homes are older, but unlike their counterparts in New England, many sprout signs advertising the certified mediumistic abilities of the residents. Our decision to visit Cassadaga had been prompted by a developing need to investigate firsthand the phenomena of "spirit communication." Supposedly, the local mediums could see beyond the physical world in ways that might help us in the widening search for answers to our spiritual puzzle.

It was early afternoon on a mild October day in 1977 when we parked the car in front of a small house with a little screened porch. Doug's mom had been there before, and had returned to Orlando amazed at the accurate information given by the medium, Mae Graves Ward. Spurred by Muriel's positive reaction, as well as by our intensifying desire to go beyond an academic approach to psychic investigation, Doug and I decided to have a go at a reading by an honest-to-goodness Spiritualist. What could we lose?

Mae Ward came to the door and asked if we were the two o'clock appointment. After introducing ourselves, Doug and I were ushered around the porch to a side room where the readings were given. Mae is no youngster, but maintains a tremendous sharpness of wit. Her personal opinions are strongly stated, but with humor and honest conviction. With a fifty-year involvement in the Spiritualist movement, she had numerous stories. Explaining how she once had rankled a group of visitors with an accurate description of a very personal situation, Mae raised her voice with a warm laugh and said, "Hell, if they didn't want to know things, why did they ask?"

It seemed strange sitting there with this obviously good-natured woman, wondering if indeed she had a special linkage to the world of spirit or if she was simply a clever fraud. Could she see and hear things in that room that actually existed beyond the normal senses, or did she live with a series of daily hallucinations? Whatever the answers, our doubts left us with feelings of uneasy anticipation and some discomfort.

As the initial small talk continued, Mae's breathing became labored, and a cough shook her body. My immediate thoughts were that this session just might be cut short. It was becoming difficult for her to communicate, when suddenly in a clear voice she asked, "Do you know anyone who died of a chest ailment? I feel someone very close to you who was unable to breathe." Doug sat bolt upright and stammered that his grandfather had passed away in just that manner many years ago. Continuing rapidly, Mae pointed to Doug and indicated that his grandfather was with us, and that he wanted Doug to know how proud he was of the work that Doug was doing. Then, holding up her hand, Mae said that she could see Doug's grandfather holding up his hand and pointing to his Masonic ring. "He's letting me know that you come from a good family," Mae said nodding toward Doug.

Without allowing us time to react, Mae kept the perceptions rolling at an incredible rate. Not hesitating for a moment, she described the intensive care unit at the Naval hospital where Doug's father had died. Supposedly in communication with Doug's father, Walt, at that point, Mae explained that he too was proud of the work that Doug was doing. Intrigued, Mae asked if he was a teacher. When Doug answered, "Yes," Mae explained that somehow she saw his students as being big, like adults. Of course the description was perfect, since Doug was working only with adults in his capacity as the training director for the school system.

Swinging her attention to me, Mae asked if I knew Henry. I could hardly believe her words. My great-uncle, Henry, had died just weeks before, and here was this woman giving me a message of greeting from him. As if that weren't enough, she went on to describe the number, ages and sexes of our children. Then, quizzically, Mae looked at me and

An Encounter with a Medium

said, "I see medicine all around you." With my father, cousin, grandfather, great-grandfather, and four great uncles all physicians, I could only agree that her visions were quite correct.

She now asked both of us, "Do you know William?" Mae went on to explain that Doug's father was telling her that he had brought William with him. We were both puzzled until Doug, remembering, said, "Of course, William was Dad's father. He died when I was a year old. I never knew him." At her usual breakneck speed, Mae then explained, "Doug, your father says that your brother isn't doing too well. Is something wrong with his head? Your dad says that he spends a lot of time near your brother and that sometimes he wishes your brother could join 'them' on the other side. Now, why would he say that?" My heart went out to Doug. His admission that, recently, his severely retarded brother had been near death on more than one occasion must have cut through him like a knife. Doug's depth of feeling for his brother usually remains unstated, but his eyes and the silence that surrounds the subject tell a story all their own.

On and on went the information from Mae Ward. Most of it made perfect sense with only small portions that didn't seem to fit. Finally, the session came close to ending with Mae saying, "Well, I don't see any big problems with you kids. Things will be even better in three years. I see you two selling your house, and Doug, I see you changing jobs. Yes, a step up in fact. I see you selling something, Doug." Now, that was a laugh. The last thing in the world Doug would be involved in would be sales.

As we stood up to go, Mae stopped me and said, "Lettie says to take good care of that little girl. She says especially to keep her out of drafts and to watch out for her ears. There's some problem in that area. Oh, and also you've got a clock that isn't working. Look for it to start again soon." With that final admonition, we bid goodbye to a very interesting lady and began our short trek back to Orlando.

"Who is Lettie?" Doug asked as he started the car. "Lettie was my grandmother," I replied, "Grandpa Hill's wife who died in 1955." Two years after that brief conversation, we would have cause to remember the words of caution from Lettie when Nicole developed a chronic ear infection that eventually led to surgery.

Mae Ward had been a virtual whirlwind of surprise information. The first few minutes on the road were very quiet as our minds tried to adjust to all that had occurred. Finally, Doug broke the silence to ask if I had given Mae our names, phone number or address when I made the appointment over the phone. I reminded him that Mae had not asked for any information. Obviously, he was referring to the history of certain fraudulent practices whereby fake mediums carefully research their clients ahead of time and charge exorbitant fees for their services. In this case though, there was absolutely no way that Mae could have researched us. Even if it had been possible, the time and effort required to find out such detailed information would have far outweighed the small amount of money that we literally had to press upon Mae at the end of our session.

Then again, we could have been witnessing a classic example of telepathy. Doug's reading on that subject had left him halfway convinced that Mae could have been picking information out of our conscious minds, genuinely believing that she was in touch with a spirit world. Suddenly, Doug remembered that his grandfather's Masonic ring lay carefully packed away in a box at home. Even with telepathy, how could Mae have seen something that Doug had forgotten? Perhaps as another theory goes, telepathy might be a subconscious activity as well. Then again, even if we had been witnessing telepathy, that in itself moved our understanding of communication into a new and exciting realm.

The many notes that Doug took during our trip to Cassadaga were carefully rewritten and filed away for future reference. It was obvious that going beyond the telepathic explanation could be done only by validating some of Mae's predictions. If future events were to occur as she had said, then perhaps some other phenomenon was at work. In fact, this didn't take long. One day, a few weeks later, an old wall clock that had refused to run suddenly sprang to life and kept perfect time for two years. It would be three years, however, before verification of the other predictions came about.

2

Death, the Searing Reminder

DURING THE LONG SILENCES on that drive back from Cassadaga, thoughts of Dad kept popping into my mind. What if Mae Ward had actually seen his spiritual essence, as she claimed? I shifted uneasily in my seat remembering the night he passed away. Barb seemed just as deeply absorbed in thought, and I wondered if she too was recalling those long hours of helpless waiting. Several years had passed since that time, but as the miles sped by, Mae's visions began to prod my memories into startling clarity. Before long, I was reliving each excruciating moment of the torturous days that preceded and followed Dad's death.

The incredibly vivid reflections placed me again at Orlando's Naval Hospital on a humid night in August of 1975. The dim light in the small waiting room added little cheer to the strained atmosphere of the intensive care unit. Dad was dying, and we shuddered with that unspoken knowledge. The tight cluster of concerned Navy medical personnel around his bed gave us little hope, regardless of the doctors' assurances that Dad was still hanging in there. Mom's fearful eyes followed the life support equipment and nurses flowing past our small cubicle. Barb and I could do little but hold her close and try to put the unthinkable out of our minds.

Reports of the operation's success that afternoon had thrown us completely off guard. With great relief, the three of us journeyed to the base exchange for lunch and an impromptu celebration of Dad's victory. Our joy was short-lived, however; on our return, the doctor quickly took us aside. With Dad conscious now and watching some distance away, the doctor explained that a blood complication had arisen leading to serious trouble. The shock began to penetrate as we listened to the terrifying details. His final comments described my father's psychological condition: unbelievably calm and rational.

Although Dad's pain was obvious when we approached his bed, he smiled as he always had, regardless of his own suffering. His concern was for those around him rather than for what he was enduring. Donning our masks of encouragement and confidence, we tried to match his bravery, but piercing drops of acid-like fear began to eat away at each of us. Soon, somber nurses interrupted our desperate attempts at unity and hope with their need to get on with life-saving preparations. Dad urged us to leave the room, not so much to make way for the nurses as to spare us further agony. Such was the nature of the man and such were the circumstances in which we would last see my father fully conscious.

Walt Dillon, that tower of quiet strength and fountain of loving acceptance, just couldn't die! Memories of photographs of Dad as a cadet at West Point burst into my mind. Recollections of his shining military career began to merge with thoughts of him as a dedicated teacher and a devoted family man. The unfairness of it all was revolting! Why must someone who is so loved and respected be made to suffer? The world needs an abundance of goodness, yet the good is so often stamped out and crushed.

How many times over the past fifteen years had Mom accompanied Dad to hospitals? The occasional recurrences of stomach problems always raised the fear that cancer had invaded his system again. Somehow, Mom always was able to reach down deep and pull out the solid block of strength that would help carry them both through those trying periods. Their marriage was a rich blend of love, mutual admiration and support. Even the biting tragedy of my younger brother's severe mental retardation had not dulled the brightness of their lives. People looked at them and marveled at the beauty of their relationship. But now the pendulum was swinging against a continuation of that union.

What a contrast this hospital scene was to our recent deep sea fishing adventure. On that early morning, the *Dandy "L"* chugged slowly into Florida's Ponce De Leon Inlet with Captain King and his mate busily piloting our boat and preparing the rigs for action. As we neared the rough channel to the Atlantic, a fresh sea breeze caught our spirits and lifted them high in anticipation of a great catch. Once through the churning shallows, Dad began snapping pictures. His best shot showed Mom sitting in the stern, face to the wind wearing an expression of freedom and security that would not be repeated during the next several years. One of our own photos captured Dad and his two young grandsons in a smiling union that would be stamped indelibly on our memories.

Murmuring voices in the hallway leading to intensive care jerked me back to the bitter reality of the present. A check on Dad's condition produced no new information. Thank God for the understanding warmth in Barb's eyes each time I returned to the waiting room. It made the transition to being a supporter for my distraught mother much easier. Underneath, I knew Barb must be struggling to maintain her composure. Just a few short years before, she had lost her first husband to cancer under similar conditions in a V.A. hospital. When we first met, she couldn't bear to watch medically-related stories on TV. How she was able to be a support to both Mom and me now was beyond my comprehension.

As the dark hours crept by, we continued to huddle together like children hiding from a storm and from the hot lightning flash that was sure to come. At Mom's insistence, we prayed in the tiny makeshift chapel across the hall, but my lack of religious conviction made this last-minute appeal to God seem shallow, even pointless. If indeed there was a God, why should he heed this "Johnny-come-lately"? I knew that Barb shared much of my discomfort, but the compassion in her eyes for Mom pressed me to at least go through the motions. Pray, I did, but strangely, with my thoughts directed more toward Dad than to some Supreme Being.

Barb and I had similar church-related experiences as children. Regular worship in cities, small towns, and military bases across the country was a standard part of both our service-oriented backgrounds. Somehow though, the spiritual import of what we were taught passed through our consciousnesses without much residual effect. The rebellion of our teen years, coupled with an awakening intellectual development, moved us to put religion aside.

For both Mom and Dad church attendance had gradually declined with my refusal to participate in the Sunday ritual. We never really talked about spiritual beliefs until this point. Soon though, I came to understand that Dad held no firm religious convictions. God, life after death, and the divinity of Christ were questionable concepts to his way of thinking. The contradiction, however, was obvious to all who knew him. Here was a man who actually lived the virtuous "Christian" life, even though his theological views weren't in step with his actions. Dad's second career, teaching high school physics, had simply reaffirmed his logical turn of mind. Yet, Mom would kid him about his psychic inclinations. This he denied heartily, since to him, the psychic was as unreal as God or U.F.O.s. Logic aside, Dad still had to admit that his ability to see a haze around all people was indeed mystifying.

What was he sensing now, if anything? Was he lost in a maze of drug-induced dreams? Was he still a part of the unconscious form lying there connected to every imaginable kind of apparatus? Was this Walt Dillon, or was there another essence of his being somewhere beyond that tortured body? How could such a good and compassionate man be made to endure so much? Was his reason for being only to suffer through life's tragedies, ending his existence as an appendage to plastic and metal? My fears and questions were now going beyond the immediate circumstances. I was coming face to face with my own mortality.

Upon leaving the chapel, we returned to the waiting room and closed our eyes to catnap fitfully through at least some of that long night. Heightened emotion and the lack of sleep produced half-waking visions in my mind. At one point in this dream-like state, I could see myself trying to pull my father out of a huge, bottomless pit. Over and over again, he would struggle up to the edge of the abyss with his hands in my grip only to slide away again into the darkness. It was then that the full realization of his impending death hit full force. "He can't die," I screamed into that imaginary pit. "He has so much of the world left to experience. He must see his grandchilden grow." The emptiness that met my argument was answer enough, until thoughts seemingly apart from me said, "He *will* see all of these things, but through your eyes." Even as the words brought a strange comfort to my agony, the rational side of my being mused, "Damn! The strain has gotten to you. Now you're having a conversation with a hidden part of your personality, creating psychological balms to ease the pain."

The occasional note of a bird's song lifted me out of my dream analysis into the uncomfortable reality of dawn squeezing itself through the blinds of the hospital windows. Soon, the early morning clatter of life resuming in the corridors nudged Barb and Mom awake. A cart of breakfast trays rumbled across the open walkway outside as the first full shafts of sunlight bathed portions of the Naval hospital in the yellow glare of yet another of the world's workdays.

The doctor's entry into the waiting room, accompanied by his

Death, the Searing Reminder

head nurse, seemed to intensify the glare coming from the windows. Antiseptic scents mixed with whiffs of early morning breakfast added conflicting touches to an increasingly unreal situation. As the doctor tried to explain gently that Dad was gone, fear for my mother and what she was about to undergo shot through me. The wide-eyed terror that followed, confirmed my fears. Rejecting the doctor's words, she turned to me pleading for a different ending to this incredible horror story. A sedative, and the efforts of Barb and the base chaplain helped me to calm her, but the hours and days ahead were to be filled with the agonies of shared grief and the adjustment to a tremendous vacuum that would be with us forever.

The return to Mom's empty house shattered her fragile attempt at self-control. It was simply too much to bear. Her racking sobs erupted time and again during the next few hours. Barb and I were with her, but parts of this battle would have to be fought alone. Only exhaustion finally triumphed. As Mom drifted off to sleep, I sat in a chair by her bed and tried not to think. I must have dozed off for a few minutes when suddenly awake, Mom took my hand. With a distant half asleep look in her eyes, she calmly told me that she had seen Dad in her dream. When he spoke to her, he simply said, "Everything is fine so don't worry." With that she went back to sleep, leaving me to wonder about the nature of dreams and reality.

The whirl of visitors, phone calls, funeral arrangements and legal matters merged the next few days into a blur. Thank God for Mom's friends, the Winterlings and the Brewers, who came to her home as soon as they heard of Dad's death. Their presence was critical for Mom's stability and greatly helped Barb and me to orchestrate the many details that had to be handled. This was no time for me to face my own grief. Too much had to be done, and grief would only sap the strength needed by others. My time of full realization of Dad's death came days later in the dark of the night. With Barb holding me tight, the tears withheld burst in a full release of anguish and acceptance.

During one of those hectic days soon after Dad's death, a shiny blue Air Force car pulled into the driveway of my parents' home. Two very somber sergeants, well-practiced in the ways of grief and the details of military benefits, stepped out of the shimmering August heat into the coolness of the air conditioned house. Sid Brewer, a family friend and retired Air Force officer, was there to guide us through the detailed procedures. Sid and I sat facing the two sergeants over the dining room table, by then covered with documents. The exchange of necessary information droned on for a while, until my attention was diverted.

"Whoever's blowing that damned car horn had better cut it out," I thought angrily. The noise continued, until I finally got up and opened the front door. Now the sound blasted through the heat, further stirring my anger. No strange cars were visible, just the Air Force vehicle and Dad's empty Ford parked under the oak tree a short distance away. The blowing horn was coming from Dad's car! Sid and I opened the hood and pulled out the wires, resulting in exquisite silence. "Must have been the heat that set it off," Sid commented. I agreed, but somehow the event jarred my already unsettled psyche.

The next morning presented a raft of estate-settling tasks. My plans included using Dad's Ford to make my rounds of the Social Security and V.A. offices, but I hated to drive without a horn. Just on the chance that the problem had rectified itself, I reattached the wires. No exploding repetition of yesterday's noise, so with a couple of test honks, off I went to downtown Orlando and my list of appointments.

The Social Security office was overflowing with people. When my turn finally came, the representative was helpful and efficient. Briefcase in hand, I was soon out the door, walking toward the parking lot. Dad's car was angle-parked only a short distance from me, and in a few steps, I was directly in front of it. My mind was a jumble of sadness and financial details, when suddenly the car horn went off with another continuing blast that shook every fiber in my body. I was stunned. For an instant, I froze in mid-stride, and automatically looked for a driver sitting in the front seat. No, no one was there, just me and this crazy car blowing its brains out. Once the wires were disconnected I continued my errands but with an uneasiness that could not readily be put aside.

The settling of the estate was one thing. Facing the boys with their grandfather's death had been quite another. "My God, what have we done to prepare them for death of any kind, no less a central figure in their lives?" was my panicky reaction. "What could we do to help them through this difficult passage, if we haven't really faced the issue ourselves? What was death? Why must people die? What happens after death?" Mustering love and logic, we launched a caring but stumbling attempt. Greg's silent tears and Fred's cries of anguish burned through the thin veneer of our adult superiority. Helplessness in the ultimate sense crushed us with its unyielding weight.

Beginning its upward arc towards the northeast, the big 727 broke through the low-lying clouds over Central Florida. West Point on the Hudson was now only a few hours away, where family and friends would draw together for the final salute. Thankfully, Mom's old friend,

Boots Beers, was with us to help her through that terrible period. This friendship stemmed from those early years when Dad and Boots' husband were still cadets at the Point. Boots had recently lost her husband, and now her depth of character was supporting Mom's disintegrating spirit. Mom was going to need all the strength she could find to withstand the upcoming ritual of a military funeral.

How many times had I seen it portrayed on TV? As a youngster on military bases, I vaguely remembered funeral processions moving at a snail's pace down the main avenue, and, as for many people, the death of John Kennedy burned the process into my mind forever. Those memories were sad but distant. That distance was closing rapidly as our staff car left the chapel and moved through the West Point cemetery. The deliberate cadence of the drums seemed to accentuate the agonizingly slow pace of the car. Mom's grip on my hand tightened as we neared the burial site.

Family and friends were waiting. A row of empty chairs stood ready. As we sat down, I looked at the face of our seven-year-old son, Greg, and wondered what was going through his young mind. He loved his granddad so very much as did my older son, Fred. I didn't understand life, or death, or much of anything at that point. What was Greg feeling? Had we helped him at all to weather this storm? Fred couldn't be with us since my former wife felt that the funeral would be too morbid. Perhaps she was right. How I hated funerals, but this one had to be endured.

A gentle breeze ruffled the flag on the casket and whispered through the trees surrounding us. The drum roll, the firing of the salute, the folding of the flag, the condolences, Mom's numbness and my emptiness, all flowed together like the mighty nearby Hudson, rushing us onward toward the infinity of our own destinies.

Sometime after the funeral, Mom remembered speaking with my aunt and uncle during that trying time at West Point. Filtering out of this conversation, came a disconcerting story. The night before my father's death, Uncle Fran and Aunt Eloise saw a vision of my father in their living room, 1200 miles away from the intensive care unit. They indicated that the vision had been there for only an instant, and then vanished. Mom and Dad had often played cards with the family in that room during their summer visits to Connecticut, and strangely enough, Uncle Fran was the first relative I called with the news of Dad's death.

After hearing about my aunt and uncle's experience, I thought about Mom's dream soon after returning from the hospital. Then a long-forgotten memory of yet another death in the family floated to the surface of my mind. I remembered my great-grandfather's claims that his wife visited him during the night just hours before the family knew of her death. Chills ran through me as all of these memories reinforced a disturbing recollection of an encounter with a car horn in the parking lot of a Social Security office.

3

The Search Begins

THE EXCURSION TO CASSADAGA had evidently stirred as much thought in Doug as it had in me. The quiet, as he drove the remaining miles toward Orlando that day, reminded me of our trip to Williamsburg, Virginia, in 1976. It was a glorious release from the year and a half of turmoil and domestic responsibility that followed the death of Doug's father. The open road and the country music coming from the radio as we sped through the Carolinas seemed to give us a breath of emotional freedom. The National Staff Development Conference offered an ideal opportunity for some time together before the Christmas holidays. Even though Doug had to attend multiple seminars, there would be time for us to take part in an exploration of Colonial America as it had once been and to sample some of that highly recommended Chesapeake Bay seafood.

After a difficult, year-long struggle, Doug's mom was making a good adjustment to her loss and was helping us by caring for the children during our absence. The time alone with the kids was to at least get her out of that lonesome house for a while and definitely keep her busy. Although this second Christmas without Walt promised to be somewhat easier for Muriel, we would be home well before the beginning of the holidays and would include her in our family activities.

Lunch in a little South Carolina town was delightful. The town's only restaurant was fairly empty when we arrived around 11:30 but soon it was noisily full of townspeople. Evidently this was the only place to eat for miles, so here they gathered. In came a group of police officers, joking and laughing. Among them was one black policeman. As our food arrived, Doug commented on how times had changed. It was not long ago when restaurants in this area displayed their "White Only" signs, and the police department enforced their message. For that matter, it had not been too long ago when public water fountains in our own Central Florida bore the "White" and "Colored" designations. With all the outward changes though, we wondered if people were truly any different.

Once on the road again, we talked happily about the upcoming visit to Williamsburg. Plans for this trip had been made for months, but we could scarcely believe that it was actually happening. This was our first extended journey together since our marriage, four years before. Doug's career had blossomed since then and his position of director of the staff training program for the Orange County Public Schools now brought him as a presenter to this national gathering.

As the miles wore on, Doug decided to nap rather than listen to my harangues against a group of truck drivers playing auto tag. When I finally escaped their madcap games, the peacefulness of driving gave me a chance to be alone with my thoughts. Ever since Walt's death, the hectic pace of life had run away with us, and times for reflection, like these, were rare.

Somehow, my mind kept returning to the morning Doug's dad died. Hospitals were dreaded places for me. In addition to a clear foreboding about Walt's prospects for recovery, I had too many memories of days upon days in hospitals watching my former husband lose his battle for life. Everything that occurred brought back bitterly painful memories of those times. Endless hours of waiting as the clock labored onward, five-minute visits to the intensive care unit, heroic efforts to maintain a human existence, and the unending fear all reminded me of what I had tried so carefully to forget. There was also the gnawing concern for my son. My former husband was Greg's natural father. How would this seven-year-old child react if his granddad were to die, after losing his father just a few short years before?

In the agony of those early morning hours when Walt lay dying, I knew that I was pregnant. No doctors had yet confirmed it, but there was an inner certainty combined with the inevitable nausea. How I wished that I could tell Walt. Perhaps somehow the prospect of a new grandchild could give him an edge in his fight for survival. Unfortunately, my certainty failed at the last moment. Before we were finally ushered away from his bedside, I watched that incredible man smile and tell us not to worry. Even in those final hours, his concern was for others. In his eyes and smile, I felt that somehow he knew I was carrying a child. All I could do then, however, was to hold his hand and tell him how much I loved him. Why do we always wait until it's too late to say the things that should have been said long before? A strange sense of life and death weaving themselves into a pattern of existence before my eyes was to become a permanent part of my consciousness.

As the night wore on and the medical activity around Doug's father began to take on the familiar appearance of last-ditch efforts, I distinctly felt that death had already occurred. At that moment, Doug's mother asked us to pray with her. Doug's glance intercepted mine, and in that split second, we both knew our fighting against the inevitable would do little good. Unsettling remembrances of my former husband's dramatic return to religion soon before his death, however, urged me to join in prayer as a support to Doug's mother. She and Doug would need all the help I could give regardless of my fears of feelings about the futility of religion.

How Doug was able to generate so much strength then and in the excrutiatingly painful days that followed Walt's death remains a mystery to us. He loved his father so very much, yet the need to undergird the family's stability was paramount in his mind. From the wellspring of his compassion and emotional strength, we were all able to draw vast amounts of courage. Doug's father had indeed left him a rich legacy of personal attributes that blossomed to their fullest under the most difficult of circumstances.

Confirmation of my pregnancy came soon after the ordeal at the Naval hospital. The months before the baby arrived were full of changes, and in the midst of helping Doug's mom adjust to her loss, my mother and grandmother arrived to take up residence in Orlando. Getting them settled flowed into the Thanksgiving holidays, but eventually we were able to start our own house hunting. Since owning our own home had been a long-held dream, the excursions into the world of real estate became an almost constant activity. The prospect of finding a home in our price bracket dimmed until soon after Christmas, when we stumbled upon a housing development that suited our needs and our budget perfectly. The building site was a large, beautifully wooded lot on the banks of the Little Wekiva River in Altamonte Springs.

As our home grew, so did my stomach. My wonderful family didn't help my self-image by jokingly referring to me as the "Preggo." Completion of the house was scheduled for late March, and the baby was scheduled for mid-April. Doug had always been quite an organizer, but such close timing was ridiculous. Luckily, all schedules merged without mishap, and Nicole was born on April 26, weighing in at a petite nine pounds, fifteen ounces.

Classes at a local hospital had prepared us exceptionally well for controlling the labor pains through natural childbirth techniques. With Doug holding me and acting as "coach," we launched a new being into the world and watched in amazement as another thread in the pattern of existence fell into place.

Our selection of Hope as a middle name for this beautiful child clearly identified the feelings and needs which had been stirred since Walt's death. With this new little lady among us, what would we do differently? How could we be better parents? Among the questions, an uneasiness bubbled to the surface and stood naked in the glaring light of honest self-appraisal. Neither Doug nor I had a formulated spiritual philosophy or belief. Admitting this to each other was disturbing. We had existed quite well over the years without such a crutch, so why let it bother us now? Recalling our awkward attempts to help the boys deal with death, we concluded that much of our children's development, as well as our own, was being ignored. A shallowness of purpose and lack of understanding suddenly overwhelmed us. In the crucible of our joint conscience boiled a definite decision to search for at least some of the answers to life's mysteries and to some day share our findings with our children.

The change of climate as we progressed northward on the Interstate provided an interesting contrast to Florida's lush greenery. The leafless trees dotted with mistletoe and the rolling hills of the Virginia countryside heightened our sense of anticipation that this trip would indeed be a true break from our daily existence in Central Florida.

The sign ahead indicated Jamestown was just a short distance away. The history teacher in Doug took over the steering wheel and, as a result, we veered off course to visit the site of the earliest permanent English settlement in America. It was cold and cloudy when we arrived that afternoon. The light, misty rain kept sensible people away, but in the interests of historical revelation, we paid the admission price, shivered our way out to look at old foundations, and read the descriptive plaques. The grounds were empty. I never really cared much for the study of history, but as we stood there, arm in arm beside the murky James River, a sense of linkage between the past, our lives, and the future shot through my mind like a whale blasting up through the ocean waves. Somehow, we seemed to belong to this place. Doug's look reflected my feelings, and we were both to maintain this sensation throughout the remainder of our Virginia excursion.

The official Christmas season of this Bicentennial year was to open in Williamsburg the night after our arrival. The firing of the guns would be the signal for the lighting of candles in windows throughout the town and the beginning of many days of special holiday festivities. The sounds of fife and drums came to us across the cold crisp air as we walked up the dark cobblestone streets that evening. Crowds were starting to gather in the town square, and red uniforms were visible now as soldiers of colonial England paraded through the streets. The rumble of the drums could be felt full force as we joined the crowd, but soon all was expectantly quiet. With cannons and muskets carefully placed around the restored section of the town, anticipation grew. Firing mechanisms were checked and powder charges inserted.

The sharp military command broke through the darkness, followed by volleys of thunderous explosions that peeled back the night. The smell of gunpowder floated past, and pinpoints of candlelight began to spring alive in all the windows, offering a caressing warmth. History was reasserting itself, and finding its rightful position in all who watched. As the last echoes of cannon fire faded into the distance, the fife and drums resumed, and the happy crowd began to drift away in all directions. Christmas had begun in Williamsburg.

Up the main street lay numerous shops and taverns. On our way to the King's Arms for dinner, we stopped at one of the many tall, iron baskets filled with burning wood. The light and warmth were welcomed by an increasing number of people attracted partly by the fire and partly by the spirited bagpipes being played nearby. The crackling flames painted flowing pictures across the faces of the crowd and the night edged deeper into the past.

The nearby Apothecary Shop held a special fascination for me. With so many doctors in my family's history, I just had to peek inside. Bright candles cast shadows on the shelves and across containers marked with obscure terms. From the doctor's office in the back of the shop, we could hear the beginning of a lecture on long-forgotten medical procedures. As we drew near the small group listening to the speaker, thoughts of Grandfather Hill crept into my mind. His country doctoring was over now, but no doubt in the early days of his 102 years, he had seen similar sights and practices. It had been much too long since I had seen that grand old man, and I wondered if the opportunity would ever present itself again.

A glass of wine at the King's Arms chased the unaccustomed cold from our Florida bones, and the candle on the table wavered as costume-clad waiters rushed by with steaming platters of prime rib. It had been a good day. Doug's presentation had gone well, and a visit with a girlhood friend had brought back comfortable memories of my life in nearby Norfolk, where my father had once been the commanding officer of the naval dispensary. Those were such good years that I considered driving to Norfolk while Doug attended the conference, just to recapture a portion of those remembrances. However, Doug's caution caught me off guard. "Reliving history here in Williamsburg is one thing," he said, "but returning to Norfolk may prove somewhat disappointing." After carefully weighing my motives, I decided that he was probably right. Sometimes it is best to let the rosy glow of days gone by rest cozily in memories' archives. I wanted nothing to disturb those precious childhood recollections.

Our conversation turned to a book, titled *Life After Life,* that Doug was reading on the trip. Obviously, it had quite an impact on him, for he talked at length about its fascinating accounts of people who had survived experiences that brought them near death, and had then related tales of unusual happenings during those nearly fatal moments. The consistency of the stories and their authorship by a physician impressed Doug and his very logical approach to life. If his logic could be influenced by something "supernatural," then it was my turn to be impressed. As we analyzed the stories and their patterns, the first tiny sparks suggesting alternative possibilities of existence began to radiate deep within our beings, and another piece of an unseen puzzle gently slid into place.

We hated to leave Williamsburg. A strong sense of belonging had become a permanent part of us during those few days. When we toured the beautifully restored buildings and sipped hot rum in cozy taverns, our sense of time seemed to blur, linking with our gradually emerging desires to understand the nature of existence. Colonial Williamsburg and Jamestown, for us, had become microcosms of life, regardless of their points in history. The past began to appear more alive and purposeful. Consequently, our perception of life itself began to change, with hints of depth and design that we had never before dreamed possible. With the glow from this adventure still fresh in our minds, Doug pointed the Chevy south, towards home and children.

Once back in Florida, the Christmas of 1976 swept over us with the usual flurry of happy activities. During that holiday period, the boys spent a day with Doug's mother and returned ready to reactivate the presents that had been left behind while they were visiting their "Nan." In the midst of their noisy re-entry into the family circle came a bubbly story about a Ouija board. Spying Nan's old "talking board" set, the boys decided to give it a try. I remembered playing with a Ouija during my childhood. Joking attempts to contact Napoleon and giggling accusations as to which of us was really moving the pointer could always dispose of a rainy afternoon. This time, the accent was somewhat different. Both boys excitedly claimed that the pointer kept indicating their communication was from their grandfather, Walt Dillon. The messages contained details about Walt's life, as well as words directed to Muriel that simply said, "I love you."

Our reaction was mixed, but the recent events in our lives had given us cause to treat their story with a light and open attitude rather than to completely negate their experience. Besides, even if they subconsciously manipulated the pointer to create this communication, what harm could it do? If their inner needs dictated that being in touch with their granddad was important, then this fanciful activity might fill the void left after our inadequate attempts to explain Walt's death. In usual childhood fashion, the boys left their story hanging in midair and returned to their Christmas gifts and everyday rampaging. Only the adults were left holding the particles of a questionable experience that seemed to gently stir the newborn embers of their own innermost needs.

A casual talk with Doug's mom revealed that the boys had indeed somehow produced messages via the Ouija but, to her, the transmission of love from Granddad was just a bit unsettling. Muriel had always been the strong believer of the family in things spiritual, but this struck awfully close to home. In times past, she had been needled mercilessly by the family for her consideration of psychic phenomena, but now a slight discomfort settled over all of us.

Most of 1977 was spent in the usual hustle and bustle of a young family meeting the daily challenges of life. For such a small creature, a baby certainly can expand its influence to absorb all available time and energy. Nicole Hope began to toddle over all creation and develop her personality to the point that we called her "Miss Nikki." Time was always at a premium, and moments alone with Doug were rare. Occasionally, after the kids were finally bedded down and the kitchen confusion put behind us, we were able to sit back and talk of our developing interest in probing the unknown aspects of life.

Since the trip to Williamsburg, Doug and I had increased our awareness of the written word regarding things spiritual or psychic. Articles in the newspaper, a few volumes from the library, or a paperback from the bookstore became topics of casual discussions during our late evening, child-free encounters. That casualness began to change abruptly, however, soon after I brought home a book for Doug called *Seth Speaks,* by Jane Roberts. Doug's every spare minute was spent devouring its contents. Something within this book had certainly caught his attention.

Seth Speaks contained the writings of a supposedly deceased personality named Seth, coming through the author in a trance state. Doug's standard response to this kind of psychic demonstration was strongly rooted in the logic of the science of human psychology, and its argument that trance personalities were simply repressed personality traits exhibiting subconscious knowledge stored away in some dark recess of the brain. This time, however, Doug went beyond the source and became deeply absorbed in the material itself. His rather self-conscious explanation was that, even if science proclaimed the author of *Seth Speaks* unbalanced, he was benefiting from her writing. Responsive chords were being struck beyond his comprehension and he was at a loss to explain why.

As we both studied this book, I came to understand its attraction for him. Its depth, beauty, and logic were so impressive that we sought other books by Jane Roberts. As soon as they were off the press and into the bookstore, one of us would burst excitedly through the front door with the latest volume. Over the next few years, the Seth books became part of our lives. Virtually by default, we came to accept the validity of Jane Roberts' trance state and Seth's existence. We were amazed when the full realization hit us that we were now taking as a matter of course, the existence of a spiritual world and an exchange of communication between that world and ours.

Through the Seth material, and other readings, we found that sleep and the dream state were important to spiritual, as well as physical growth. With some concentration, we were able to remember bits and pieces of our dreams, and we began recording these recollections. Doug laughed time and again at what he called my "soap opera dreams," which were continuations of a single dream from night to night. Since Doug had more difficulty remembering his nocturnal journeys than I did, his humorous attitude was chalked up to pure jealousy.

His turn was to come in April of that year, however, when he awoke with unusually vivid recollections of having dreamed about exploring an ancient Egyptian tomb. Doug remembered that while looking over the many varieties of long lost treasure, he had come across a small book. Its cover was overlaid with gold leaf, and its

The Search Begins

exquisite beauty was dazzling. While browsing through the various rooms and looking through the golden book, Doug wished that parts of his exotic travels could be brought back to the family. As in many dreams, though, the exotic seemed to change into the everyday, and he was ushered from the tomb through corridors filled with people in modern dress. Doug recorded the dream experience, but we were not to comprehend its meaning fully until almost three years later.

During that same period of early Spring, the Ouija board was brought out in a spirit of levity, slightly colored by anticipation. As Doug and I sat across the coffee table from each other, the embarrassment of playing with this child's game got the best of us, and we collapsed in a mass of exploding laughter. Remembering the boys' experiences with the board, and after properly admonishing each other, we placed our fingers on the pointer. It moved! Slowly at first, and then with deliberate swirls, the pointer circled the board. Accusations flew back and forth. One of us had to be consciously manipulating the movement. Starting again with serious determination and sworn pacts of non-interference, a message was spelled out that said, "Uxpmu kd tlf befk fh," and other equally unintelligible gibberish. So much for direct contact with the spirit world.

We were to find out later that advice against use of the Ouija board was widespread. Some believers in the spiritual stated fearfully that evil or low level spirits might enter the picture and cause untold havoc. Neither of us could accept the concept of evil spirits. We were barely within the realm of believing in anything spiritual, no less an evil aspect. Besides, we totally agreed with the Seth philosophy which simply states that reality is created within your own mind, and evil is more in the eye of the beholder.

The obvious failure at Ouija communication resulted in better use of our time, but eventually our interest resumed. In August, a startling message caught our attention. "Will you try harder?" it scolded. Doug was certain that this was my way of persuading him not to be so easily discouraged with the Ouija, but that message certainly hadn't come from my conscious mind. When we hesitatingly asked questions about the source of our scolding, to our amazement, the following exchange took place:

Q: Who are you?
A: Fred Tegus.
Q: Where are you from?
A: Dresden, Germany.

Q: When were you born?
A: 1848.
Q: Were you married?
A: Yes.
Q: What was your wife's name?
A: Rosalyn. She died.
Q: How did she die?
A: Ruptured appendix.

The board was put away for the next three weeks. Careful self examination ensued. Doug and I are very self-critical people, but if indeed, we weren't consciously prompting this message, then what? Obviously, it had to be subconscious muscle control coupled with long buried memories of something read or experienced in the past, or so the more orthodox approach stated. Our response to each other was an acceptance of the subconscious possibilities while keeping an open mind.

In early September, we tried again. This time, however, only one word came through, "Walt." This was much easier to explain. Our love for Doug's dad and the boys' experience had uncovered our dormant desire to once again communicate with that wonderful man. Yes, that was the logic of the situation. Two weeks later, we tried again. During this attempt, the name Salley Kruger came through with this message, "I have received you. Keep a close entry in your family dreams."

At the completion of the note taking for that message, I noticed Doug looking at me intently. "Ah, is something wrong?" I asked. "Hair out of place? Spinach between my teeth?" He didn't smile at my effort to be funny, but very quietly explained that he was seeing a small misty blue cloud above my head. Our reading included explanations of auras, and we wondered aloud if this was the case. Again, attempting humor, I explained to Doug that he had just seen my halo, and it was indeed about time that my true nature was discovered. "Let's ask Salley," was his unexpectedly serious reply. Ask Salley we did:

Q: Is what Doug saw an aura?
A: Yes.
Q: Why did he see it?
A: You are gifted.

The Search Begins

Over the next several months, our spiritual experiments with the Ouija produced varying results. Usually the attempts were late at night, after a full day. The more tired we were, the more unintelligible the messages. Our records, however, show the following excerpts that kept us going:

1. "Ever keep digging."
2. "Be big of heart."
3. "Will be hoping to keep in touch."
4. "It is the light of the guide for you to have the hidden knowledge."
5. "Try picking good seance."
6. "Keep your private views. I will have gentle words for you—a way to work with life."

On one occasion, a very specific communication seemed to capture an essence of something considerably more than we had been receiving. These few words literally thrust themselves through the other labored transmissions and flowed with an ease and beauty all their own. "Raw intellect delving into drops of time," it stated. The thought seemed to be pointed directly at us and our efforts to unfold the unknown aspects of existence.

4

A Closer Look at Reality

WITH THE PRESS of Doug's responsibilities in the school system and our active family life, precious little time was left in the year following the Cassadaga experience to resume our pursuit of psychic experiences. Only toward the fall of 1978 did we begin to feel a distinct need to try the Ouija board again. Most of the results were disappointing and discouraging almost to the point of our giving up. Luckily, two messages kept our interest alive even though their meanings seemed somewhat obscure:

1. "Walt owes you a way of knowing. One avenue you knew. Before he died, you had Walt commit a way. At very ill point, he was with you. Can you be free? You need to be rover to get past inner barrier. Walt focused us."
2. "Vox is the way. This nil to see."

Vox? Did this mean voice? As always, the questions outdistanced the answers. At that time, it seemed as if there were almost no answers. Little did we realize, however, that a gradual change in our methods was to lead us eventually into a torrent of communications, answers and even more questions.

Much of our reading during that period seemed to be revolving around an alternative communication process called "Automatic Writing." Part of the history of spirit contact involves this method, and, as with the Ouija board, there seemed to be both positive and negative

A Closer Look at Reality 35

aspects of its use. Finally, our pioneering traits won out in a decision to give it a try.

According to the literature, most Automatic Writing was simply a result of an individual sitting down with pen in hand and allowing it apparently to move over the paper of its own free will. The free will movement of the pen seemed laughable to us, but the possibility of a subconscious linkage that might produce communication did make sense. Involuntary muscle control by the subconscious could move the pen and if messages resulted, perhaps we could learn at least a little more about our selves. Beyond that, maybe the subconscious was a connection to a higher self or some other state of being.

We began our experiments on separate occasions. Doug would sit minute after minute and nothing would happen. After the initial attempts, he would dabble with it, but his heart wasn't in an effort that couldn't be under his direct conscious control. With my first try producing the same result as Doug's, the forecast was for a future locked into a slow and reliable Ouija board.

Still, the idea of Automatic Writing fascinated me. On those rare occasions when the family was off in other directions, out would come a pad and pen for yet another try. Finally, something happened. The pen moved. Just squiggly lines at first, then barely legible letters were formed, and eventually a few simple words. Having an intellectual understanding of the power of the subconscious is one thing, but watching your own hand write words apparently separate from your conscious self is quite another. It was downright weird!

When Doug got home that day, I excitedly showed him the results of my work. He looked at the paper first one way, then another and asked "What's this?" "That," came my proud reply, "is my Automatic Writing." His suspicious look spoke volumes even though, "Yeah, right," was forced through a suppressed snicker. I guess it did look a little strange. The results were about on a par with Nikki's two-year-old markings on her wall. With great restraint, I sat my well educated husband down and explained each mysterious slant and curve until he could make some slight sense of what was written. Slowly, his amusement turned to excitement. From then on, his encouragement was an ever present factor that continues to this day.

Over the next couple of weeks, my experiments began to produce a large flowing script with identifiable words and the beginnings of unpunctuated sentences. The more comfortable I became with the process, the more clearly words seemed to flow. With Doug's assurances that we would treat any information that was produced just as we had the Ouija board, I began to practice in earnest almost daily. Our agreement was simply to let the information flow and to evaluate it over a period of time in relation to how useful it appeared to be for us.

With our own punctuation added, a reconstruction of some of those early messages is included here for your review:

January 2, 1979

"Your hand is the way. We now awaken everyone about another life. We give to you a way to go. You are ever a way for us. Look to Heaven every day. Soon we will near a point of all attainment. You are about to see everyone's goals as we do."

January 3, 1979

"Enforce your self esteem. I am Agnes Williams. I was born in Belfast, Ireland in 1933 and died in 1938."

January 5, 1979

"You forgot your past entities. Now you will all see. You are part of another world. I knew Doug in Ireland. His name was Thomas Bunn. You were his sister. He was born in 1911 and died in 1938. You were born in 1918 and died in 1919, eight months after you were born."

January 6, 1979

"Agnes has her helper here. Doug is her helper. He was help to her before. He always had friends for her to help her to be in touch with the other side."

January 16, 1979

"Open up. Erase your egos. I'm elite and so are you. You are both reassured that every single grief needs to you be given. I open the other ways. Love is a very avenue to seeing about self."

January 17, 1979

"Everything has an explanation. In place of your alter ego, you must elite yourselves. I expect elite things of you and Doug. Elite means one thing to me. It is a person who has a single goal and has the ability to explain about another life. You and Doug are elite in two ways, and one day, you will see how I see you. I see that all of your levels of oneness are elite with mine. If you will find a path to allow your ego to take, then you will find every experience a fulfilling one. Enter one of the levels of consciousness that you haven't entered before now. I see you on the way to evolving."

January 18, 1979

"I will go to the elite ones before you. How one goes forth in time evolves around the apparent ego to give away its boundaries. I think you're both taking the right steps in finding a table to channel elite areas of communication."

February 15, 1979

"Agnes is living in death. I open the door for you to see your true image on the mirror of time."

February 27, 1979

"Isabella is here. I watch sudden exchange of other beings in this reality. I said 'realm,' not reality. If you elect to pursue a path which allows your freedom of thought, then you must have all the real scenes in vision. Doug has been very well in his approach to span of knowledge. He is seer of your thought. In Walter is a peace not obtained on your plane. I will give you the answers to all of your questions in time. Be patient, as you need to approach the lot of life slowly. I shall help you to relax with death. I endear you to our existence along with Doug."

A strange and interesting sense of cautious excitement began to surround each of these sessions. Our busy lives permitted only sporadic attempts at continuing this experimentation, but somehow, thoughts of the brief messages filtered into most of our daily activities. The expressions of hope and encouragement seemed so very genuine that negating them or maintaining a coldly logical distance was difficult. Accepting the possibility that I might simply be displaying suppressed quirks, Doug and I reaffirmed our decision to wait and see. If nothing else, my subconscious had quite an active and comforting imagination.

Thoughts of trying to validate the historical aspects of our writings and the Ouija material passed through our minds. Doug's interest in history and his love of detail almost got the best of him at times. Once, he even gleefully started planning the investigation of each name and date. With the press of time and better judgment, however, we decided to leave that method of operation to others. Validation, we still concluded, was not always wrapped up in names, dates and places. If we expended our efforts to research each fact, a lifetime could be spent resulting in only a mass of disjointed conclusions. Our validation would come from either the positive or negative effects on our daily lives.

The writings and their talk about feeling comfortable with death must have stimulated memories of my grandfather and the realization that at his incredible age of 105, life couldn't continue indefinitely. My last visit to his home in Illinois had been so long ago, and now I wasn't sure whether I would have the chance to return before it was too late. Rummaging through the family budget proved that finding enough cash for a family trip to the Midwest was impossible. The need for me to see Grandpa Hill became so intense, however, that Doug and I scraped together enough money for me to fly to Illinois in early May.

Life for me then moved very quickly into an even higher gear than usual. How my wonderful family would survive for a week without total motherly supervision and care was hard to visualize. The only thing to do was to fool-proof the household by freezing meals, cleaning every crack and crevice, ironing every shirt, and nailing down, with the babysitter, all the details of her responsibilities. That effort left no time for philosophy or much of anything else. The rapid pace of activities seemed to stop only when I finally sat back and watched the trees and lakes of central Florida disappear below the wing of the airplane speeding me toward Illinois.

What a switch! Doug was usually the one flitting around the country by himself. Now it was his turn, for once, to pack the kids home from the airport, wash the breakfast dishes and get ready for lunch. In fact, this little trip would probably do them all some good. Fending for themselves for a few days just might bring tears of grateful appreciation upon my return. Savoring that rare moment of release and mock-revenge, I ordered a cool drink from a passing flight attendant and relaxed with my fellow free spirits. There was indeed life after housework.

My moment in the sun was experienced fully for only a short time when a few pangs of guilt crept into my mind. This was my first trip without Doug since our marriage. I wanted very much for him and the kids to be able to share this flight and the visit with my grandfather. But, in addition to budget considerations, they all had such intense allergies, that staying in the house with my grandfather's housekeeper's cat for so long would have been deadly.

The see-saw of my emotions bounced up and down until stabilized by mental images of Grandpa Hill as I remembered him ten years before. What a grand old man. Had he changed? Was his memory slipping as much as my father had told me? Would this be the last visit?

A Closer Look at Reality

The relentless questions eventually focused on the purpose of this trip, but the answers weren't there. Somewhere below the surface of my mind lay an unidentified force that was driving me in pursuit of my grandfather. The feeling went beyond love, or compassion or the simple need to see him once more. Perhaps it was Grandpa's precarious age or my developing spiritual awareness, but whatever it was kept building inside me until tiny particles of understanding began to form soon after my arrival in Illinois.

The change of flights in St. Louis drew me back into the real world, and the short hop to Springfield's small airport offered little opportunity for further reflection. A hearty welcome from my dad and his wife, Dixie, provided a much-needed link into my grandfather's world. Interestingly enough, Dad and Dixie coincidentally planned their visit from California during this same time. Even the airline's loss of my suitcase couldn't overshadow my excitement and anticipation.

As we drove from Springfield to Athens, Illinois, Dad was in his glory pointing out historical landmarks, new buildings and even locations of his own childhood exploits. Now, there was a thought. *The* Dr. Harold H. Hill, age 74, retired, might actually have been a child. That shift in time and perception heightened as we pulled onto tiny Main Street in Athens. It really hadn't changed since my last visit. In fact, I had the distinct impression that it hadn't changed in sixty or seventy years. There on the corner was the home of Athens' beloved Dr. Tolbert Hill just as it appeared in ancient family photographs. Except for dirt streets, hitching posts, and my grandfather's horse and buggy tied up in front, that scene was a replica of early 1900.

No street numbers exist in Athens since there really isn't any need. With only 1100 people in town, everybody pretty much knows everybody else. Since old Dr. Hill was once the town mayor and had officiated at the births of most of the inhabitants anyway, he and his home were a local institution. In fact, people all over the state marveled that he continued to practice medicine until the age of 96, and had delivered more than 2000 babies. Even though honors from the state legislature and medical society phased him little, I couldn't help but wish that the American Medical Association could research the possibility that he might be the oldest living doctor in the country. Seven months after that trip to Illinois, the A.M.A. initiated a search at my request which resulted in my grandfather's receiving a congratulatory acclamation as the oldest known living physician in the United States.

Walking through the front door of Grandpa's yellow wooden house on that day was like stepping through a fine warm mist into another world. Why was it so different this time? There he was in front of me just as I remembered him. Perhaps minus a few hairs on top, at 105 he looked better than many men twenty years his junior. I instantly felt an uncanny rapport with that sunny smile and those eyes crinkling behind thick glasses. Slender and handsome, he wore a suit and tie as he had every day of his life for many, many years. As we hugged each other, I seemed to be in touch with a part of myself that had been missing for a very long time.

Those days in Illinois were filled with talks, excursions, and the deepening of my appreciation for life. When my suitcase finally turned up, brought from Springfield by one of Grandpa's "babies," I quickly dug out the cassette recorder and preserved most of Grandpa's conversations. Those priceless tapes contain the thoughts, stories, loves, disasters and triumphs of an age that can no longer speak for itself. I felt compelled to capture those things for Doug and our children as well as for myself.

Grandpa loved sharing the past. He seemed to need to talk about his accomplishments, especially in the light of his now less demanding retirement. His alertness was incredible but it appeared that the further in the past, the clearer the story. As for many elderly people, recent events made little impression on his memory. For him, the past was probably as alive and pulsating as the day it was lived. I understood much of the medical and psychological aspects of aging but sitting there listening to him brought me a sense of connection to his past that was truly uncanny. At times, I had the feeling that an unseen part of my Grandpa was guiding and teaching me in ways that I was just beginning to understand.

It wasn't long before I dove headlong into Grandpa's photos, albums and hundreds of other keepsakes. The two of us bounced merrily from item to item like two kids on Christmas morning. What a profound delight! How fascinating to leaf gingerly through a weathered journal and read names of patients long gone from this world who visited my grandfather near the turn of the century. Of special interest in our time of economic concern were the rates per visit that varied from 25¢ in cash to all types of trade goods.

Out of the memorabilia popped Grandpa's grade report from Rush Medical College, 1899. Well, after all, he was born in 1874! There were photos from that era, pictures of individuals and full family portraits. One particularly large picture showed my Grandpa fresh out of medical school, his four brothers, all doctors, their wives and children. In the middle of that handsome family sat Great-grandmother Hill who

A Closer Look at Reality 41

looked as though she could handle anything and anyone. What a contrast and series of contradictions to look at those likenesses staring up at my grandfather as he held that picture. To me, time was somehow becoming so collapsible. The now and then weren't making quite the sense they used to. Looking into my grandfather's soft brown eyes gave me fleeting impressions of the possibility of his instant interchange with that young man in the picture. The living reality of the past pressed itself against my fragile understanding of existence.

Sensing my developing interest in the historical, my father quickly seized the opportunity to provide a guided tour. Getting me away from Grandpa wasn't easy, but Dad and I were soon greeting old family friends in Athens and eventually making our way toward Springfield and New Salem, Illinois. Obviously, my learned father was going to lead me down Abraham Lincoln's early pathways. We saw them all, the museums, restored historical sites, and other places of special interest. Every minute was fascinating. If someone had told me a few years before that I could enjoy history, I would have questioned their sanity. Now, I couldn't get enough. What a change.

The full impact of the day's events reached a peak with our arrival at the Springfield Cemetery. Now, cemeteries are not exactly my favorite places but seeing Lincoln's Tomb and then walking over to where my ancestors lay, reminded me of those recent talks with Grandpa. Before me sat the tombstone of Dr. Green Hill, my Grandpa's father. According to Grandpa, Green Hill and Lincoln were friends. Lincoln even called Green by a special nickname, "Greenberry." To me, Abraham Lincoln and the Civil War had always been just so many pages in dusty books. Sure, they were important but not terribly relevant to my world. Then and there, in that cemetery, the full realization began to hit me. My great grandfather knew Abraham Lincoln and my grandfather was born only nine years after the end of the Civil War. History really wasn't that distant after all.

On the way back to Athens, I had a chance to assimilate much of what had happened since my arrival in Illinois. The bombardment of new perceptions blended with the rushing river of my own spiritual development. Those experiences appeared to form an intricate web revealing a definite pattern. The contrasting mixture of age, youth, past, present, birth and death was not as chaotic as I once had imagined. Time now seemed so much more pliable. Even the placement of people, events and relationships demonstrated such a definite purpose that I wondered why I hadn't seen it before. Beyond that, specific thoughts or words to express the strong feelings within me failed to materialize. How do you explain, even to yourself, an inner sense of knowing that flows not from tissues in the brain but from some vast reservoir beyond consciousness as we know it?

Lying in bed that last night before my return trip to Orlando, I couldn't help but trace the pieces of the spiritual puzzle that had fallen into place since Doug and I visited Williamsburg. The experiences in Illinois were such an important part that I hoped to help Doug grasp at least some small portion of it. Planted right in the middle of these thoughts was a very strong desire to pursue our psychic studies and the Automatic Writings. I had to know more. Once back in Orlando, we could take additional time and seriously investigate those intriguing messages that we had been receiving.

For some reason, once the plans for expanding the psychic investigations were set in my mind, thoughts of Grandma Hill were waiting next in line. Even though she died when I was only eight years old, that house seemed so empty without her. If only I could see her, talk to her. Maybe, just maybe if all this psychic business had any validity, I could see her spirit, if there really was such a thing. Something visual would seem so much more tangible. Then admonishing myself with comments like, "Right Barb, let's play Halloween and call in the spooks," I managed to make myself feel a little childish. With logic in full control, I quickly checked out the darkened room just to make sure that an apparition wasn't waiting to say goodnight. No apparitions, but there was a slight glow in the room. As I watched, the glow turned into a small bluish light. It sat there in midair slightly away from the foot of the bed. I couldn't believe it. "Must be my eyes playing tricks or a reflection from outside," I thought. Averting my gaze and shaking my head did no good. After a few minutes, the strange blue light gradually disappeared.

There I sat in the middle of a darkened room, wondering what had just happened. Investigation showed no possible way that a reflection could have occurred. Besides, it wasn't a reflected light that I saw. Then what was it? There were only two choices open to me. Either my mind had created the vision or I had actually seen something beyond our reality. Again logic conquered. Yes, indeed, the intense desire to see my grandmother produced a hallucination. Then again, why did I feel so happy? Why was a piece of me still saying, "Maybe your logic isn't worth a darn"? The fact was that whether or not my mind created the event, my emotions gave the benefit of the doubt to the remote possibility of an actual spiritual contact. Satisfied and comforted, I happily drifted off to sleep.

The next day was full of goodbyes. This visit had enriched my life in

A Closer Look at Reality

such a dramatic way that it wasn't easy to leave. Once on the plane, I again was struck by the realization that this was probably the last time I would see Grandpa. One of his last comments to me was, "I'll go when the Good Lord calls me." The simple calm of that statement accentuated my newly acquired sense of the beauty of existence. For the first time in my life, I felt comfortable with what we call death.

After an irritating lay over in Atlanta, I was finally back in Orlando, scrutinizing my family to see if its ordeal without Mom had taken its toll. It didn't take long for me to become immersed fully in tales of interesting meals cooked by Dad, battles fought with neighborhood kids, and the thousands of other important events of the past week. Surrounded by love and chatter, I was whisked home from the airport so that Doug and the kids could show off the house. Yes, it was still there and spotless. Laundry was undoubtedly lurking in closets and hampers somewhere, but outwardly everything was perfect. Survive they had, but with enough verbal diplomacy to let Mom know that she was still sorely missed.

Adequately sharing my feelings about the Illinois trip with Doug was a little more difficult than I had hoped. So much of it seemed impossible to express. It wouldn't be until the writing of this chapter two years later that I would be able to better explain those emotions and events.

With my interest in the psychic heightened by all that had happened in Athens, the desire to delve more deeply into our Writings increased day by day. A review of the Writings reminded us of the reincarnational information recorded in January. That brief encounter startled us at the time, but planted a seed of interest that we were to see grow as the Writings continued. If the descriptions had been overflowing with famous names and places, we would have rejected them outright. But Ireland in 1918 and my supposed demise at eight months of age was just about as inglorious as you can get. If my subconscious were trying to create fascinating past experiences, it certainly had fallen flat.

Soon after my visit to Illinois, Doug and I found an evening with household chores done and kids in bed. Grasping such a rare moment, I grabbed a yellow pad in one hand and Doug in the other. Grinning broadly, he knew what was up. Settling back into our easy chairs, I asked Doug if he was ready. He laughed and asked if he had a choice. Shaking my head in mock solemnity, I knew he was just as eager as I. Then like two expectant fishermen casting lines into a secret pool, we plunged into a Writing session. As soon as the pen touched paper, the large flowing script began to fill the page. Unlike previous times though, I knew instantly what the words were before they were written. The following is a major portion of that information:

May 20, 1979

"Isabella is with you. I lived slowly and I died fast. One has to be able to live as if the *existence will forever be present, as it is in actuality true.* You and Doug have touched upon the true meaning of existence. If you continue your search for truth, you will find many doors will open to you both. If you believe in another existence than your own earth existence, you will prosper to great heights.

"I was also a carpenter in one lifetime. I enjoyed life as a man of abundant wealth. If you place effort in the right direction, you, too, will find yourselves very wealthy. See yourselves as beings who are not merely existing for the present time. About yourselves, place things which are meaningful to you. Don't be afraid to let go of earthly possessions in order to obtain further oneness with God. If you do this, you will find existence to hold more depth for the two of you. I will try to be more specific. If you try to be of a level of consciousness that is difficult to obtain, then perhaps by giving up some earthly possessions which really hold little ultimate value, you will be further ahead in your search.

"I lived in a time of strife during oppression and hunger. It was all at a time when women were eager to live a type of life that appealed to the other men who lived also. I was one of those men. I only evolved around earthly possessions as I was never at a will to be otherwise.

"See if you can understand what I am about to say. I will be with you if you will be with me. If you choose to be elsewhere, then do not call upon me to write through you. Open your channel of communications. Then you will be at an advantage. I will allow my soul to be free to help you find your existence in your sense of the word. However, if you do not try to open the lines of communication, then you will be allowing yourself to be open for less meaningful existence."

5

Touching the Unknown

DRENCHING RAIN pounded the roof while sharp bursts of approaching thunder echoed up and down our neighborhood streets. The commotion outside, punctuated by flashes of lightning, made us giggle self-consciously. A haunted house was the only missing ingredient as we sat down to again probe Barb's Automatic Writing ability.

Time's elusiveness continually had frustrated any serious thoughts of expanding our psychic efforts since Barb's return from Illinois. Now, however, hopes were high that this fourth of July vacation would give us ample opportunity to further investigate those intriguing messages. If only Mother Nature would give us a chance, we could get on with it.

Hoping that the storm's clatter would lessen, we paused and talked about the difficulty in decoding Barb's flowing script after each session. At first glance the material always appeared to be alphabet soup. Only by drawing slash lines between recognizable words and adding our own punctuation were we able to decipher exact meanings.

Dreading the thought of again plodding through pages of material in that very slow manner, we decided to try an alternative approach. Noticing that she was increasingly able to picture the words mentally before they were written, Barb recommended that she simply speak them as they came into her mind. In that way, she felt I could take notes on what was said. If it worked, we just might develop a smoother and more rapid translation process. For some reason, our new method of transcribing Barb's material seemed familiar. It wasn't long before we realized that our "invention" was very similar to the method Jane Roberts and her husband, Robert Butts, used to transcribe the incredibly articulate Seth materials.

Vowing that any man could take dictation as well as any woman, I armed myself with my own pad and pen. There we sat, comfortable, yet poised for action. With hollow cracks of thunder still bouncing around the house, Barb's pen haltingly began to move. With gentle arcs, it gained speed and words spilled onto the paper. As quickly as the words were started, Barb amazed us both by delivering this verbal message:

"I am about to unveil a very slight stopgap in your open life; a spark in the flame of eventuality of all people on your level of open communication. The outer offer is a very true existence that yours must face in a time of a very spiritual control. I will you to follow a path of outer existentialism which will alienate you to be free.

"I am trying to form a pattern in which you can follow to open the door of the spiritual sphere of training the soul to be free in your self. Your soul is a very complete linkage to the finality of existence. If you search the books, you will find this to be true.

"In this existing relationship, follow my thoughts as you are with a spirit guide not just a subconscious effort which wills you to put down its thoughts. I am new to this communication. I will have to be experienced in this way before I am able to be a total help to you and Doug. I am a spirit, not a sport!"

Our laughter at the last sentence broke the intensity of the delivery. Welcoming the comic relief, we sat back and looked at each other. Our new method was certainly working well but the rapid flow of Barb's spoken words created the distinct impression that someone else had joined us and was just warming to a full-blown lecture. Labored Ouija transmissions and Automatic Writings couldn't compare to the sense of personality that now filled the air.

Barb's self doubt began to show through at this point. I had to admit that, as intriguing as the material was, her subconscious could well be working overtime and even defending itself. But, then again, if by some chance it wasn't her subconscious, perhaps we had stumbled onto something. Agreeing that we both were probably downright crazy, the decision was made to press on while keeping very careful records. Settling back to try it again, I asked Barb to request an identity for this supposed spirit guide. The response was as follows:

"I am a spirit who is at a level of consciousness to reach out to one or two of you in your realm of existence. Give me some space to open myself to you as we are only beginning our relationship. I am Ollie Lopez of Acapulco. Sally informed me that you and Doug are looking for some new existings in your lives as you are not satisfied with your current existence. I am here to help change these things for your evolutionary process. Let me lift you to the heights, attuning yourselves to a new found spiritual existence.

"I especially think that the way you are handling the messages I am sending you is a very sound way of interpretation. I'll let you know if you are not receiving images correctly. If you have doubts, then be careful to let me be able to answer. Sort the questions you have at that point. If you are afraid of being laughed at, then don't be afraid of asking me as I will not laugh."

"Thank God somebody won't," I blurted out. "I can't seem to see myself going back to the school board offices next week explaining to my colleagues that my wife is speaking for the other side of reality while I take notes and ask questions." Barb's laughter was interrupted by the kids trooping in to ask for sodas, snacks or whatever could be scrounged from the old folks. Fred and Greg looked quizzically over Barb's shoulder at the flowing words but said nothing. Whatever their thoughts were, psychic investigation yielded for the rest of that day to the noise and the further demands of family life.

Over the next few weeks, snatches of time were stolen here and there to tap into the source of what we were now calling The Writings. Each day at least four or five handwritten pages would be produced, leaving us even more eager for the next encounter. Whatever we were in touch with was clearly not coming from Barb's conscious mind. Most of what was recorded dealt with very personal issues such as family relationships and especially the need for our continued emphasis on spiritual development. From time to time, however, we asked specific questions about matters of special interest and recorded these fascinating responses:

Q: *Barb's perception seems to be changing when we do these writings. Is this significant?*

A: "She is allowing the freedom she feels to penetrate her body and mind. This has not been an effort which was used frequently before now. She has not had the ability to free herself and totally absolve her earthly problems. You, Doug, have changed this for her. She has allowed you to place her freedom at a higher value. Her present sense of being has been altered and will carry itself eventually into other stages of her daily routines. She is seeing a fullness of light and will learn to interpret this in time. You will see her in a trance at times as she will lose herself completely to our voices and penetrate our souls with your communication. We will favor you both as having these powers. They are increasing and this is what is being felt by Barb."

Q: *Is it possible through this communication to talk to Doug's father?*

A: "Walt is not able to be of assistance at this time as he has other important developments for his soul to achieve. However, he wishes me to assist him in these questions that you have. I really wish to be of some service to you about Walt as I understand the trauma that you all went through at the time of his death. Be cautious not to be pulled in by means of communication which does not involve me as it may not be the actual existence you are searching for.

"Walt is growing but the learning of your existence did not allow him to grow enough. He will be back again someday and you will see him to be an entity of love and compassion. He may not appear but instead be a newborn child. He is a highly developed soul and you were fortunate to have been entwined with his earthly existence."

Q: (From Doug) *Why was my brother born retarded? Why must he and others be so afflicted?*

A: "Your brother, Doug, is at a loss of foundation at this point of his existence. Should he become aware of the situation he is now in, he would lack a powerful role of existing structural development. He is and has been a child in many ways although the spirit is in full cooperation in his physical manifestations at this time. He is about to become a fully potential being, as we know that being to be here on our plane of existence.

"Do not be sorry for him as he will be your friend at another point in time. He was your own father at a previous existence, Doug. Be cautious not to let this influence your daily life now. He is serving the purpose for his soul to become a higher being.

"Retarded people seem to overcome their existence from within and reach toward a higher form as they seek to challenge their own instabilities. Although their physical alertness has many times dwindled, their spirits are filled with relaxation. Acceptance of these individuals must come early from you as we will work with them in an affordable manner. Your future involves many experiences with these people. Their purpose is to develop a way of existence beyond yours. They have already learned to need much of emotional values but fear little. Their openness to you has been useful for them as they close out all concentration on trivial earthly needs. Their linkage to us is closer than yours. They have been shown a way of development which far exceeds many who live 'normal' lives. The lives of retarded individuals will change as they progress here. Some may never change but have a reason also for this. They are available to our world as ones whose capacities of learning are exposed and will accept our thoughts here more readily."

Q: *What is the soul?*

A: "Give me a chance to open your minds as we develop the definition of the soul so that you may comprehend what I am about to say. I will tell you that a soul is an opening in the light of the spiritual realm of thought. He is the core of existence on this realm due to the fact that he is the one way of light and the one way of time as you know it to be. The soul is developing slowly through space and time."

Q: *Barb and I feel that we have known each other forever. Does that indicate some sort of linkage beyond the physical?*

A: "You have known each other before, many times, in many places. You are not new to each other and are a soul's existence in the reality of love which is a powerful source of energy in itself. You are both a more attuned couple than you have an idea as you were born to be in the world you are now in. Be thankful to your souls as they chose the existing circumstances for you many years, as you know them, ago. Be at peace with yourselves as you are both in the eye of God being here with us. We will make the union more concrete.

"You are both a part of a very complex unit. It is not a usual thing to be able to evolve all personalities at will and therefore I do not know all the answers for you.

"You are specifically a part of each other yet not a part of each other. You are a soul whose purpose is one which you both understand individually but not necessarily in collectivity. You are about to become more aware of your patterns of existence with each other. You are twin spirits whose purpose is one and not two. You must serve each other in order to fulfill this requirement for your soul to be fulfilled. You are a soul to be born on this planet at other times in your earthly lives, however long that may be. You will see other souls before I am here with you again. In that way, you will be free to use the earthly memory in your times after death in order to benefit your souls. However, the soul's overture of existence will not preclude the entirety of your earthly one. You have a bank of memories there but you have a will to obtain it here. Your desire for each other is abundant. Use it as a method of advancement for your soul. It is not coincidence but a useful measure to help your development.

"You are both facets of the soul's seeking forces. Be careful not to be at a will of acceptance that you are the only two forces in control of its destiny. I examine your souls to be a complete unit with one another. However, this does not eliminate the need for outside assistance in helping you to obtain wealth of a sort which is extremely valid in your own path of existence.

"See the nature of reality as it is and not as you wish it were. See it as though you were not a part of it only as a soul peering through a looking glass. The soul is only attached to the earthly plane for a short span of time. You must be aware of this if you are able to truly function in the capacity you wish to. Be aware that these capacities are also short-lived in various ways. The methods used to obtain various ways or patterns depend on you and your soul's outlook through you.

"You exist in a reality of total awareness as you see it to be. However, this awareness is shallow. You are only aware to the point of earthly existence not of other existence totally. You are always in touch with other existences but you do not always carry this information with you. Be in contact with yourselves more and expand the area of reality you now comprehend.

"See yourselves as progressing, not stagnating as you have been. You are not alone in this as many on your plane are stagnant. That is too bad as they will not progress as you are. They are of another soul, each of them. You must find your way as they must find theirs.

"Be calm as you have shown me you can be. Do not be too aware of yourselves as they are merely shells of time abounding in places as the shells in the ocean.

Q: *You have mentioned something before called the "Patterns of Existence." Please explain what they are.*

A: "You are a part of my learning patterns.

"Be aware that the patterns are an opening to your understanding our ways of communication with each other. The ways are unlike your own. We are not what we see but what we feel through various forms of communication. We reunite our soul together in order to be a more perfect union. You are reunited already. At the present time, you are still the opening for many who strive to be of a more perfect union.

"I am with you both, and I see your souls united in this plane.

"The patterns of life are not only patterns of existence. You are aware of this already. You see the color at other times which radiates from you, but they are not really made of color. The light hues are of a pattern in themselves, but you cannot see this pattern. Be careful, but be wise as you won't understand this now in totality. The color is a form of a visual aid to help you see the spiritual existence of life at your level. Only in a colorful atmosphere would you accept its existence.

"Patterns of existence are modes of color that are transmitted by the two of you. There is a way to show all the patterns of your spirit's connections. This is known as aura but it is not a pattern in itself. You must have knowledge of the soul's purpose to be understanding of the aura in full.

"The purpose of these patterns is to be a further development for your soul's communication with others. The bond between you and Doug, Barbara, must set an example for us to see here and others to see on your level. These are not always seen but always felt by others' souls as they near your surroundings. They have the ability to see your own still life. You do not always become aware of it as time has a different effect on your existence. You are aware of my intent, even though the understanding is muddled in your minds. The soul's comprehension is much more lucid. It has great abilities but you are limited."

Q: *What is God?*

A: "I am not sure exactly what God you are referring to, but I assume you mean the total awareness that only one can hold in total power. That which you are understanding of on your realm has a different vehicle of magnificence than is actually true. The glorification that earthly beings put on a God is a false interpretation.

"He is an ally to you as you are to Him. He is but one and not so much as a particle of glory. The idea is to be found here on higher levels as to the composites of His being. Although I cannot witness these higher levels now, I am working toward that field of development later on.

"Each level holds different interpretations of God as each holds its own progression toward Him. He is not known to you to be the last being in the system but is the being which makes the system. He is us and we are Him. He is not a unique being. He is suppressed in the state of consciousness that you know now. He is not free with you and yours, but you are beginning to be free with Him. Be careful not to be taken in by misinterpretations as they will only confuse you. Be at a will to accept my general statements as those of clarity and brilliance."

Q: *Tell us about Jesus Christ.*

A: "Go to your source of power and concentrate on what I am about to say. The Son of God is not the Son of God. He is but a figure of imagination in many people's lives. He did exist but did not represent God as he is but another soul as you are. He was sent as a teacher not as a Son of God as you and many conceive him to have been.

"He is not here with me at this level. Go your way and see that

I am right. The level of your 'Son of God' is not here as he is another higher soul still on a journey, however, his journey has not ended. It will continue for some time as he needs to further develop his soul as many others in his position do.

"He was seen by many but known by few. He was but a spirit-guide to a flock of people. He was human but only for a short while. He was then materialized as a spirit-guide, respected and worshipped by many. Do not perceive him to have magical powers as he did not. The powers which were shown were misconceived in the time of Christ and have been carried through the ages of time that way.

"He was not a source of magic but a source of power as I mentioned before. He was here on my level long ago. He is no longer in need of the things this level can teach. He is a highly developed soul and is in communication with others at a very high level. He will be back to your plane at a time of chaos when people will accept him as a way to accept themselves. They need a teacher to be able to function in this capacity. They will see him as a teacher who will be sent to relieve them of their own foolish mistakes."

Q: *Was there a particular purpose for our daughter Nicole being born into our lives when she was?*

A: "Yes, there is always a purpose for the birth of a child. However, your child has been planned to arrive in your lives due to her abundant source of energy and love. Both of these facets of her being are extremely useful to your purpose. You will and have drawn much of her psychic energy into your beings. She has become a source for you as her gift is one of planned still life of ideas and thoughts. By this I mean that she holds the key to your peaceful existence. You have acknowledged the fact that Nicole is a hopeful body and mind for you as noted by her earthly middle name, Hope. She is always loved and will never hunger for it."

With each of these messages, we became more intrigued but, eventually, a concern for validity began to temper our fascination. Where was it all coming from? Who had experience with this sort of thing to guide us? In the midst of the endless questions came this direction from Ollie:

"Shelley's rosters share some conclusive evidence of my being. She would be able to show them to you soon. Shelley is another name for your friend Millie. She is your link to me at some point of trouble in your lives. She will seek the truth from me and give it to you.

"She will be an open link of power communication at times. She is an especially nice person whom you have already met. Yes, there is the evidence you need for my being. Here is more. She will let you be of a choosing if you so desire her, to be a friend to you. Do not feel that she will come to you alone. You must approach her also. Here is why. She needs not to help you as she helps many others. She needs to be of assistance to you still because that is her path. She will be of a comfort to you in many ways if you let her. She is here with you at times also but is not able to be here as I am now. She is a spirit guide in your world."

Shelley? Millie? The only person we knew by either name who might fit the description was Millie Stephens, a former neighbor. Before she and her family moved to nearby Apopka, we talked briefly about religion and the spirit but in nothing more than light conversation. How could we possibly approach her and casually explain that she was "recommended" by some spiritual entity coming from Automatic Writing? Besides, everything we had read regarding spirit guides indicated that they were always people who had died and were returning to help those still on earth.

In tune with my "generous nature," I recommended that Barb be the one to call Millie. After all, she knew Millie better than I did, and I could always claim that unknown to me, Barb had simply lost her marbles. Writings in hand, Barb uncertainly approached the phone in our bedroom. "Are you sure we want to do this?," she called. "Of course," came my fearless reply, "go to it, kiddo." Soon she was chatting with Millie and warming to the main thrust of the call. Hesitatingly, she outlined the development of our writings and read the part about Millie that had just come through. Barb's jaw must have dropped far enough to crack her toes when Millie jovially admitted that indeed she was a spirit guide and deeply involved in work similar to ours.

After the call, chills ran up and down our spines as Barb reviewed her notes on the conversation with Millie. If Ollie was a subconscious manifestation, then Barb's subconscious had produced results that were clearly extrasensory. That fact in itself catapulted us both into a state of awed confusion. Experiments and armchair philosophy had jumped suddenly into the big leagues before we knew what hit us. Our little psychic verification would probably seem insignificant to those used to such events, but we sat there utterly flabbergasted.

Millie's invitation to join her for an in-depth discussion the following week beckoned us like a quiet harbor in the midst of a hurricane. With everything swirling about our heads, we definitely needed some help. Just how much help we wouldn't realize fully, however, until a few days before seeing Millie. During the night of July 15, 1979, Barb had an experience that needs to be told in her own words:

"While sleeping, I somehow felt and heard Nikki come into our room. Upon waking, I thought that she needed my help or that she was sick. At that point, I could feel her move onto the bottom of the bed and crawl up toward me, which she often did. Her little hands pressed against my left foot and leg on her way up. Just as I was about to turn over, I felt her blowing in my ear. It was a very irritating and steady stream of air that annoyed me considerably. Ready to pounce on my sweet daughter for playing games so late at night, I started to turn over but to my horror, I was paralyzed. I absolutely could not move.

"There I lay with my eyes wide open, unable to move. The blowing continued until I finally mustered all of my strength and was able to force myself to sit up. The blowing stopped. Nikki was nowhere to be seen. Doug was fast asleep with his back to me. Within a few seconds, Nikki awakened in her bedroom and called to me. Until I actually saw her in bed with the covers still in place could I believe that she hadn't been in our room at all."

Now a physical manifestation was a little above and beyond our already overflowing cup of experience. When things get to be downright spooky, you really begin to wonder. I never doubted Barb's perceptions of that event but it did cross my mind that our interest in the psychic could have caused a dream condition to simply flow over into her mind as it became fully conscious. That thought lasted only a very few days when, late one night, I suddenly awoke, aware that something in the room was quite different. Barely audible footsteps on the carpet stopped at the foot of the bed. Gentle pressure on the edge of the mattress was followed by light indentations moving up the covers between Barb and me. Whirling around, I could see nothing. That sequence of activity was to happen to both of us on random occasions for the next year.

Before going to see Millie, we decided to ask Ollie about Barb's particular experience of feeling something on the bed. Here is the response:

"You (Barb) were not aware physically of what of what was happening to you. It was a source of extreme confusion in your mind. I am referring only to your physical mind not your spiritual existence which was manifesting itself at the time. You saw only a part of the actual experience. Prior to your knowledge, there was a defined experience. Nikki's soul or spirit was with you before. You have only recently opened the door for experiencing such circumstances now. As I recall, you were startled and scared. The feeling was not new, but it was a new experience. You need not have any fear as it will happen again, and you will be more aware instead of afraid. Therefore, you will learn more than you did this time.

"It was an experience to show you both that actual astral projection (the spirit leaving the body) does exist and is not a figment of all psychic authors' imaginations. Ollie's opinion is that he feels you are now prepared for further projections. He sees you following the lines of psychic communication of which he has been speaking to you before. Your paths are extending themselves into another bend. The other thing I will mention regarding the other night's experience is that it was profoundly real and that is why you were so scared.

"Nicole is a soul as you are and she has earthly needs as you do. Therefore, if she can't reach you through earthly ways, then she will, through her soul. It is evident to me that need was a strong one the other night. Nicole was a bit frightened as you were when she awakened and found herself in bed alone as she was with you just before. She is not alone any more. If she needs you, her soul will enter your realm and take cover from earthly overtures of negative existence. She will learn much from you as you already have learned from her. She will show you spiritually the ways of further development as she progresses in earthly time. The time is not going to be long from now as she is already a highly developed soul. Note that she was a vehicle of communication in your experience. Go to your child and see her as she is. She is the way for you both to be bound together at all times. She gives the stability of life to each of you through her own source of power. She is able to communicate with others through this same source."

The meeting with Millie couldn't come soon enough for either of us. Unfortunately, we weren't able to get a baby sitter that evening so over we trooped seeking guidance with kids in tow. The Stephens family greeted us with their usual warmth and delight at seeing the children. As always, good food and Southern humor abounded as Millie and her husband, Bruce, settled us into their comfortable home. Even with the incredible burden of their two adult handicapped children, they are always cheerful, caring and full of fun.

After exchanging pleasantries and family news, the kids sped off into adjoining rooms, and Bruce decided to ease out of the picture himself. The conversation was beginning to shift toward the psychic and according to Millie, Bruce very definitely puts no stock in that sort of thing. So the three of us were left sitting at the dining room table moving word by word into the true nature of the visit.

Casually, Millie mentioned that two prominent psychics in the Orlando area came to her during the same week we called. This, she claimed, was simply a natural fulfillment of her role as a guide on earth as well as in the world beyond. Another startling assertion was that ever since her childhood, she had been able to see into other realities, as well as actually being able to leave her body at night in order to consciously travel as a spiritual entity. In that supposed spirit body, Millie remembered serving as helper and teacher to the living and to those who have passed on to the next world. In turn, she was a student learning from higher beings during part of these nightly trips.

Millie's absolute belief in what she was saying was astonishing, especially to an old sceptic like me. No matter how much Millie philosophized or what our writings said, proof and validation had to be much more tangible. Maybe all of us were merely letting our imaginations run wild. Impatiently, I asked Millie if she could give us specific impressions about Ollie, the Writings, our lives or anything that might help us get some answers and direction.

Smiling at my need for details, Millie said that all my proof would come about eventually. As she talked, though, her eyelids lowered considerably and she began to rub her forehead. With a softened voice, she began to explain the surging images that evidently were coursing through her mind:

"You are truly in touch with those beyond. Don't doubt Ollie. He is very real and is trying to help you. Ollie is especially trying to open Doug to the possibilities of existence. I can see Ollie here with us. He is very dark, a short man, with black hair and dark skin.

"Barbara, you and Doug are soul mates. Your relationship goes back 1700 years. The two of you have been together during many reincarnations, and you often were married to each other. You both are old souls and are much more advanced than you know. That is why the Writings and experiences are coming so easily. The work is not new. It is now time to bring back the ancient stored knowledge.

"Doug, you and Barbara attend classes at night in your spirit bodies. One night, I took you both by the hand and led you to one of my own classes. Your friend Ollie also has been a student of mine. You and Barbara go out of your bodies a great deal but are only now becoming aware of it. When you both have felt something on the bed at night, you were out of body, and what you felt was your daughter also in an out-of-body state.

"Doug, I see you changing jobs. You and Barbara will one day work as a team. I see you, Doug, doing something very enduring with Barbara's help. Your financial condition will eventually improve, and I see you buying a new house. Doug, you will sell something.

"Doug, have you ever thought of being a writer? You will be a writer one day. You will write children's books. You and Barbara will begin teaching the children, then the adults. Your psychic writings are a preparation for the writing of books."

Millie looked so very tired. Giving this information seemed to drain her visibly. Just when we thought the session was over, she continued by saying, "I see something blue in connection with your Writings." Blue? We couldn't figure that one out until I suddenly realized that we were keeping the Writings in a blue notebook. Of course!

Looking straight at Barb, Millie then zeroed in with a certain determination that was lacking before. With two or three short sentences, she uncovered something hidden deep within Barb's mind. An ancient fear unknown to anyone but herself burst into uncontrollable tears and sobs. Still intense but with warmth and consideration, Millie very deliberately assured Barb that her fear was unfounded.

Regaining her composure, Barb rather self-consciously admitted the preciseness of Millie's observation. The release in that admission seemed to lift a burden of incredible proportions. To Millie and me, the problem seemed insignificant. But as with most of the rest of us very human beings, Barb must have let the issue build inside her until it seemed so terrible that closing it off from the entire world seemed the only alternative. Our reason for not sharing the details of Barb's fear in this book is that it involves an individual who is still living and who would find that discussion an understandable invasion of privacy.

After that first session with Millie, Barb and I decided to ask Ollie for his thoughts about Millie's information. Here is the reply from the evening of July 19, 1979:

"Ollie is back. He is a servant again. He was by your side last night as the visions were coming through Millie. She is quite a woman. She has many abilities, some you are aware of, some you are not. Be careful not to expect too much from her as she will tire in her body soon.

"I will see her (Millie) again tonight as she travels to this level. Her teaching is a much desired form of existence here. There are many who envy her position but few who are ready to attain it. You are now aware more than ever that you and Doug, Barbara, are in communication with me, Ollie. I am here as I told you I was. Until you actually see me to be in your vision, Doug, you will not fully believe. However, I am patient and understanding so be at a will to continue your current lines of progress in my direction.

"I am not lonely any more as I have found the two of you are believing more in my existence. At the right point, you will confirm my existence through your own efforts. We will then form a perfect union.

"Are you going to accept what Millie told you as truth or will it be weighed as a lot of fresh fruit? We are surprised if you don't weigh everything, Doug, as you have the ability to decipher many trashy things from the beauty of life. You are not really offended, Doug, as you know me as yourself, don't you? We are alike in many ways, however, you have abilities which I don't possess. You are above my level of intellect on the earthly plane.

"In regard to last night again, and I will be making many regards, you were very impressed as you should have been."

Millie's friendship, insights and gentle guidance continue to be an underlying source of strength for us. Millie was to call us one evening about a year after that first session in her dining room with the news that a friend of hers in New York kept getting a strange name through her Ouija board. The name seemed to be associated with Millie so the friend called her to ask if she knew anything about the name "Shelley." About that same time, Millie began having a great deal of trouble with her heart and over a period of time lost a great deal of weight. She also developed cataracts on her eyes and underwent an operation for their partial removal.

During that same year, following that initial session with Millie, Barb's method of delivery while transmitting information from Ollie changed slightly. Soon she was closing her eyes and doing nothing more than doodling with pen and paper while speaking the words in a low, sleepy voice. At least twice a week, we held sessions and by Christmas of that year had recorded over 500 handwritten pages of notes.

The information seemed never ending. At the same time, our experiences were taking us far beyond the written word. During the writing sessions, I occasionally would see muted colors and lights around Barb, and twice I saw distinct grayish shapes of roughly human size near our chairs. Ollie casually confirmed that, as we progressed, our perceptions would increase. According to Ollie, the forms that I saw were the spirit bodies of living persons who were asleep and traveling out of body. They were simply observing our work. What was simple to Ollie, however, was certainly startling to me.

Barb and I also began to notice that our dreams had become increasingly vivid and more easily remembered. On many occasions, we even dreamed the same dream. In the morning, one of us would start to tell about a dream only to have the story finished by the other.

Out of all the strange happenings, perhaps the most fascinating were those of the precognitive nature. To have a waking vision and then to see it actually take place in the physical world has to be one of the most intriguing experiences a person can have. When you actually can perceive an event that occurs in the future, you begin to seriously question the concepts of space and time as we think we understand them.

Early one Saturday morning, Barb awakened remembering a dream about a man with a full beard and curly hair. A few seconds later, she opened her eyes and looked up to see what apparently was a chubby, stuffed Teddy Bear floating in the air. Thinking she must still be asleep, she closed her eyes and opened them again only to see the bear still happily sitting in mid air. Then, almost instantly, it disappeared. Later on in the morning, she related all of this to me including a detailed description of who I kiddingly called her "Dream Man."

Well, a Teddy Bear floating in the air on a Saturday morning was just a little much for me. Not wanting to disturb Barb's apparitions, Nikki and I soon scooted out of the house on our way to the movie theatre. The "Muppet Movie" was in town, and Nikki had been waiting anxiously for old Dad to take her. The night before, she had asked me to tell her a story about the movie before she went to sleep. Not having the slightest idea what it was about, I fabricated a wild tale about Nikki and Daddy going to the theatre and being physically caught up in the beginning of the movie. Those opening scenes, according to my story, were to show beautiful clouds and blue sky that would then fill the theatre for Nikki and Daddy to fly through. She loved the tale as it expanded into other silly events, and I patted myself on the back for my never ending ability to get kids to sleep with wild tales.

Our early arrival at the theatre, armed with popcorn and sodas that next morning allowed us to grab good seats and chat as we watched the theatre fill with excited children and grown-ups. I kidded Nikki and asked her if she were ready to fly around and through the clouds. She giggled happily through her mouthful of popcorn and finally the house lights dimmed. Kids and parents alike hushed as the screen brightened. Brilliant white clouds appeared against a baby blue sky. My soda almost fell into my lap. From a stationary position atop those clouds, the picture changed to an increasingly rapid movement as if the camera taking those pictures were mounted on an airplane skimming the surface of the clouds. Nikki and I sat there wide-eyed, in disbelief as we visually swept over, through, and around the puffy whiteness on the screen.

I couldn't wait to get home. This was going to blow Barb away. Bouncing in the front door, I pulled her aside to recount the experience at the movies. Shaking her head, she sat me down and added a postscript. A new plumber had come to fix an obstinate toilet while Nikki and I were gone. He fit Barb's "Dream Man" description with full beard and curly hair perfectly. If a double-header precognition weren't enough, the next day Nikki came home from a visit with my mother dragging behind her a huge, chubby Teddy Bear.

Now one or two such experiences might be written off to coincidence, but when it happens more often, the law of probability begins to rule against mere chance. My visit to the University of South Florida in January of 1980 confirmed that fact with yet another peek into the future.

The Directors of Teacher Education Centers for the state of Florida were to gather for their regular meeting at the university in Tampa. This meant an hour and a half drive down Interstate 4 with lots of time to think and relax. After weaving through the downtown Orlando traffic, my thoughts drifted to landscaping. That back yard of ours was nothing but a mass of weeds, crabgrass and mole crickets. Maybe if we just covered the entire mess with thick cypress mulch, that would do for starters. As part of my imaginings, I could see large branches and sections of hollowed out trees strategically placed in many sections of the yard. Sprouting from all those bare trees were brightly colored bromeliads and other types of tropical air plants. What a beautiful scene that would be. No doubt, we would win the Garden Club's award for the best resurrected yard in our part of town.

Blinded by my own creative genius, I almost missed the turnoff to the university. It wasn't long before I was through the small community of Temple Terrace and looking for the Holiday Inn where a block of rooms had been set aside for our group. After finally spotting the motel and completing the registration ritual, I drove slowly around the side of the building looking for my room. Glimpsing the pool area to my left, I suddenly hit the brakes throwing my briefcase to the floor. Instead of the usual lush St. Augustine grass around the pool, were hundreds of square feet of thick cypress mulch, hollowed out bare tree stumps, thick branches and beautiful bromeliad plants hanging everywhere. That scene was a perfect replica of what I had thought was my own mental creation.

Direct experience can be a great teacher. It leaves a mark on you forever, but sometimes with all of its deep impression, it gets pushed aside. Such was the case when certain predictions made in our Writings did not come about. Statements were made in the Writings about supposed future events. I forced the issue over Barb's objections and asked for infinite particulars. If indeed these events were going to happen, of course, we should know who, what, when, where and how much. When some of that information didn't pan out, we began to question the validity of the Writings.

Doubt is a deadly emotion. Closely allied with fear, it eats away at you. Only occasionally did we try our Writings after that. Even then, we looked askance at everything that came out. If nitty-gritty predictions were wrong, then maybe it was all wrong. Maybe we were just fooling ourselves about all this psychic business. Confusion reigned. Unfortunately, we also visited a local establishment billed as a psychic information organization. The well-meaning people there confirmed our connection with a world beyond, but seemed to emphasize the possibility of negative vibrations surrounding our work. Exactly what that meant we didn't know, but it certainly didn't lessen our discouragement.

March of 1980 came, and with it came the flu bug. Both Barb and I were hit at the same time. Luckily, the kids were spared, but we couldn't shake it for almost two weeks. Daily, our fevers climbed above 100 degrees, and fitful coughs seemed never ending. Taking turns feeding the kids, we would then collapse back into bed or on a sofa. "A virus," the doctor said, and no amount of medication seemed to help. Rarely have either of us been so sick.

After the first week of flu misery, Barb and I noticed an increasing number of dreams during hours of feverish sleep. In these dreams, we both repeatedly seemed to be conversing with a great many others as well as being deeply involved in various learning processes. The exact memories would elude us but gradually we began to feel an overpowering need to understand what was happening. It was as if a significant meaning were being pushed to the surface of our minds for reconstruction into a sensible unit.

As Barb and I talked and compared notes, we began to sense some sort of relationship between our sickness and the dreams. Somehow, an explanation of this illness was seeping into our sleep state. The more we explored the issue, the more certain we became that an answer did exist. Strangely enough, the more certain we became, the better we began to feel until finally the fever left us entirely.

After recuperating for a few days, Barb and I decided to hold a writing session and ask about the illness and our dreams. Unfortunately, the response was wordy and confusing as had been many of the limited Writings from previous weeks. For that reason, instead of quoting the information directly, listed below are the major points that we were able to decipher:

1. A person's state of mind and spirit can cause physical problems.

2. When you allow your conscious mind to contradict what your soul knows to be true, physical problems arise.
3. Our intense flu bug was created by our lack of understanding and follow-through with the Writings. We had allowed other people's inaccurate perceptions to sway us, and we had placed too much emphasis on predictions. In effect, we were negating what we knew we must do, thereby creating an internal conflict. That conflict in turn led to illness which was simply a way to force us to take note of our actions. The dreams were giving voice to our own knowledgeable inner beings as well as showing us our actual communications with those beyond the physical world.

So, we caused our own sickness. Now that was a little hard to swallow. Psychosomatic illness was one thing, but a virus strain that hits millions of people was quite another. Hard to swallow as it may have been, we definitely were stimulated to return to our Writings and to question the nature of our existence. In fact, looking back on that experience is like looking back on a dam breaking wide open. As difficult and confusing as that time appeared to be, it was an absolutely necessary part of our growth pattern.

A visit with Millie soon after those days of thermometers and antibiotics was to shed even more light on our wayward thinking. Patiently, Millie reaffirmed the source of our information as being valid. She perceived nothing negative about our work and solemnly lectured us about listening to other people unless we knew a great deal about them. Her rather terse comment was, "Sometimes people can only see their own negativity and are often jealous of your abilities."

Regarding predictions, Millie just laughed and explained that spiritual sources are on different levels and that our source needed a little more maturity. Evidently, our "lower level" communicator had a lot to learn. Many of the predictions would eventually come true to some degree, she felt, but not in the time frames given since time perception on the "other side" was so different than ours.

During that same week, Barb and I decided to write to Sandy Gibson, author of *Beyond the Body*. Barb's enthusiasm for the book came from an identification with the author's own struggle to understand her developing psychic abilities. Hoping that Sandy might give us a long distance appraisal of the events in our lives, we sent her a lengthy letter including samples of our writings.

Within a week, Sandy's reply was in our mail box full of warmth and encouragement. Using a cassette tape, Sandy gave us an extensive analysis of our writing and our source that fully confirmed our positive spiritual linkage and was almost an exact duplicate of Millie's information. To see such a marked parallel between two psychic individuals totally unknown to each other was both amazing and reassuring. Sandy's guidance was reinforced further when she went into a trance on the tape, giving this fascinating reading, as she calls it, for Barb through her own sources of spiritual communication:

"We have here the records for this soul. We have here a soul who has lived many previous lifetimes on this plane. This soul is nearing the completion of the series of earthly lifetimes. There have been particular lessons chosen for the series of earthly incarnations. The soul was once studying on the higher planes and learning much advanced material. There was, however, the lack of appreciation for that which was learned. There was the lack of interest in the ability to appreciate the opportunities there. The soul therefore chose a series of earthly lifetimes to better appreciate the higher planes.

"There were chosen lives of hardship and service. The soul has appeared as a servant and slave of others in various lifetimes. There have been the harsh punishments from the earthly realm. There was the resistance to the earth in the early lives and the dissatisfaction with the soul's choice. Over time, the soul came to love and appreciate the earth. There was improvement in the lives. There were greater opportunities. The soul served as a mother in a number of lives. The female lives were most common in this middle period as the male lives had predominated in the early period. In the later period, the soul slowly grew in the appreciation of the higher knowledge and began to seek this knowledge. Because of the opportunities scorned earlier, the soul now must turn and strive for the knowledge to be gained. In the present life is the final stage of the earthly existence. Here is the return to seeking higher knowledge. The way is not easy and is slowed by the earthly restrictions and doubts. Yet also are available the friends and helpers from higher levels to guide the soul through these times ahead.

"The soul needs to fully overcome the resistance to acquiring the higher knowledge. This will come slowly yet is the path at hand. In the times ahead are far greater opportunities to acquire the deeper knowledge and to use it in the help of others. The soul is completing karmic obligations through the marriage and children of this life. As these obligations fulfill themselves, there will be greater pull to use the psychic work for the help of others. This is the path ahead chosen by the soul.

"For now, the lesson to be acquired is that of faith to seek deep within, to learn to trust the personal guidance, to have confidence in the self's path and to believe in the higher forces and their guidance in life. The soul must return to a state of seeking higher truth and spiritual growth. Keep the focus throughout this life on the seeking of spiritual growth and higher truth. Do not be distracted by the superficial displays of psychic powers. Pass these by for the greater spiritual truths ahead.

"There is much love and sincerity within the soul. Learn to trust in these and the guidance will be clear."

6

Probing with Some Age-Old Questions

THROUGHOUT THE FIRST YEAR of our Writings, we seemed always to be fighting the potential validity of that communication with logic, self-consciousness and a great deal of old-fashioned doubt. Continually, Doug and I tried to force the messages into certain preconceived molds in which they just didn't fit. Surface belief often seemed to shatter on the hard doorstep of credibility. It finally took Millie's calm assurances, Sandy Gibson's long-distance insight, and a painful but revealing bout with the flu, to stimulate a surprisingly calm acceptance of this developing channel into an alternate reality. Laying the unfulfilled predictions aside for future reference, we realized that some very helpful and interesting information had been delivered that couldn't be ignored.

It took time and a few nudges for us to understand that our penetrations into the unknown, if they were to continue, would be creating their own blueprints rather than conforming to some existing system of thought. This was a little scary, especially for me. After all, that stuff was coming directly out of my mouth, not out of anyone else's. Twentieth century society has its adopted ways of accumulating knowledge, but our method was definitely not one of them. Then again, society certainly didn't have all the answers. You only had to look at the constant negativity of the six o'clock news on television to see that, so who was to say what was best for Doug and me? Repeatedly, we asked that same question, watched the news, looked at the Writings and answered, "If it works for us, who cares?" It was a very intimate leap, onto what our inner senses told us was to be a difficult, yet correct path.

Fully accepting the possibility of subconscious material infiltrating our writing sessions, Doug and I agreed that we were either in touch with a higher part of my spiritual being or some separate entity inhabiting another plane of existence. The totality of our experiences, mixed with the messages from the Writings, seemed to shift the balance naturally from a fuzzy, apologetic semi-belief into a smiling recognition of just how fully we were beginning to accept the actuality of our connection with a spiritual existence. The change in Doug was the most striking. From his original stance of objective analysis, he moved to a position that said, "Let it flow. I sense something beyond the usual, rational approach to life. I don't understand it, but there's a validity within what's happening to us, that has to be lived instead of inspected piece by piece." His views mirrored mine perfectly, and from that consolidation of our beliefs, we proceeded to absorb useful tidbits from periodic, but satisfying, writing sessions.

Like it or not, I had to admit that this transmission of information was a communication through a light trance state. Almost asleep, I would verbalize in a low, drowsy voice those words or concepts coming into my mind. Seldom did I remember what was said, only that it either seemed "right" or "not right." It felt as if I were almost shifting a portion of my conscious being, leaving an openness for the conveyance of information. Doug and I strongly suspected my subconscious as the actual linking agent with that other level of reality. As always, Doug was the dutiful recorder, scribbling down what I was saying at any particular moment.

Over the three-year period since we had begun receiving messages directly from an alternate reality, we have accumulated over 1000 pages of Doug's abbreviated, handwritten session records. The manner of communication is very unlike my normal communication style, with its involved sentence structures, flowery wording and periodically veiled meanings. Sometimes, I'll just sit and thumb through that material as if I had never seen it before. As I look over the information, most of it seems to be very personal encouragement and instruction directed at both Doug and me. But then again, we were able to satisfy at least some of our natural curiosity by inserting those inevitable questions that have been asked countless times over the centuries by many other inquiring people. After all, when unique insights about the world are at your fingertips, the temptation to do a little probing is hard to resist.

In thinking about the structure of this book, Doug and I realized

Probing with Some Age-Old Questions

that our curiosity was probably little different from your own. If you'd been with us during some of those sessions, you might well have been tempted to ask similar questions. With that thought in mind, the remainder of this chapter is devoted to a consolidation of such inquiries under a heading loosely called "Age-Old Questions." This material will provide a compressed look at the wide variety of topics we've pursued over the three years since those communications began flowing. Our insertion of "Age-Old Questions," at this point in the book also intentionally begins to separate those early days of uncertainty from the last two years of solidifying belief.

This is the first of several opportunities you will have to digest a large portion of our trance messages as a unit, without interruption from either of us. Put yourself in our position as the receiver of this information and draw your own conclusions. Only one personal observation before you begin. The full meaning of some of these passages takes a little effort to absorb. That can be irritating at times, but we've found this style of delivery almost intentional, as if it were saying to us, "Slow down and think about what's being said here."

Q: *What happens at the point of death?*

A: "You are apt to return to this level primarily by choice. As in any period of adjustment, your soul must replace one level with another. Out of sequence at times, this change will seek to deliver a new period of consciousness for your learning period to become a layered reality.

"When your physical death occurs, your spiritual entity remains intact. It is not partially linked, as suspected, but will remain at a point nearby for a period of time. Should there be a strong spiritual need at that time to complete this process, your spirit will flow according to the entity's purpose. Your compassion, therefore, for a spiritual entity will be established as a primary motivator. The body, in actuality, leaves the spirit. It (the body) does not reverse itself since the body's parts are limited, but the spirit is not. Should the spirit then be cast as a prior image of return for physical life, he will then begin to prepare for this new existence. Away from his own earthly problems, his growth period is now freer to establish the higher knowledge that is needed to acquire full physical respect from any entity that rebounds itself.

"Should your entity (on earth) be placed in a position of wealth, this is a prior choice. For you, what is occurring is a growth process through purpose. Thus, similarly, a spiritual entity on this realm must maintain a process of growth. We are open to outside forces as we are all-encompassing. After a physical death, these forces begin to control our observant needs, thereby placing them into a priority position. Your physical relatives and friends who are passing through our realm also shall be a comfort to newly passing spirits.

"Your willingness to perceive this period (death) is the primary motivation, again, for its occurrence. Their (those who die) growth patterns are also a way to help you, showing their needs are entrapped through yours. Thus, as your spirit travels here, to greet you, will be your friends, as wished by your self's supreme being. As your lesson of earthly fear dwindles, the entity then releases these spirits as a need quickly fulfilled.

"The aspects of each layer of death surrounds itself with an act of credibility, thus releasing any previous fearful commitment. 'Thy will' is done at that point, you see, as your proposed circumstances have then embarked on a new journey beyond that which was totally committed as a goal before your death. These layers are grounded in a reality of pre-conceived surroundings. Their placement has a purpose, thus eliminating fear and doubt of past suppositions.

"While observing a pattern through a demise of earthly concepts, you will learn to accept a more perfect value system, thus eliminating fear entirely and enjoying trust as your only guide in this reality. Be willing to adopt this philosophy as yours: Death has no meaning within itself, but does promote an energy that surrounds its happening, thereby releasing a 'quick-start' for the soul's re-entry program.

"I have astounded many who have come to know a reality beyond death, to form a more useful experience than had previously existed. I welcome this opportunity to share a layer of thought with you both tonight. Waiting for life to explain itself has not become a purposeful unit of message here. Life's net will hold many a thought to awaken a spirit and find a new growth beyond self-righteous physical existence. •

"When death occurs, your soul begins to change form with life's dwindling earthly existence. Slowly, an active partition begins to form a film of recovery for your spirit to cling to. This (film) is placed by your spirit prior to the last entry of that lifetime. Between layers of acceptance, your image passes through a period of waiting for further instructions. This comes as a means of support for your opening into a new reality. This reality then awakens eventually to find a pattern of new experiences for your further awakenings. These patterns are circulating rapidly, thereby decreasing past reservations of challenging unknown presences.

"You (Doug) teach the philosophy of death during your sleep periods to many who have passed over in recent times. They look to you for reassurance that all is well on this plane. Your students on earth have been your students here. They are with you on both planes for two purposes. One is to develop the physical mind and the other is to develop physical rejection of life. Your duty here is to help others understand, as I am helping you.

"Your concept of 'death' has no purpose by itself other than to remind your soul that it was only a transactional relationship through existence. Here, death, therefore, has become a starting point for each soul to witness as a link between a future and a past. This point is necessary, but its lingering effects are slim and easily adjustable. To your soul, this period disposes of a previous existence, while acquiring a new transition back to our realm, leaving a path partially completed, only to return again.

"While attaining a purpose here, you must find a way to expose yourselves and believe that all will end (death) shortly, as you see 'all' in the physical sense. This I have said, has short ramifications in itself, so others must understand that while their lives show neglect of spirit, they will perplex themselves by discovering their nature within, and explore their potential. We find that death has a wakening effect on those who seek a contact with it. They return to know aspects that otherwise would not have asked for their audience."

Q: *Tell us something more about the soul.*

A: "The usual perception is always different for a physical entity to conceive, due to the speculative ventures that one physical being takes and spreads to another, thus, then re-creating another structure unlike the first.

"The soul is the only structure of a physical being. Its inner penetration portrays the exact linkage that each physical part must have to survive within. A soul has, again, the ultimate linkage with another higher plane of development as it progresses through various levels. Its aggravations and joys become multitudinous in style. The soul's actions are penetrable into other souls. Therefore, the concept of a circular vision has merit. These souls are all grouped into a passageway that allows their unification to become gratifying. Only through this participative, progressive state will each soul then become reincarnated to serve multiple choices of its designation.

"Your placement has now begun as a choice by your own souls. This placement has determined your future direction also. As your souls are older than some, and newer than others (Doug and Barb), you are appropriately placed at this stage of your development.

"Each level of a soul's perception changes within itself. By this, I mean, that a level is not totally predestined to serve exacting purposes. Its structures have been set. However, the advancement of each entity through these levels may alter this structure as a device to embetter the soul's purposeful needs at this point.

"The division within each soul creates many angles of perceptions. These divisions are made and then redivided many times. Each division then reaches out toward its own private destination. Your present reality encompasses more than one of these realities. This is because of your inner soul's need to reincarnate several of these divisions at one time into two entities whose release then becomes an imperative step for this (your) soul's structure. Being cognizant of this will allow your freedom of thoughts to flourish. The accuracy of these thoughts will then be recycled back into other divisions. Therefore, your purpose serves other divisions other than your own combined ones. As each soul's decisive points of reality are shown to be controlled by an inner core, you are shown to have the basic choices of freedom from this directive within your own power. The ultimate guidance still remains within the core, however.

"As you seek to deliver this message to others, reach out and see that their division may indeed be a part of yours. The finality of the soul's construction is non-existent. Its opportunities are never ending, therefore the construction is never exact in its nature, either. To place a physical form within view of each physical mind, you must relate to that which encompasses a realism for your particular being. If each person depends on others' interpretations, he will then become lost through confusion.

"Your angles of perception are decisively accurate for your personal advancement. Thus, clinging to these perceptions is useful for your own devices. Being comfortable with your own construct is most important. The physical terms are useful only to those in physical bodies. Therefore, the ultimate reception of a physical construction is not going to be complete until the physical awareness stops and begins the spiritually intellectual beginnings. After death occurs, your beings seek a higher knowledge of the total conception of the soul immediately, to be used as a comforting device. This is understandable."

Q: *Tell us some more about God.*

A: "Your determination of originality in this particular concept depends upon your ultimate perception of belief. As each individual sees an ultimate source of guidance in various ways, your narrowness of physical minds will themselves to form a structured ideal for their own personal grasping. This alternative is useful for them to grow, but will not provide the cushion which many seek. Your own beliefs in a 'God system,' provide a moral adjustment to pnysical embodiments. These standards are basically self-influenced. They are not created by a source of 'God.' Your own inner conflicts with this position are actually guided again through physical means of repercussions.

"Tracing your ancestors, you will find that only through worshiping a particular means of spiritual entity were they able to perceive any form of ultimate reality. If they chose not to believe in an entity, such as this, then they became objected to by many around them. Subsequently, they divided their minds into two parts. One was actual earthly living according to their own needs. The other was according to their own perception of God's needs. This served then, a direct purpose for their lives and their own ancestors.

"You are now in a period where short answers are not acceptable. Do reconsider this when your books of religious literature are read. The Christ concept is no longer easily explained, as it was during these previous lifetimes, for again, your angles of perception are higher throughout the world.

"As you will yourself to a higher existence level, you shall seek to dwell with and upon an ultimate concept of belief. This, then, will provide the inner workings for your 'God.' If your persistence of a belief structure is necessary to you, then your needs are ultimately correct. However, your physical perception again may be colored, due to the infinite amount of exposure within your physical surroundings. Be patient with this concept, as you are not full grown as yet."

Q: *Is there a Heaven or a Hell?*

A: "Your 'Heaven' belongs with me, as I teach your areas of reasoning, thereby incorporating all pleasures and punishments directly. A pre-requisite for such a joining (pleasure and punishment) was established as a planned link with your future, before you were born. You will see that a 'place of detainment' from life is neither a 'Hell' nor a 'Heaven' yet the concept stems from within a selfish nature to achieve fulfillment for all negative needs.

"This 'placement of bodies' has not been determined by your soul, but indeed its vision (of Heaven or Hell) has been impressed on your minds by other people. Your own individual placements of these 'areas of adjustment' are open to controversy, as others will annoy themselves as efforts begin to formulate in their minds to diminish the importance of long-held life value systems.

"Heaven has not really been purposely placed forwardly as an aspect of reality. It was simply never meant to be. Our realities are ever changeable, therefore a place such as demonstrated through a 'devil' has neither impressed the soul, nor changed its perception of reality. Only attitudes which *desire* a negative influential power, will proceed to abandon a soul's comprehension, as its awareness extends only through a shield of self opposition. If a party *decides* its (Heaven or Hell's) necessity is valid for their own opportunities, then it will be so. 'Heaven' has no place, except as a conscience pacifier."

Q: *Tell us something about reincarnation.*

A: "The term that you use as a physical being shows total accuracy if used within the guidelines of the soul's purpose. Many other souls' individuals do not adhere to correct understandings of the total concept. Reincarnation is only a beginning process for future self discovery. Its term implies another point of living that one looks forward to. As this part is true, it is not complete. The interaction of lives depends again, entirely upon the after death sequence that involves so many other parts of the soul's travels through other realities. Your friends on earth will be born again to rediscover life if their pre-chosen way is to partake in another venture of this kind. Your limitations are not set in order for the pure pleasure of knowledge of rebirth. They are set in order that the penetration of the soul is again enhanced through each physical existence.

"As your lives teach many lessons important to the soul, they also discard much outer frill that does not seem necessary as a functional growth. Each partition of lives has an important part in the development of your soul, also. It creates a waiting period of observation for your soul to choose. This period often proves successful to itself as direct choices are placed in each lifetime, then reviewed within the same period. You will begin to see more of your past lives through dreams, thus recognizing your self-importance as other individuals who also become linked with you.

"The future lives are always as important, as they will transform parts of your soul into a regressive period, thus reconnecting each one with the past. The final regrouping of all physical existences performs a continuous whirl of experience for the soul to derive from. Your souls are always choosing pathways of varied choices. This may mean that your choices are expressly designed for their usage at another time. It may also mean that your soul has so many lives that it did not choose to ignore even a pinpoint of each one for its usage.

"Your avenues of discovery regarding these past, present, and future lives will be tended through their inner core of your soul. Should you choose lessons beyond the earthly existence to take a priority, then you will seek higher integration with your own soul's guides. These lifetimes provide many learning experiences that will expire only when your soul's choice is given a reality. Become aware of this, as you see, the earth has provided a partial placement for

Probing with Some Age-Old Questions

your soul's mergers with others who desire the same incarnative periods.

"Your personal earthly guide is also very important in each lifetime, as a choice is always determined by the soul, ultimately. However, the individual physical choice is bound to his own private destination. Therefore, become aware of your own total existence within your own reach. If your soul's choices involve the demise of another person, this will ultimately influence your path greatly. The spiritual concept is not meant to be used for negative self-advantage. The soul will make up its own progressive stages, however. Relying totally on its wisdom, without earthly infiltrations of choice, will not consume the total ideals for a soul's growth. This must be clear. Your earthly choices are most important. Your soul does not create each one for you, but as a part of your soul, you must choose each one according to your own physical desires. Thus, you see the possibility of alterations within the soul's periods of embodiments.

"As you are apt to be sustained primarily through physical surroundings, you are also aware of a partiality toward another unknown. Hopefully, your faith within yourself will show enough guidance to give to each lifetime, thus bringing about the final course for your soul only to begin anew. Be wise and accept this, as you are all part of my teaching. I will learn much from each lifetime of yours as a swirl around mine."

Q: *What are ghosts?*

A: "Ghosts are actually visions created by a mutual agreement between parts of your souls, or parts of other souls and yours. In order for your physical adaptability to enlarge itself, your visions of these beings are accurate, as their presence is always present. Belief in these 'ghosts,' is actually a higher concept that provides a necessary step for a spiritual/physical overflow between realities. These visual concepts are important not only to the physical person who sees this image, but also to the image itself, as again, it is part of another being who is exercising the choice of materialization only to a minute degree. Here we have an image that is self-created, by the fact that each image is in control of itself from within another form of its being.

"The inner workings of a vision, divisions of the soul, and your physical entities, are unified at certain points in order to relieve the fearfulness of many who need this removal. As images appear to people after deaths, they bring with them certain reminders of faith that usually will promote calmness instead of fear. They are prepared for this lesson ahead of time. Both sides again grow from these experiences.

"Your concept of the soul's growth must include these visual concepts of reality, as with blinders on, you will not see them and your particular area of growth will not occur. If you shall release your own earthly image to a point of a possible merger within the spiritual realm, you will begin having visions of spiritual entities behaving in a pleasurable way toward you. Their power is not within you, but yours is within them. Therefore, your control is satisfactory in disarranging their presence, if necessary, to a later time. As you regard their presences as ultimate particles of life, be aware that their particles are only adjacent to yours. They have mighty divisions within themselves also, for each is able to create according to the need of a physical body to see a familiar shape, person, or surrounding."

Q: *How did man originate?*

A: "Man was not created. Man was evolved through time as a mortal object, to be prepared for eternal object lessons. In order for full spiritual attainment, man was sent to evolve through many, many periods of adjustment, thus requiring specified realities to change and mold his self development.

"A valuable time period was through Atlantis when people began to discover their own intelligences as a vital link through soul contradiction. Your uniqueness is not the first power that was given to you. As a mortal, you, physically, are only recreated to serve as a power beyond all animalistic forces who bend with their own natures. *Your personal growth is needed for a soul to become unique, yet merged with other souls.* This vital growth will plan a course of its own to become installed as a precious level of understanding.

"The evolutionary process is but a start in the entire system of physical eventuality. The evolutionary process has taught many of those who seek a need for reassurance. Be careful not to evaluate this material as a prime motivation for belief in all unions of life, as they all create their own souls through a pattern of undeniable resistance to one another's penetrations.

"Should an evaluation be necessary, then create from your own remembrances a process of evolving. Upon this level, you will find that over and over was a process repeated by an arrow of direction. This same force was gathered as an entity once planned his own evolvement here. As your guide, I was also evolved throughout the same process.

"Once completed, a soul may re-enter this evolutionary chain by recentering his grasp on other levels of independence. "Becoming" an ape-like character would not sufficiently serve a further purpose. But, your soul may cohabit with that being and create a most useful product, that of an intelligent human awareness who created himself through a soul's preparation.

"Your cohabiting is an actual entity process that begins

through a lower level of nature that provides a womb for thought to begin expandings and products. Through that relationship will grow the expansion of human actualities that process themselves.

"Alleviating this stage of development will not alter the form of your animal inheritance. It only acknowledges the existence of one's tendencies. Be quiet and learn by these teachings as they are your own and will become more established."

Q: *Tell us something about Atlantis.*

A: "Weakness has temporarily destroyed that land mass that was once beyond your visual interpretation and acceptance. That soul group remained at an adjusted level for a period which now exceeds most others. Your (people) remaining (on earth) denotes a link between a past experience, as through your eyes were visitations of beings from this previous realm of thought.

"Atlantis remains an indelible cloud of mystery to many whose understanding is limited. However, don't forget to place its existence in perspective. It was released of its duties through a common bond that was planned prior to acceptance of its origin. Neither of you (Doug and Barb) will visit this crust now, as its present purpose does not include yours. So shall you be limited in its encompassing purposes.

"Atlantis was once a part of an undeniable structure that purposed itself in remaining as a memorial to help others look in a directive pattern. Through this, will come a way to understand the future destruction. The destruction of Atlantis came when many were unprepared for this visual concept. However, technology was outwardly noted for encasing a deluge of thought and placing this as an actual physical transformation. Behind these thoughts, though, were neglected patterns of receptivity toward physical demise."

Q: *Tell us about the possibility of life on other planets.*

A: "Your realms are yet to open into the release of barriers. You will have to discover the various aspects of life that lie beyond your present one, prior to fully comprehending others that share your common knowledge on other planets. Should you desire to expose this knowledge before you are positioned to receive it, then a recall of ideas would necessitate a quick reduction of information, thus validating your previous existences.

"I, too, was born on a planet of change. This was a necessary pattern for me to place myself, as through this pattern, you see, I was left to recharge the plans of development for further lifetimes. There, I saw a way to deliver forces (a group of people) that opened themselves to quieter, yet brighter, existences. They (the group) are as yet unchanged in this way.

"We will begin a teaching class with this group, as on your planet, there are several whose existences were sparked by a previous other reality from which life's teachings came. We recognize the need for acceptance from your current status of this present existence, but be not excited to a point to find these other places in space. Your opportunities will come beyond most of those who cannot yet understand the reality of possibilities beyond their own comprehension."

Q: *Through history, even from biblical times, come stories of unidentified flying objects seen in the sky. Tell us something about these so-called UFOs.*

A: "Your UFOs are areas for concern for your present level of understanding. These objects are valuable lessons for your period to absorb, but will not be placed directly into full view of mortal comprehension. Face value is only acceptable when one has ultimate understanding and abides by his inner nature, thus unraveling any prejudices of incomprehensive passivity.

"Unidentified objects are only that. They have resounded themselves during a period of unacceptance for a reason to be discussed later. However, in part, this reason will be explained now. As we watch, our periods become more sustaining, and other periods of time are merged with each level of understanding. This creativity takes on a form of an object which seemingly is unusual, thus unidentified. Its scope of perception is not any different than yours, but will maintain a vital pointed interest in obtaining a particular message for those who are ready for its observance.

"Your youthful advantages are obvious. This stage of acceptance has flowed into areas of others who always deny the obvious. UFOs are part of this obviousness to be reconciled with your thoughts of acceptance.

"This form of deliberateness (a UFO) takes on an area of firmness for a reconcilable union with that thought, thus eliminating any pressure on the mind to draw a configuration. Its own appendages are seen through the eyes of a mortal being who also draws mortal qualities from another period. This interlocking has a valuable key and is explained as a partial relinkage to a present/past/future time period. As a mortal, the observer will see himself evolving as a witness to his own presence. He will seek to destroy this unidentified image in his mind and fear its own reality.

"As it (a UFO) begins to transform itself into a solid mass, it will carpet the mortal's object. Becoming placid will help to remove any tremors of fear. These people (observers) who use these objects of time release will always evolve together. They are interrupted by needed pursual to recreate an image that was once lost.

Probing with Some Age-Old Questions

"Reasonable reactions towards this interlocking will remain a secret for each soul to achieve in its time of goals and thus remaining a clue for our own future.

"UFOs will always be around. As your spirits become evolved to a point of lessons, always be sure to use their (the lessons) material, as a purpose is critical for further growth and development in an odd situation. While appraising these magnificent objects through spiritual means, you will develop an area of righteousness that demands a promising return.

"Objects of identity always serve external purposes, but outside aptitude actually has never penetrated absoluteness of wisdom. Periods of unseen forms are all around your beings and yet have not become a shared physical awareness to a point of understanding. Seemingly, this is sad, but actually it is not. Your beings are not in preparation in this period for futuristic complications. However, your spirits will lead you through those times of actual visitations and increase the melody of such a relationship. Working toward a union with these prospects is inviting and should be entertained by a majority. However, your spirits (Doug and Barb) will not relate totally to identifiable patterns of thought resistance. Be sure to implicate all who derive a pleasurable attribute from searching these reasons behind the 'object.' "

Q: *Why is there so much pain, sickness and disease in the world?*

A: "When you enter a place of desirability, you maintain a circumference of vulnerability. This vulnerability permits various physical organisms to penetrate your wall, because, through this penetration, will lessons stem. As a painful experience will psychically enhance your depth of perception, so will the challenge of physical displeasure.

"Your beings are never totally adaptable to environmental situations, you see. Therefore the changes that alter your personal preservation are usually seeded to purposely interrupt the flow of life. While your changes are being transmitted through these periods (of pain and illness), you will seemingly reflect upon yourselves. Actually, this is only a crevice of time from which you will seek other guidance.

"Pain has a will that is stronger than ours to release its facets through a channel of pulsations that will themselves to become noticed and observed by all who experience their vibrations. You are surely adept to pain as a stimuli but prefer to remain on a consciously aware level of pleasure. This proposes an inadequate way of formulating your psychic vibratory state, thus allowing a false moment of truthful existence to fade throughout unpleasurable reasoning.

"Neither those that shall release their earthly tensions through the bowels of time, nor those who pleasure themselves in returning to this stance shall awaken to find a painful existence beyond their present one."

Q: *Senility in the elderly seems such a waste. Why does it occur?*

A: "Their (elderly people) oppression is maintained within themselves. Their lack of clarity is due to their own dishonesty with self and a physical reality that demands a truthful existence. Because of due course, events (physical) proceed their ways of neglectful actions, thereby disregarding all other presences that may otherwise become vivid.

"Should your own minds become wary of such negligence, be safe and adjust your paths accordingly, in order to detour this problem position. Neither acceptance through senility, nor adherence to its concepts will benefit the soul. Its importance, however, lies in the fact of rejection. This physical ailment has been placed as a welcomed sight for escapees (from life). Their tendencies to avoid natural physical sequences has enabled a method (of escape) to arise out of their fears.

"While attending a school of thought, many observe themselves in this sleep state. Wandering from their own conception, they permit their selves to dwindle as their escape seems necessary.

"Purpose unfolds as a natural cause. As a physical being changes its form, a plight for survival becomes all encompassing within that physical self. A lessening of wit derives its origin from a token of past dissolvements. A purpose of leaning toward these pasts becomes an importance to this physical reality. Designating yourself as a peaceful entity will enhance that aspect in you to a permanence, which will decrease your own fear of senility in yourselves.

"Be prepared to learn, however, that through aging, a one-time youngster will then only appear old as his mind adjusts to past incarnations and wishes to return.

"Your purpose (Doug and Barb) is altogether similar with others, only yours is enhanced through a unique spiritual system of guides, thus providing the necessary leadership that is critical to use in evaluating a person's presence and ultimate values. Your promises of less senile aging will not be brought as a comfort to many whose fear has already overwhelmed their bodies, but their minds will still react in a useful, ultimate way, thus helpfully conserving their energies and permeating their spirits with contentment. Your (Doug and Barb) understanding of this period will provide a basis of love and cooperation with fear, and your apprehensions of old age will thus be eliminated. Be your own guides of self, as you are."

Probing with Some Age-Old Questions

Q: *Why is poverty seemingly a standard condition of much of mankind?*

A: "Your adjustments to these facts are not always useful, nor easily imposed on your mind, but I will try to impress your pictorial section (of your mind) and completely surround your emotions with factual knowledge to comprehend this area of reluctance.

"Your poverty means nothing, as it reflects failure, which does not exist as an act of truth here. It only surfaces to compel those who flourish within their nature to fall before they climb. They are beyond a point of recognition with themselves, as their failures are enhanced through their repeated efforts to fail again. Their opposition to this problem existence will not suffice to enhance their position ultimately. However, their opposing position will be recognized as an act congruent with their reality.

"Beings who entertain this position of poverty are made aware that life's only goal should not be wealth or materialism. Therefore, they maintain a certain level of understanding and peace. As they share hardships with one another, they advance through karmic outlets to be installed as a permanent endeavor through that time.

"To behold a poverty-stricken group is to know of wealth in a way unseen by others. Its aptitudes are not failing, but its self-afflicting opinions are temporarily destroying their purpose of objective fulfillment.

"As your souls (Doug and Barb) turned this lifetime to choose a better financial position, so will those in poverty at a time convenient for enhancement of their own development. I actually demanded of myself a place in a poverty-stricken circumstance on my own path. Many times was I stricken with grief as I sat before others whose nourishment was less than mine. I too, however, was placed as a servant to those who enjoyed watching poverty eat through the masses.

"Your conception (Doug and Barb) of being must be altered to a higher state of realization. This will become a critical find for your work and appeasement of others. Should your relationships grow with those who may not fear their financial loss, you will begin to thoroughly comprehend my meaning.

"Poverty is merely a state which is acquired through a multi-dimensional process of learning. Through this agonizing reality (physical), apart from others, people will cope throughout actual hardships and remain anonymous to souls of a higher mortality. These periods of seeming unfairness will be lessened throughout lifetimes of riches, thus bringing the circle to a close once again.

"Your masses will be met from all angles of poverty and wealth, thus adjusting to a finer definition of creativity and life. Your mortal sense will not be decreased throughout these changes. They (your senses) will help to eliminate fear and doubt while showing a constant growth pattern. I have allowed your knowledge of wealth to become apparent for you, as your own choices will be lingering in the depths of your minds.

"While retaining the compassion for those who want and want not because of a physical outcome from poverty, these people will change. As they challenge a newer, higher existence, their willingness to increase their bodies' pleasures will also change. The likeliness of privacy for these individuals is shallow. Their existence is known and used seemingly against them. On the surface, this partition between rich and poor will display a negative reality. But, do not overlook the fact that this course has been proposed by a majority who see the challenge as a beautiful growth, thus ending all agony from its physical turmoil."

Q: *Why do earthquakes occur, often killing so many people?*

A: "Your reasons for earthquakes are yet required to become a known loss. They (earthquakes) are handled with a precise, decisive manner. While they appear to be happenstance, your purpose (Doug and Barb) in this relation, I see, is to challenge their necessity. Your beings are awake, but many are dead.

"It is not known to the people involved with earthquakes (consciously) that all of their possessions along with their lives would be destroyed. But, their purposes become self evident before their return to our plane of existence. While obtaining a purpose for their existence, they will see a physical change in their reality.

"Through a multi-dimensional experience, they learned to adjust to a promise that was made before their return to that physical place. It is through this promise that they become readjusted more easily.

"Earthquakes are only a magnification of fear which migrates through a land process. Should you waken to your fear of these experiences one day, you will then employ one another for self appraisal and hope to relinquish these thoughts. While admitting that a purpose, en masse, is there, your psychological minds will portray a much gloomier picture—a mind's rebuttal to natural truth.

"Reasons for so many people being killed always have a purpose that will come as a surprise to your actual comprehension through a network which comprises many facets of learning abilities."

Q: *Can you give us any perspectives on disasters, such as, on the recent tragedy when so many people were hurt and killed at the Hyatt Regency Hotel?* (Saint Louis—July 17, 1981. A walkway crashed onto a very crowded dancefloor.)

A: "Your adventures of life will pass by many experiences, such as this, with the one understanding that this young world will change as each evolvement purposes itself toward that direction. A period for adjustment in the remaining lives (relatives of those killed) is necessary to promote a more divine approach to one's self, as each spirit is lifted from its shell. An explanation of grief is sent by those remaining. However, in an ultimate sense, their grief is only known as spiritual growth. This multitude of people who willingly die was sent as a way to strengthen the bonds between your world and their ultimate one.

"Every 'tragedy' purposes itself for a banner of freedom. This awareness must be felt by those who are left behind to await their own rejoicement in continuing life. Our ways do not share a sadness with yours. Only through accepting this will you appear to grow. Callousness is not a part of this acceptance, as compassion for others must remain a primary concern. Through the inner knowledge of learning and adjustment will you see the souls of all who were involved as being intertwined with one another's process of growth. Shouldering a path for another soul is not intended here, but many of those remaining will sense this duty, thus responding in this way.

"Finally, let's help them cope through their own adjustments. Some who were there were also capably aware of the spiritual world, thereby helping others, comforting their physical needs, and will continue to imply that their spirits are maintained individually from their physical bodies.

"A few doctors were there who sensed a release from the physical through an ultimate experience of fear. This now will enable them to seek highly developed pathways to understanding. Your own reliving of an experience that may have affected your beings will not become overwhelming. This life has exchanged such a tragedy for others but will not have influenced your souls. Prior to this, your involvements were one of many who became such an exchange. This period was a familiar one, as for others who suffer, only remaining to grow again through their spiritual belief."

For Doug and me, those quick dips into such engrossing aspects of life were always tantalizing, but also a little uncomfortable. The disturbing side of the answers was a constant drum beat, which kept saying: "Everything happening in life is purposeful and is the result of a selection process by all the participants." This was also the continuing theme song of those more personal messages from our source. We couldn't seem to escape the idea that the individual, through his own spiritual linkages, has some ultimate responsibility for whatever takes place during his life. Intellectually, the concept fit with some of our reading, especially the Seth books. But, saying that our daily existence is a result of our own choices, perhaps totally—now that took a little thought.

Although the philosophy of the buck stopping with the individual had a definitely acceptable logic to it, only experience would forge a total acceptance for Doug and me. Oh, surfacely, in those early days of the Writings, we would say, "You create your own reality," but, it was always easier to apply that belief to the people down the street rather than to ourselves. When another disaster blared from the evening news, we began to accept the fact that those particular people involved might have selected their entanglement for some spiritual purpose. But, when the disasters hit the Dillon household, it was just plain old bad luck, or somebody else's fault. We passed the buck very neatly for a while, until finally, the intensity of our lives and the guidance from our sources forced us to look behind the events of daily existence, and to question the "coincidental" and "accidental" happenings around us.

7

Life and Afterlife as Learning Concepts

THE SUNSHINE SKYWAY BRIDGE stretching over a portion of Tampa Bay loomed before us. Roadways reached gently upward to disappear into the towering maze of steel girders at the summit. Our lane of traffic was diverted to the left-hand span of the bridge, turning what was usually a one-way flow into two-way movement. Progress became sluggish as we began the slow incline, leaving the road to our right vacant and strangely lonesome.

Brake lights flashed as Doug guided the car towards the crest of the roadway, finally bringing us to a full stop just inside the entrance to the huge metal structure. Looking toward the right, we stared at a chilling sight. Abruptly ending in the swirling sea air over Tampa Bay was the twin span of the bridge, leading nowhere. Stretching for over 1000 feet, that bridge, normally used by southbound traffic, no longer existed. The kids, minutes before, had pointed out the twisted wreckage lying on the sandy beach. But, sitting there, stalled in a line of cars, the view of that incredibly empty space to our right, forced the awesome impact of this disaster to etch itself into the family consciousness.

Several months before our trip, a barge, pushed by hurricane force winds and blinding rain, rammed the bridge. In the furious storm of that early morning, the structure collapsed, sending cars, a bus, and tons of metal crashing into the bay. More than thirty people were killed, some of them small children. If the timing had been right, we could have been among them, and we shuddered.

Closeness to catastrophe often stimulates a certain amount of introspection and questioning. We were no exception to this process, but, unlike most people, we later went to our trance communications to capture whatever explanations might be offered:

Q: *Tell us what purpose was involved in the Skyway Bridge Disaster.*
A: "Everyone has to find a play for existence in this realm. You (Doug and Barb) are too attuned to desirable ends with your lives. This purposeful circumstance will show more meaning in your time. But, be sure to weigh yourselves carefully, as each event is connected with another set of circumstances that will also be headed as 'tragic' one day.

"While your friends of life are encountering these disasters, they are playing their role as indicated prior to times onset there (in physical reality). Your feverish anxieties are still being held as a way to unravel existence. This I see as a token of myself, as I too was once exploring possibilities of death around my arms' lengths.

"You are both (Doug and Barb) being able to complete this hazard, in a form which will softly open others' ideas to history, as yours are freeing themselves now. Be quickly observant and understand that these people (bridge victims) are uniquely placed, as each has a silent marker on him in time. These (markers) help to distinguish a path for each who comes to know astounding differences in life's ways.

"Those who are closely related (relatives of the bridge victims), are a part of a mass who need ultimate understanding. These people (bridge victims), therefore are chosen to show a mass that the way of life is death.

"Shower yourselves with these thoughts as they will help to control your emotional reactions. These events are 'disastrous syringes' that penetrate the developing psyches of all on your plane. Be quietly patient and advise your peers that while these deaths were painful, that pain is lost as they (the bridge victims), are freed from their continuous efforts of being in your society of ideas and practices.

"You need to uncontrol your web now, as it has tangled your vibrations of understanding. Peace will come to those who appreciate my aggressive research from within their realm of reach.

"While accepting my ideas of death, you must also propose a solution to your own demise, as I will say that yours (Doug and Barb's) also has become a part of a plan which will end in a cycle of wonderment from others. Therefore, should you decide to answer this, your framework will become a receptacle for others to hold near."

As in many of the previous writings, the notion of intricate, spiritual purpose surrounding pain and disaster, again was laid before us. As potentially acceptable as that philosophy was in the abstract, our physical nearness to such agony and loss of life forced us to wonder if this understanding would actually help those remaining family members of the bridge catastrophe. If we were the ones facing that loss, would the pain have been any less, or would our abilities to recover somehow have been enhanced because of our knowledge? In all honesty, Doug and I just didn't have adequate answers.

The incessant harping of our trance communication about all life events being learning experiences under our own spiritual control, was a sweet and sour proposition. On the one hand, perhaps human existence wasn't as chaotic as it appeared to be on the surface. Perhaps, we do place ourselves in certain conditions for growth through a selected series of life circumstances. Instead of being awash in seas of God's wrath or being flung willy-nilly into a random universe, perhaps we were the ones driving our own vehicles of fate. But, then on the other hand, wouldn't we partially be at the mercy of some sort of unconscious design on the part of our spiritual selves? Certainly, conscious planning by the victims of the Skyway Bridge incident hadn't caused their deaths.

Back and forth we wrestled with the practicality of such a philosophy. If adopted, it would mean a certain acceptance on a daily basis of personal spiritual responsibility for every life occurrence. That in totality was still hard to swallow. In the midst of this struggle, Doug and I wondered how other people would react if given a source of information similar to ours. From that curiosity then grew a realization that possibly others could benefit from our gropings into the unknown. Millie and our own Writings hinted time and again at some organized method to share our understandings. Could a book be written about all of this?

A book? On the surface, the idea seemed a natural carryover from our extensive trance records, but its reality just hung on the edges of my mind and kept slipping off. Neither Doug nor I had any experience or training in such a literary adventure. Besides, did we really want to open our very private lives to the world at large? Periodically, those questions raised their heads until a continuous, quiet certainty covered them with the inevitability of writing such a volume. Logically, we realized that it might never be published, or even if it were, perhaps no one would read it. But, Doug and I determined that no matter what, our children, at least, would inherit a complete record of their parents' searching venture. Even by itself, the idea of a legacy for the kids was enough for us to begin drafting an outline that would take over two years to complete.

Perhaps it was that initial commitment to write this book, coupled with the Skyway Bridge episode, that brought back an even more intense focus on the aspect of practical application. For us, in Doug's terminology, it became a time to "fish or cut bait." We had been presented with a philosophy of spiritually pre-planned life events, as well as with a series of disturbing predictions from our Writings that had not yet been fulfilled. Those predictions hinted at some very unsettled times for the entire family. Early in my experiences with Automatic Writing, came this statement, "You are both assured that every single grief needs to be given to you." Added to this, at a later time came the trance messages with forecasts of: a time of upcoming troubles; illness and multiple deaths within the family; Doug leaving his long-held career in the school system; Doug being involved in a business venture; and our deepening involvement in communicating psychic understanding. What a mixed bag of information. What if it all happened? If it did, had we actually made those selections on some super-conscious level? How would we react?

At this writing, it is September, 1982, two years after our trip across the Skyway Bridge and our decision to write a book. Doug left the school system over a year ago and entered a business venture from which he has just now disengaged. After months of agonizing conflict, financial loss, and nervous exhaustion he left the business. Needless to say, our financial state is barely above water, with many family members pitching in to keep us afloat. Our son, Greg, has suffered severe allergic reactions to an unknown substance, and my father has been seriously ill. Three deaths occurred among Doug's family and mine last winter. Our house has been burglarized twice, and Greg was robbed and threatened with clubs by two boys who were later arrested.

There's a lot more, but why go into it all? Chapter Nine, "Death Experiences Viewed Differently," does, however, provide considerable insight into one small segment of that period. Physically, psychologically and financially, these events taxed us to the limit. Having those predictions finally come true in one way or another hasn't given us much cause for celebration. So, why did we know about any of it ahead of time? What good did it do? The results were the same. It was a "time of troubles" and still is, to some degree, no matter how consciously we pursue more positive aspects of living.

In the quiet times between crises, Doug and I wondered about the philosophy of events being purposely and cooperatively planned on some spiritual level. If life and all of its difficulties were supposed to be such an educational process, were we learning anything through our own sequence of adversity? Were we surviving any better because of our understanding and linkage with another realm of existence?

It has taken a lot of objective introspection, even recently, to conclude finally that the preparation and continual guidance, through the Writings, definitely helped us endure. Now, we know that understanding doesn't always protect from pain, stay the tears, or forestall poor decision making, but it does provide a sense of purpose that shortens the agony and at least partially clears the vision.

The multitude of observable, individual learning sequences that crisscrossed during the last two years makes that period appear as a complex spider web. The pains and the joys did indeed interlock, in some flowing manner, moving each of the many participants along paths of comprehension.

For Doug and me, the string of events reveals a definite pattern. First, we had to test our newly-developed belief system and the guidance from our trance communications under withering fire. Second, great amounts of material for this book came directly from that period, including the title, *An Explosion of Being—An American Family's Journey into the Psychic*. Third, Doug's separation from the school system and then from business, led to our absolute focus on the writing and publishing of this book. Interestingly enough, Parker Publishing Company offered to publish this material only two months after Doug severed his connection with his company.

A definite sense of comradeship is probably the best way to describe how Doug and I relate to trance communications. For three years, the source of this information has consistently, patiently, and with almost loving care, helped us to comprehend our own beings in relationship to more than one reality. Amazingly, in this assistance, we discovered a somewhat parallel course of development on the part of our source. In that "other realm" from which the trance material flows, there is apparently a genuine striving for improvement, understanding and knowledge. Evidently, life beyond the physical is also a learning sequence with various stages of discovery and understanding. From what we are able to piece together, this growth process is sometimes directly dependent on positive interactions with our earthly reality.

How strange to think that by working with us, our source was growing through our personal development and experiences. But such an idea consistently crept into the messages over the years. I suppose the strangeness comes from some cultural mystique that tells us that if there is a consciousness beyond the physical, it must be all wise, all knowing and complete. From what we can see, that just isn't so. It's as if someone superimposed the multiple variations of maturity in the physical world, from childhood to adulthood, on whatever realities that exist beyond this one. Consequently, Doug and I feel a sense of responsibility to "their" development as well as to our own. Each trance session then becomes a very interesting two-way street.

By now, this chapter may seem like a mish-mash to you. If so, I apologize, but there is a definite pattern that perhaps can be seen only through the trance communications themselves. As Doug and I looked at this chapter, we recognized that only by living through those messages over the past three years with us, could you really begin to grasp what has been happening. By carefully putting together selected messages, maybe we can paint a picture for you of a highly complex interchange of mutual benefit between realities.

Beginning in July of 1979 and ending August of 1982, these quotations from our records are offered to you as a chronological synopsis of a patient guidance and concern emanating from somewhere beyond our full understanding. These are some of the private communications that have served as a tranquil pool of assistance in which we have dipped many times. Again, I urge you to develop your own conclusions as you read this information. But, be aware within yourself of any subtle sense of familiarity that may seep into your mind. Look at these messages as if they were also directed to you, in relation to your current life circumstances and thought patterns. In that light, you might find your reactions as varied and interesting as we have found ours.

From the name given as Ollie, to the simple terms, "We" and "I," you will see how our source has shifted its identity from a separate personality to some sort of collective consciousness. Even when addressing us in the first person singular, look for our contact to serve apparently as spokesperson for a multitude of others, using the terms "Our," "We" and "Us."

July 5, 1979

"I will begin by telling you both that your troubles will not be of a minute nature, but, instead, large ones. So, be prepared for the worst to happen. The one way of channeling your efforts in the right direction is to be aware of these events and take them well emotionally. We will be together, so do not be afraid.

"You will be put to many tests that are of a lot that is difficult to maintain elasticity. I will be with you at all times. I want you to be prepared for the eventuality of your lives, but, I also hope that you will not run from the hurting moments. They will turn to other paths of joy at a later time, which will be hard for you to understand. I want you to believe this very much.

"You are about to become a new factor in the life of existing experience on this plane. You both have the potential to become a new form of communication for us, from this realm to yours. You will be a pole of strength in the psychic world of communication if you so desire. Be careful, but do not be afraid."

July 8, 1979

"Good day to you both. I am here with you again, in the modification of life at its best for you right now, as each step provides a surface of promise. The openness you extend to us, indeed helps to deliver the messages you will want to savor in your lives. Be joyous at that, as the everlasting impressions are here with us now. Be clearly advised that we are here to help, not to hinder your development.

"Be careful not to go too far in your rejection of us or of your acceptance. We are trying to lead you, but we are not always at a will to do this in a manner you will understand. Therefore, do not accept the concreteness of your words or thoughts to be valid at all points.

"Be continued with us. Do not let go, as we will be of great help to you both in your lives. We will be understanding and sympathetic with your lack of tolerance for us. We are here also for development in your world of existence.

"You are living in an earthly position of an intelligent force of being. I am staying here on this level as I need to be here filling the gap between you and the still life of mankind. Here is 'still life' explained. It means that which is not living. It is a form of soul transmission unto itself. Some of us are not yet at that stage of development."

July 9, 1979

"You are not going to be caught in the web of spiritualism at the level you know it to be."

July 10, 1979

(Directed to Doug and his career as a school system administrator)
"See that you are now positioned in a factory of ideas and that you are only one smokestack. You are similar to one who is chained, but not in a reality of earthly sense. You abide by the rules given you, but you do not accept the inner workings of the factory. You are set in your ways, but your ways are good. You are to use those ways in an area which will benefit people to the inner sense of development. Now, you are only helping them to be guided in a superficial way."

July 14, 1979

"You are able to perceive only what you wish to perceive. Therefore, your turmoil of this existence is affecting you. But, you are not totally responsible for such actions, as you were placed in those positions before birth.

"*You placed yourselves* in these positions. You were guided by many of us, but your final decisions were yours. The circumstances surrounding these decisions are not too clear to me. They were made when I enabled myself to be free from you.

"You are not the only ones who will prosper through my communication with you. There will be many, as you are the linkage between me and them. Their psychic abilities will come to light also, as they become aware of what you are doing with me.

"At the right time, you will see a path. If you were to see the path now, you may not accept my validity. There will be a time when your readiness will be announced by me. It will be of a purpose to inform you to move ahead to the next step. The next step is not known now, as your decisions have not been made, and further, you are not ready to make them. However, there will come a time soon, when you will have more interest in making these decisions, as the validity of my contact is impressed on your minds. You will want to share my contact with others. Know the reason I cannot answer questions now, as there will be many paths to take when the time comes. The final decision will be yours, not mine."

July 15, 1979

"You are a part of an intricate circle of souls. These souls make up the larger mass of a oneness with God. Be at a will to accept this in some way. You are accepting, but not in total awareness. Be aware of the source which is instilled in each of you. It is the same power which exists and maintains your soul. It is now partially being expressed as you communicate with me. Use that source gently, as it will be a comfort to know that many stems of energy will prevail in your future as you and Doug pursue this field more thoroughly."

July 16, 1979

"Be cautious that you accept only the ones of us who can benefit your patterns. Otherwise, there will be other spirits who will enter without your intent to accept what they offer. That is wise, as they may only offer what you don't need. The need for ESP as you define it is not important in itself. However, many people seek this as a way to prove their own importance. You will not fall prey to spirits who are trying to convince you of your abilities, as you are already aware of them."

July 19, 1979

"I am not what you call within some of your philosophies, a Master. But, you are developing quickly and will receive an open communication from ones who deem themselves to be Masters. You are fortunate to be able to experience this occurrence in your lifetime, jointly. There will be times when both of you will be contacted by a Master in unison. This will be helpful to you, and at a later more developed stage, will provide some comfort to others. Masters will come to you and the feeling, you should know, is always manifested in a physical way. You are now being approached here at times by Masters, whom you will later recognize. They are training you for the physical transformation that you will receive in the future. While sleeping, you are both in training. Allow yourselves freedom of expansion in your beliefs, as you will then promote the Masters in their efforts to free you further."

July 23, 1979

"You are of a nature to be free. However, your ideas and thought patterns allow this to be challenging to you. You are not as free, as you place restraints on your ideas and thoughts. This will indeed be changed as you grow. You are linking such ideas and thoughts together with my projections."

July 24, 1979

"You will be allowed to travel into a form of communication which is unusual to most people. You are to explore the possibilities of psychic awareness and transfer these abilities to others. You will seek advice higher than you now know. This is inclusive of myself. You will be able to transfer part of your power to others who seek an awareness that is beneficial to their individual paths. It will be your responsibility to seek out these people and help them."

July 31, 1979

"You have many abilities to perceive us in your dream state. We are only as accessible to you as you will permit us to be. We have powers which go beyond yours, but they cannot always penetrate the stubbornness of the mind to relinquish all physical attachments. The openings to which we are ever hopeful, occur when you both have reached a peak state of being within your communication range. This happens only if your receptivity is clear. However, if your body is tired, then we must make preparation for refreshment. This occurs in a sleep state which takes our own level of concentration to be able to form the patterns of relief, to which I am speaking. You have seen these patterns (in dream images), Doug. They are representatives of trials of effort which we place before you and your powers of vision.

"You have only seen us through these patterns. We are showing you an alternative reality. This is a concept by which you are able to control thoughts through patterns. We will show you many of these patterns as you are surely impressed, aren't you, Doug?"

August 1, 1979

"You have given this choice to us, as before your present birth, we were chosen by you to be the instrument of communication for your purpose. You have begun fulfilling the agreement now, and we are pleased. This is only a part of the agreement, however, so do not feel that your task is complete. We will enter your beings for a long, future time and process our correspondence with you in command. The events which will take place are part of our union with you, as they will confirm our existence."

August 2, 1979

"We have always allowed those who seek to obtain justice (fair understandings) in your world, to reach to us for guidance. You have always been promoted as a couple who attained a high station of ideals. We are forming your future ideals, along with your own perception and conscious efforts. This will help the future, as it will indeed depend on beings who are able to transform various negatives into outright hope, and to transfuse the wrong into the right. This I understand is a matter of perception, but I am one who now has the ability to perceive that you have helped me in this area, as your abundance has been transferred, in part, to my spirit.

"We are in better communication than many who have offered themselves, but have only received verbal abuse. Our souls are one with each other in this respect. Please do not misunderstand the need I have with you. We have learned much from each other. Thus, your feelings at night, as we draw the blood of ultimate life from each others' veins. I hold your veins to be a part of me, as you have held my form to be a part of yours. You have seen me as you also have readied a form yourselves. This is not an omen, but a fact.

"We are proud of our forms and will not totally relinquish these to earthly beings. The light which prevails is a reflection of our form. This seeks acceptance, as the light holds a significance that is only remembered when man can see no other concrete being. Therefore, light is accepted as a way to transmit our form. Man has seen light to be an awareness in his religious cults, therefore, it holds a communicative device for us. We use it to formulate an awareness and acceptance of the

Life and Afterlife as Learning Concepts

naturalness of the world which lies beyond yours. We are encompassed, virtually, with your world, as you are a part of ours. Be patient and, someday, you will see it attained. But, before you do, we must prepare you for this journey. This will be an active way for you to seek your purpose. Your teaching will bring you closer to our world, and we will learn from you.

"Upon your release from us, you will find measures which will take you to worlds far beyond any writings you may have accomplished at that point. We have been selected to bring you both to our higher teachers. They will help you, as you are helping us, but, in a sense which is now beyond your comprehension."

August 3, 1979

"We will filter out the threads which prevent your growth and replace them with direct lines of communication. You will sense a growth that encompasses your entire being. Therefore, this will erode a portion of existence which will allow you to direct and channel into distinct areas of evolvement. This will transpire as your awareness becomes more acute.

"You have already begun to develop your own powers and abilities. They are streaming forth toward your ventures yet to come. We are sharing your enthusiasm as the powers develop. Have patience with yourselves, as your sense of time is lingering and is not immediate.

"You have watched yourselves participate in a circus of life. Now, this is over. You are in the arena and we are watching; not as critics, but as learning spectators. We have waited for you. Now, open your act and complete your purpose.

"Be cautious not to allow your own search to depend upon us. This will limit your vision as we have not encompassed all areas of growth as yet. But our teachers have traveled further and are therefore able to control their source of advice in a more organized fashion."

August 5, 1979

"You have an accordance with our beliefs, as you are our own sense of immortality. You have an awareness far beyond ones that hold the key to our development. By this, I am saying that in your visits with us, our development is apparent. But, you have yet to find the key to your own development. We have lost a part of knowledge which is now being replaced by your efforts."

August 6, 1979

"We hope you are aware of the places you have passed, as are we. This is vital for your growth. Those who encounter experience and never look back are facing an unfortunate reality to come. This alleviates all tension, as the past has shown its path and must be annointed by respect. If you have lost respect for the past, then you will not attain the future's assignments as they are intended."

August 7, 1979

"You have established a pattern which is not unlike our own. We have learned that our ways of life were not always beneficial to our souls. This was difficult for our perception at the times designated for our earthly survivals. However, now we are coming upon future alternatives and will establish a desire to use these lessons in a changed way on earth, when our time to be reborn is near. This has not been designated for us as yet. We feel that our learning here has much to offer both of you and, of course, ourselves. Hopefully, your correspondence will ordain the right for us to promote a stability within our nature that was never there before."

August 8, 1979

"You have been a beautiful couple to work with, but I am not to be your sole advisor any longer. We, ourselves, will branch out and you must do the same. The openings are coming your way fluently, so take advantage of them. Do not misuse your own souls, however, as you will not find all of the proposed answers. All of your questions will be answered, but not simply by your earthly requirements now. The answers will not always satisfy your needs to curtail the questioning, but soon you will learn to adopt new ways of proposing the questions."

August 10, 1979

"You both have challenged the realms of possibilities and are reaching toward a goal which is slowly surfacing. I admit that my soul is not ready for such a venture. You will seek a higher plane soon, as my plane is beginning to become boring to you. Do not feel amiss with this information, as the course of advancement depends on such changes. We will be here together, for a while longer, but the change is coming soon and your preparation will be an intricate piece of your puzzle which will allow this learning to be recognized.

"We are your friends and guides. We go to school, as do you, on this level and obtain information from those who teach and are beyond our knowledge. There are forms here that also teach the teachers, as you are so used to dealing with, Doug. The levels divide themselves through the schools; as each school has its own level, each level has its own school.

"You are awaiting your next step with a guide who is a teacher like

Millie. This guide will be beyond us and will formulate your plan to reach a higher point of contact. I will no longer be with you at this final point of contact, as when a Master guides you, the place for me is lost. I, of course, will try to follow your travels and therefore change my present perception, but I hold little faith that my course will follow you into that realm.

"We have no direct control over the earthly details which seem to bind you. This is not our realm of problems. You must deal with these in due course, as they raise their heads.

"I am set to awaken your souls to a reality that only exists as you deem it to. Have patience with your mind, as it is the seat of the soul and you will find much stored there which will help your future to unfold. Be careful not to jump ahead rapidly, as you both tend to want. This is not meant as a warning, but only as a friendly plea of concern."

August 13, 1979

"Take time to reflect upon your own relationship as one which has only begun to unfold. This is the beauty of a twin spirit, as time is its master on earth and each petal will only open when readied by the soul. You are both now ready to open a new petal. Allow this process to develop in your mind and it will repeat itself many times."

August 15, 1979

"You are both willing to challenge many people and their inborn decisions against accepting us. This will not create as many 'friendships' as would appeal to your natures. However, the friends that you will make will help to spread this work as an ocean spreads its waves upon the beach. Allow these friends to perpetrate their desires upon you, as they will grow from their experiences."

August 16, 1979

"Believe yourselves, as the self is crucial to existence. Without belief in self, one cannot function, as he has lessons to learn that are only partial, and have not succeeded in meeting the whole."

August 18, 1979

"You have observed that all of our understanding is not on your level but does pertain partially to your level. This is due to the last embodiment that was discovered by our beliefs, and the effects have not been totally reduced as yet. We are looking toward a day when we can absolve all earthly attachments and place an honor of higher systems in our paths. This will eventually happen to you also, and it will seem that you are constantly plagued by inner revelations. This is a course of study which enables you to maintain the level of desires that must accommodate you before you will turn to us and completely accept our knowledge as your own."

August 19, 1979

"Within each entity is a portion of energy which alternates between this realm and yours. We have watched this portion become increasingly influential to your existence. Be careful not to acquire a form which will only find a release for energy, as this will not be purposeful. Energy itself, is composed of matter which injects a force beyond control of any known quantity. Without energy, we would not function, as it is the base of our formation here. We are aware through our energy, we comprise the ability to change our environments."

August 25, 1979

"Ollie has erupted, so behave as you would under volcanic conditions. We are now attending a conference of ideas and have purposely set forth ways of incorporation. We will seek to allow former representatives of areas unknown to you to belong with our group. They will obtain our area which will manifest important tasks. They shall uncover new ideas and forms of life.

"You are a part of our conference as we are unfolding you all together. I will oppose any spirit who enters our realm without due consultation efforts prior to our gathering. We will seek to share all that arrives before us as you have sensed a need for expansion with our presence.

"Stakes of high ideals will now serve both of you instead of your serving them. They have begun to unfold before your nature and have penetrated every ounce of your spirits' knowledge. We are waiting for your translation of these ideas to become effective soon, as we develop our paths further.

August 30, 1979

"You, Doug, are to be a facilitator in another world of communication, such that would not be accepted by many of your colleagues (in the school system) now. You will not lose sight of what you wanted in your teaching career. It will be better as you are away from it. It will take a different form as you progress in your psychic training. Your field of teaching will not go unnoticed. You will be able to perform for others in a similar role. However, it will not be at a factory (school system) as it is now. You will respond to ideas, thoughts and manifestations of your nind. This will become more transparent as you get closer to the time of change in both of you.

"The earthly decisions, again, are yours to make, not mine. I am only aware of what they will be."

September 7, 1979

"As we are all around you both, you are sent a barrage of messages. Each will be deciphered as Barbara picks up other vibrations as well. This has not always been, as she now has become transformed to another level of a receptive channel and will hold this for a long time. I have begun challenging her efforts and have placed my values within her. I will allow many openings for her verbal commitments."

September 8, 1979

"I await your decision to enhance my being. As you come forth with various new ideas that are well received here, I shall acknowledge them as being my own and therefore place them in a proper perspective. Acknowledge also, your own potential as you become increasingly efficient in our communication. As I observe your needs, I also assess your desirable results as I do my own. Your negativity, at times, influences my sense of direction toward your attaining accurate information. Due to this perspective, I wish you to re-evaluate your own surface needs as opposed to mine.

"You are surely aware that our level of response partially depends on yours. We have long since become knowledgeable that you are aspiring to a higher level of refinement. This causes our purpose to be constantly enhanced, as through your eyes, we will function more acutely as time progresses for you both.

"As our concern for one another here develops, our insight of your world is also broadening.

"As I appear, your beings call to me, for as your guide, you seek to employ my strength as a power in this world. We will meet and have a power source between us which happens to form the shape of a starlit evening and expresses a wideness of time in alliance with our thoughts."

September 10, 1979

(To Doug)
"A friend will contact you for an offer to work with him. You will be called by him at a time when it seems most appropriate. He is not aware now what that time will be, but the future work will allow his time to prepare for you to come into his existing field of work.

"You will be partners with this man in a business venture which will prove very different than what you are now doing. This will come as a surprise to you and will be unexpected on your part. Your souls are old friends and are awaiting to be joined at a point of altered consciousness."

September 26, 1979

"As you are attuned to me, find yourselves at peace, as in my spirit, I adorn your affection. Within reach, lies a cautious pattern of unfoldment."

October 14, 1979

"Your values are needed now in order to establish certain decisions which are due to be made. If you seek to reopen all paths of memory, then your next steps are going to show valuable assets in obtaining a present course. Watch for your needs to unravel and fall behind other cares, as while we are entertaining your new ways, we have needed to substantiate efforts which are not always open. But, you are again returning, and we are glad.

"You recall our various transmissions because our anticipation has increased and our union is solidified whereby we accelerate when your cause allows the freedom to move beyond windows of silence and spoken words. Searching has now become no longer unique to you, as through your telepathic powers, we are sending you wide angles of our stages and have no longer welcomed an ongoing resistance from you."

October 28, 1979

"As you seek to find ways of developing, care should be taken to avoid ways which provide discomfort of thought, as progressive detail will fall gently into an open correspondence of enrichment. Your abiding care will offer a redemptive opening for us, so be patient as your newly developed ideas are only babes, as your culture has not offered acceptance yet. Awaken to this quickly, as while your newly developed assets are strong, they have barbs which will cause conflict."

November 16, 1979

"You are now opening a new plateau of a realm which leads to ways of attainment and options which are seemingly unlimited to your purpose. Our explanations are becoming increasingly powerful.

"Acorns are part of a tree which abounds itself to place a future with outside surroundings. They are yearly drifts which provide opportunity for further development. I also will provide such development, as your beings are drawn from within our circle. This shall supply outstanding efforts and thus abilities will increase a thousandfold from their present stance. Should your discouragement be light, I will applaud, as this will furnish a further linkage toward our own release here."

December 2, 1979

"Act as a consultant to your own persons. Don't remain on an active course that will follow active people that control others beyond their own paths. This will stifle a great deal of a promising adventure, as you are both beginning to embark."

December 9, 1979

"Weed not through your changes, as they are all necessary. This allowance will considerably challenge an area of circumstances that will arise for further discovery. Observe that you both are now accepted by a new road of developers. This shall influence your future as a pair of well developed psychics, but do not allow hesitation to follow your advice as such will only instill fearful regrets."

April 12, 1980

"You will both surely welcome our responsibilities to your attitudes and goals. We shall relieve all that has since promised actual response to your questions. Satisfied that your willingness is showing continuance, see our time has begun to nourish your breaths of freedom.

"We are with you as a group instead of a party of individual recognition. Yet, as we are clearly observing you both, your knowledge of us will appear soon to be fulfilled as an entity of great concern and passion. Keep and maintain that which will open your following. We should listen closely to your allotted decree, as you are both welcome sights to us again (after such a long absence during a time of sickness and spiritual confusion).

"Quickly remember, that your responsibilities are ever greater than are your demands. While we are one, we have control of our group. As a group, we naturally control each other. Wait for future avenues of departure before your stones are overturned for recognition. Be quiet and observe us, though your own familiar planes are incorporated with your presence.

"Should you maintain that our presence be liquidated, then follow an oath of remembrance toward your past. Be calm and careful as your plight continues to grow. *Weakness will only destroy your future ways of mind and soul.* While we are here, be kind and thoughtful with yourselves, as though your soul was open to us constantly. Will yourselves a free mind to respond quickly as one. Your aspirations are high."

May 1, 1980

"An author (in the spiritual realms) has already usefully attached himself to your work (writing books). We are astounding you by means of acceptance. As this occurs more readily, your evaluation of thought will come about quickly. Be quietly absorbent and retain this information again as an integral part of your books. They (the books) are now being recited to your minds' eyes. These and others will flow greatly, and as a term to be discovered, we will always be with you.

"Don't let us down or find your own purpose is dissatisfied with itself. Be unified in thoughts about your book and measure its wisdom through the channels meant to incorporate others' understandings also. Be sure to eliminate doubt, as this destructive force will quickly work to control your book and therefore your thoughts of reality. Be quiet and remain interested in our work as well as your own."

May 8, 1980

"Your book will become a most critical portion of communication between levels (of reality). This, you see, shall open all ways of becoming a more involved spiritual ideal.

"If you propose that we are able to welcome others, then be still and assure your readers that all has to be attained as a newness for future realities to become apparent. If, however, you see that your index of ideas has now a certain look of despair due to inadequate supplies, then don't be afraid as you will surely find avenues of thought which are yet unopened.

"Awaken your wisdom and knowledge. Know that you are becoming a spirit of wise choice for all to implicate us in a pattern which no one has surrounded with love before your commital of our world with yours. Be calm, Doug, and understand that your work has now regained an abundance of strength and identity. *Be sure of this.*"

May 11, 1980

"Weed out that which destroys ableness of mind, as these powers are not to control but to accept, teach and dwell among the many who desire the creativity which flows from within your hearts.

"Wisdom will spring into a new flower bed of realization, for your patronage of spirit has taken on a form of merry surroundings that welcome any challengeable efforts from others. If you describe that which plays a more important part to your mind than ours, be content and wise as the flow shall congeal that necessary equivalent to mold our pathways together.

"Do not despair, for further readings are available from within your own makeup, rather than performing for others' sakes. Be quiet and observe your own foundation, as this will survive and flourish into a melting pot for others' awareness avenues. Should you develop an actual contact with our guides, then be assured that you, too, will be needed to follow upon them to meet required standards of verbal commitment.

"We have hopes that your patterns are changing admirably. See our opinions corrected, as primary understanding developed through a period of negotiations, lasting through your births. When we decided to re-open this caliber of thought, you welcomed all that was contained from our world. This has therefore helped to funnel any challenging desires which are now forming a pattern within your oneness of thought.

"Be still and listen to our pleas. Don't hesitate to ask us for further understanding, as we are needed by others also, and will give that which sees a beneficial reason for thought forms converted to future encounters with our realms to enhance this communication of ours. We, then, you see, will have a fourth representative of communication that will in turn entice us for future study of behavior here, for our world has not yet been completed satisfactorily by us either. We are challenging your efforts, as you must challenge ours. Wise is the spirit which attracts philosophy, as through this avenue, you will begin a search to establish a greater need from within the body's mind."

June 6, 1980

"Your souls are attuned to outer wisdom through extra perceptive observations that are compiled of thoroughness, through your minds' reachings. Wisdom shall reflect that obvious course of handling others' influences through your vibronic state of being. The wisdom of earth's recollections are a part of yours also.

"I have allowed your paths to lead to a spot for developmental reincarnative purposes. We wish to announce your frankly observational powers to your previous observers. Be kind to your observers, as they have knowledge that will affect all that influences this writing at periods when an undertaking of mind necessitates recapping the obvious with knowledgeable thought, through wise choices of ideas.

"Calmness of mind will always enable your thought to become a more concentrated effort toward rebinding beliefs, as we create particles of ideas to entwine with themselves. Be calm. Try not to absorb your own thoughts while delivering mine. Be sure to negate every item that has conquest as its purposeful placement.

"You are to learn that while we have formed a union of identity, this, too, has begun a wide range of expectancy from your readers. We are thoroughly invited by your willingness to create a pattern for us to follow, as each of us here has a need to flourish beyond our efforts on this realm. While you are undertaking the inevitable ways of life, you are also gaining a posture from which to explore every outside crevice in each others' thoughts. Be quiet and watch as these happenings occur."

July 12, 1980

"We are useful only to others who welcome our insights as authentic ways of reaching the higher parts of their own selves."

July 28, 1980

"Why do you observe me as an entity beyond, when your entities are level with mine? Your aptitudes are just as equalized in their spectrums as are those who also stand beside me now. Though your materialization is evident, theirs cannot be reached right now, by your efforts. They want to behold your promises as their own, thereby swarming relentlessly around your beings. In contact with us, you will seek a higher plane. This, my friends, is our higher plane. As you seek to destroy lower levels of self, we derive a pleasure in obtaining a wisdom from every level. Your levels are there for our learning, and your destruction of these has permitted openings for us to behold.

"Unnamed, my spirit must remain firmly anonymous. To this, I add, that your names are showing actual importance as your soul adjusts to its present course. Your plea of knowing me will come as a certain effort to maintain a structural image. This will sense another need for an image to place a rather constricting name toward an entity of many names. Bless your indulgence of our clarity as we represent a million thought patterns."

August 2, 1980

"Your works (books) will accentuate the market for educational benefits to be supplied for many, many people. They are waiting for your benefits to penetrate their worlds and your books will supply a beginning step for their worlds to be nourished. I will publish these works in my way; contact through aspect observation, thus promoting through spiritual reaction. You will, therefore, be proud of the reaction that stirs people to continue their own independence."

August 3, 1980

"Welcome. Your arrival again is a pleasurable contact. I allow our time to be reconcilable with yours, thus permitting a joint communication unlike your own. Weaken your strengths of character, as they are sometimes false. Their avenue of purpose shall not be merely a self-fulfilling prophecy, but will spawn other levels of characteristics for you to observe. Be there as a willing subject, watching yourselves grow. I do!"

August 24, 1980

"Your openings will come as your work progresses toward helping others. They will not seek your help outwardly, but they will advance in

Life and Afterlife as Learning Concepts

your direction through their choice of a spiritual nature. We will help to promise them that their place will be assured of this enhancement. They will weigh a part of your messages, yet obtain little value surfacely. They are encumbered with much pain of thought. Actual replacement of this thought will depend on their own efforts of adjustment, not yours. Your help will decide a possibility for those few whose ears are open for such illumination. Watch their wistful eyes."

August 31, 1980

"Because of your abilities to show others of our world, your plan will come as your intentions desire their birth."

October 12, 1980

"Your abilities to comprehend our world are a comforting presence for us to relate our woes and triumphs. Be aware that your adjustment has enabled us to visualize a further way to mobilize our desires of enhancement here. Your abilities, therefore, are a source of our encouragement."

October 26, 1980

"Your purposes, Doug, will be revealed, therefore combining an interest within a soul's searching process. This tabloid of adventure will begin as a mirror to your past. As I speak, there is a 'cattleman' who will rustle your thoughts into a corporate adventure for his own learning process.

"Your books will provide a suitable course for your return to this embodiment. Our sources are interested in the promoting of this lovely material."

November 7, 1980

"Your publisher (of your books) has not yet received a purpose for his objective to merge with yours, but shall evolve with you as a particle in your purpose. Your airing of views will come as a surprise to your publisher, as he will wish to narrate the prominence of this book. Your pleasure will come as a part of his wisdom will flow into yours, thereby comforting any flaws. A publisher will respond to your request for more advice from his level. Be self-adjusting to this criticism and thankful that he is a polisher."

November 15, 1980

"Be aware that your future has leaned into an open field of color. I will undoubtedly be there to welcome your passages and thus create a new media for you to verbalize within.

"I will watch you further grow and manipulate your wisdom into a cherished pattern for all who wish control of their lives. You will not suffer from this tyranny of past pleasures but will have gathered ultimate understanding from your failures."

November 22, 1980

"Be pliable, and you will adjust quickly. Be sure of yourselves and you will lie awake, unfearful. While your turn is beginning to unravel itself, be at a will to open your minds, for I shall continue to play a dramatic role in your lives. Be aware that I will always remain with you. Your Master has approached me and waved me onward toward your future goals, thereby eliminating any possibility of other outside intervention. You are weaving a pattern that won't be interrupted. We will support your ideas and mature your thoughts."

November 24, 1980

"Our access to your lives has become increasingly strengthened. Your sources for this material are never to be apart from your soul's optional contract."

January 17, 1981

"Be calm. You will not pass this way again. Our paths will be advancing in the direct future. Your avenues are not young. They are well-learned and experienced in this area. The final contact is through outside forces. These forces will change throughout your experience as they become more developed. Your wisdom shall maintain a full balance of nature while attempting to step upon new territory. Be swift to neglect nothing that has already approached before your developing eyes.

"Your attempts to penetrate our avenues of fortune are yielding a great net for your private catch. Be sure to obliterate nothing. We shall work with your comfort, so that in turn, you will receive more valid information. My station is not permanent, you see, as I will await for your arrival at the next step that will be taken by yourselves."

January 18, 1981

"Your past faith was not always as reunited with us as this lifetime seems to be. Your willingness to recover from this error in judgment is pleasing and will prepare the way for future compatibilities with our guides. Your luncheon has just begun."

February 22, 1981

"Surviving through a period of turmoil, you have enveloped a multitude of reasoning powers."

February 27, 1981

"Be quick, yet calm to deliver these messages amongst crowds of others who attain a spiritual awareness of self.

"Your avenue of insight has become a stepping-stone for further attainment. Your power is reached through an insertive system which provides an avenue of linkage to a greater existence than heretofore known. Your possibilities of lifely acquirements are pyramiding toward an open scale."

April 19, 1981

"Be kind to yourselves and wonder not where you are going, but from where you came. Your aptitudes have created your present as they will also create your past."

May 18, 1981

"Following the flow of pages from beyond your current level of sight, you will seek to draw in the publishers (for your books). These individuals have played a part in your efforts for a purpose also. Their accompaniment through time will wait as a pleasurable expectancy.

"Your books will indeed play a prominent role in the lives and creative abilities of many others."

July 19, 1981

"Love yourselves as I will always love you and cherish your ultimate souls as your final beings. They will emit more energy than you are aware of now, but do not rely totally on this, for they are also guides for your physical bodies."

August 2, 1981

"Wise use of tenderness gives examples to the living, that our concrete purpose of being is to love and explore the senses that love shares with others. Should you all become a part of intricate love, your values open themselves unto a sea of possibilities."

October 18, 1981

"Sending waves of reality toward your level is not always a challenging effort. However, your values are seen as an indication of what messages may be released. Your values, therefore, are used as an indicator point to seek a correct flow of operating information from one point to another."

January 1, 1982

"You are not travelers of woe, but will direct a teaching seminar for those whose hopes are dwindling and are in need of repair."

January 31, 1982

"As you publish each of your books, your own needs will lessen. Be still and acquire much forethought of purpose. As a pastime of purpose, saturate your minds with this purpose of publication so as to fit others' needs into your private lifestyle.

"Be conscientious, and your books will flourish publicly."

March 21, 1982

"My love for you is not a spectrum of life, but it shows clearly the facts of all that exists from within one another.

"Your acceptance of our work will be included in a most deeply described futuristic setting. The abilities of your realm are hereby enhanced through your spirit's limitations. But, this is not less understandable. Actually, because you each conceptualize a problem, the spiritual entities here are absorbed through their own means to see why the soul's learning process at times becomes tedious. Your positions will help them to clarify their questions and absorption will then take place."

April 3, 1982

"Finalize your work as a direct passion of your arrival in this life. Your spiritual connections are leveling themselves to a direct point of reconnection, so as to perpetually stabilize your entities. Becoming yourselves has not been an easy course for any who undertake it as thoroughly as your own beings have.

"Your work (business venture), Doug, will lessen its load as your spiritual penetration involves itself more deeply within your being. This will help to accurately define a position by which you are needed now. As your pressure develops, its accuracy will show itself as a position of learning. If you persist in actual advancement of thoughts, you will surely find an avenue that takes your work through active spiritual lessons.

"I will act at times as an observer for your rambling thoughts. Direct me

Life and Afterlife as Learning Concepts

as you would them, as I will complete the answers only as you may need them for your growth period to be enhanced."

April 25, 1982

"Searching within will become one of the family's most intricate relationships. This bonding shall serve as a nuance for overtures of peace within many homes. Be still and enjoy the responsibility that you have both placed within your own reach.

May 1, 1982

"You will renounce your business efforts, Doug, after a period takes place whereby your own recognition of trials seems insurmountable.

"Your receptivity has enabled us to channel your truer natures, thus creating a fuller experience not only for your beings, but also for your readers to follow."

May 9, 1982

"When you (Barb and Doug) are masters of your own fate, your abilities will certainly increase. Be as cautious as an animal on a limb, but do not reach beyond its current growth. The course of action that you will take shall open to many."

May 22, 1982

"As you both finalize a present stage of your core existence, be open to sustaining yourselves through the negativity that surrounds you both, now. Your valor is no longer an optional trait, as you both explore the unknown.

"Your gift (expanded awareness) is being calculated not only through your own devices, but also here, has left a mark directly upon your soul and we who are working together with you, through your efforts, thus maintaining a seed from which a plant will thrive.

"A purpose that you will teach, actually surrounds the events that your souls are enduring now."

May 23, 1982

"Your aptitude will serve as a wedge against financial destruction. Surround yourselves with comforting thoughts, as they will help you to thrive throughout this trial period.

"Your trend has now turned and will begin promoting itself through another path. As your soul takes a form of outer body experiences, it will then define more clearly the entire pathway to which you will adjust."

May 26, 1982

"The avenues, of which I have spoken before, are now ever clearer as you both are at the entrance to existence in a truer form. The records have been exposed in order for your knowledge of experience to be duly increased. Every particle of sound will permeate your beings, thus creating the base platform for future promotions of thoughts and ideas. These platforms will hold many new ideas that are only a stage of expression now *for others* to follow and admit within themselves.

"Your willingness to receive and transmit our messages is clearly evident. Thank you and good luck."

June 19, 1982

"You are delving into an unknown reality that actually is known, far better than your own. You are two alone, who emerge into other realities calmly and comfortably."

July 7, 1982

"Be calm (Doug) and adjust to your loss (business) as a temporary one. Be self-adjusting, as a period will fly through this barrier quickly and softly. A temporary learning pain will therefore adjust itself to farther outcries for help of your own nature on different levels. Be courteous to yourself. Be quick to spew self-evidence into a way of being kind to you. As you love yourself, you will be furthered as a wise person who deplores any further negative constitution to hold down further spiritual attainment."

August 6, 1982

"As your books are entered into a giant area of interest, be aware that while they are being incorporated, they will serve as a pliable force in your life."

8

Children—Colleagues in Awareness

BLUE JAYS AND GRACKLES occasionally break into my thought patterns with bursts of irritation, as they quarrel outside the window. It's early on a typically bright Florida morning, and from my favorite writing position in the living room, I can look through the sliding glass doors in to the back yard. Squirrels are playing on the patio, and hungry birds swoop over the badminton net, sagging with its load of dew not yet evaporated by the rising sun. Greg is off to school, but Barb and Nicole are still sleeping. They certainly need the rest. It's been a long bout with a stubborn childhood virus, and only now does Nicole's fever seem to be broken.

So, here I sit, Indian fashion, in front of the coffee table, with papers, pencils, and folders littered everywhere. The fish tank bubbles softly against the opposite wall, and the graceful Silver Veil angel fish peer through the glass as if to say, "O.K., if you're going to write your chapter, then get on with it." But, where do I start? There's so little written about children and their psychic abilities that I have no real precedents to go by. The bookcase next to the fish tank contains over 100 volumes relating to the psychic, and only one addresses young people and their abilities.

It's been six years since Barb and I made our pact to uncover what we could of the nature of existence and to share whatever evolved with our children. In those days just before visiting Williamsburg, we had absolutely no conception of what would develop, but one thing was certain; the kids would be a part of it. Looking back, I suppose we viewed ourselves as their eventual spiritual teachers, the way many parents do, but little did we realize that the kids were also to instruct us in unimaginable ways. Through their own unique experiences and connections with boundless realities, we would learn from our children lessons of magnitude and beauty. For our family, adulthood and childhood now merge at times, and we become companions walking arm in arm down a path of mutual amazement.

Hints that children could have their own spiritual linkages came early in the game when Fred and Greg startled us with Ouija messages from my father. Then, Nicole's outright demonstration of innate psychic ability through continuous out-of-body trips to our bed crystalized a recognition that beneath the surface of young minds and bodies may lie incalculable depths of being. In explaining Nicole's journeys, Millie referred to this depth, and Ollie's explanation seemed to confirm it:

> "She (Nicole) will learn much from you, as you already have learned from her. She will show you, spiritually, the ways of further development as she progresses in earthly time. The time is not going to be long from now, as she is already a highly developed soul. Go to your child and see her as she is."

A highly developed soul? Our commitment to teach the kids began to take on a different meaning right then and there. A highly developed soul? If that were true, wouldn't whatever instruction we gave Nicole just be releasing parts of a vast reservoir of some infinite maturity? If that were true, was it the same for the boys? If it were the same for the boys, could it apply to all other children? As the questions multiplied, from our Writings came further information:

> "Children are a vehicle for your learning, as they witness the transgressions of others who are larger than themselves. They wait for your witness of their experiences and errors. Learning from them is most valuable for your spirits' growth. As children, they must forgive the parent for neglect, but accept the parental love as a tribute to their lives. Your positions as parents are thus established as prime motivators, and although you may see a rebellious attitude as failure, learning has become a product of those episodes.
>
> "Your children are actually young, yet very old spirits."

With those words, long forgotten portions of my own childhood snapped into vivid recollection. Of course! Maybe if my parents had better understood this concept, then I wouldn't have shut out those experiences for so many years. Maybe, if my parents had had this same knowledge and had applied it, I would now possess a rich early background of experiences, abilities and understandings.

One by one, some of those forgotten events paraded before my inner vision, as if I were reliving portions of my childhood.

Memory 1

"I'm three years old. I like morning time 'cause I almost always wake up before Mommy and Daddy. It's fun, cause I can lay in bed and play with my friends. Most of 'em are little. They just float in the air and go away into the wall. I can't catch 'em. They're just little animals and trucks 'n things. Sometimes they're just a bunch of pretty colors. They go 'way when I get up. I don't talk to Mommy and Daddy 'bout 'em any more 'cause they say I'm dreamin. They say they're not there, but I know they are 'n it's still fun."

Memory 2

"I'm scared. I'm so afraid. I'm six and I shouldn't cry but that dream was so bad. Mom came in and said it's O.K., but it's not. It was so real. The swimming pool was inside. Are pools inside? Oh, I was so scared. Dad and I were swimming, and then we were on the side of the pool but Dad was laying down on his back. He wasn't moving, and his eyes just stared at the ceiling. That's when I got scared. I shouldn't cry, but I still can't help it. When I looked at his eyes I heard this sound. It came from all parts of him. It got louder and louder, and I screamed 'cause Daddy was dead! But. . . how could my Daddy be dead? Is my Daddy going to die? When people die . . . are their eyes open?"

Memory 3

"Why can't anybody else see it? Am I just going nuts? Can you go nuts at fourteen? There it is again in the snow. Yup, same old thing. The street light is behind me and my shadow stands in the snow on the field below the road. Look at that! It's always there. All around the shadow, that band of white light. It must be some kind of natural thing, but when I brought Dad and my friends here last night, they couldn't see it. They must be right. My eyes just play tricks on me so forget it. It's not really there."

Each of these events shimmered before me with their own individually, iridescent realities. Of no great importance at the time they occurred, perhaps, but now they stood there, demanding recognition as evidence of what we were being told in the Writings. These were living, personal messages out of my past to help Barb and me shape a solid framework of psychic reference to which neither my parents, nor hers had any access. Our parents simply did not know. Now, the understanding had been born within us, and it became our responsibility to act upon it, but how?

In the full recognition of our responsibility to the kids came the parallel awareness that our development was somehow intricately mixed with theirs. We all seemed interwoven with each other's unseen patterns of existence, with the role of instructor being shared by everyone. Through the kids, Barb and I would learn and grow, just as they would, through us. In that conceptual light, we began to consider our children as colleagues on certain ultimate levels, bursting with their own inner, but unconscious, capacities.

But, again, how could we act on this understanding effectively? How could we begin to implement working with the children without overwhelming, short-circuiting, or frightening? Children are still children in their conscious life roles. You can't barge in with great revelations, expecting the result to be productive.

It had to be handled very delicately. Taking it slow and easy was a beginning answer. Indicators of some sort would emerge to show us the way, we felt certain. By this time, Barb and I had learned from the Writings and from our own developmental patterns, that events have ways of sorting themselves on levels other than those of detailed conscious planning. Our very first decision, then, was to do nothing but psychologically open ourselves to the depth of our children's potential, and be prepared for whatever interactive process evolved. If nothing else, that openness, recognition and commitment, whether spoken or not, would be felt by some portion of their beings and maybe, just maybe, a primary sense of security would at least allow them the freedom of a fuller self-expression.

Barb was the first to notice an increased nonverbal rapport with both Nicole and Greg. What we had always accepted as a mother's natural sensitivity to her children seemed to double and triple. A mother's natural sensitivity? Now, there was an interesting phrase. Just what did it imply? Without the use of terms like psychic, spiritual, telepathic or precognitive, it really was society's way of gracefully accepting what existed but could not be explained. This was especially true of the male portion of society that has been conditioned to the use of logic, and away from intuitive emotionalism. The result: a grudging nod, acknowledging some mysterious female trait, followed by an immediate dismissal of its value.

What Barb was sensing was quite simple. Invariably, when she thought about Greg or Nicole, they would appear. It even got to the point that Barb, when awakening during the night, tried not to think about Nicole, because if she did, Nicole always seemed to consistently come to the bedside with some imagined complaint. I've watched time and again over the years as either Greg or Nicole emerged from their rooms saying, "Mom did you call me?" And as always, Barb would look at me, wink and say, "Yes, I was just thinking about you." A simple thing, no doubt repeated millions of times each day across the world in many other households, yet so vital in its ultimate importance.

Admittedly, I guess some of my cultural inhibitions against anyone but a mother being involved in such goings on dominated my own belief system for quite a while. Oh, telepathy was an acceptable phenomena. I could see it between Barb and the kids constantly, and she and I enjoyed a lively rapport on a nonverbal level. But, still, Barb was a woman, and she was supposed to have those kinds of connections directly with the kids, not me.

Not me, that is until I awoke with a start one night and looked at the clock. 3 A.M. It was that kind of awakening which instantly transports you from the deepest sleep to the absolute clarity of consciousness. I didn't move, but lay there wondering what could have roused me so completely. The gentle bubbling of the fish tank in the living room was the only sound, but there was still a sense of expectancy. Nothing happened, but something was definitely about to happen. That's what it was. I could feel it hanging heavily in the air, as if it would drop any minute.

Lying there in the darkness, I analyzed the sensation of expectancy for an instant before the familiarity hit me. On those occasions at night, when I could feel Nicole on the bed in an out-of-body condition, the sensation that preceded each encounter was the same as I was feeling at that moment. Within seconds, light footsteps on the carpet stopped at the foot of the bed. O.K., I thought, are you really there, or are you flitting around again, out-of-body? With that, my arm began to tingle. It was as if a physical imprint were purposely being made, but why? Again, within seconds, Nikki started to cry in her room. Jumping out of bed, I found her feverish and coughing. Then things began to make sense.

Time out! Against the logical rules of literary presentation, I have to break into the flow of this chapter, to share an experience that just occurred while I was writing the previous paragraph. It's 1:30 A.M., Barb is typing another chapter in the study as I work here in the living room where I began this morning. When I got to the point in the previous paragraph describing Nicole at the foot of the bed, all electrical power in the house diminished to about three-quarters of its normal capacity. Both Barb and I could see it in the lights and hear it in fluctuation of our central air conditioning system. When it happened, I looked around, because the dimming was so prolonged, as opposed to the usual, quick variations in power that we usually have. Exactly at that point of restored electricity, Nicole let out a howl from her room. Rushing to see what was going on, Barb and I found that she had fallen out of bed. To us, it was fitting punctuation for a discussion about Nicole, kids, and out-of-body travels. Now, back to the planned text, where I had just finished explaining about finding Nicole sick in bed.

As if one experience with a sick child wasn't enough to convince me that I had graduated to psychic motherhood, another one recently occurred that shocked me into even further changes in perception. With Barb as the official family doctor, all those who are ailing come directly to her for help. Call it a culturally assigned role or attribute it to the history of Barb's medical family, but that's how it is in the Dillon household. Therefore, it was not at all unusual, when late one night, Greg woke Barb with some sort of physical discomfort. Closing the door to our room behind her, she took Greg to the other side of the house for doctoring. Very, very vaguely, I remember the door closing, but within seconds, I was contentedly sawing wood. Then, in the deepest sleep, I could literally see and feel Greg standing beside the bed. He looked directly at me and said, "Dad, I need your help." Completely startled, I vaulted out of bed, half asleep. Barb was gone. It was dark. No Greg. The door was shut. What was going on?

In sleepy confusion, I found Barb in Greg's room trying to ease his pain. He was in agony; excruciating headaches, vomiting—the works. When I walked in, they were both surprised. As with most teenagers, Greg likes to show old Dad how independent, detached and "together" he can be. It's a natural process, but on that night, minutes before I entered the room, Greg told Barb, "Boy, I sure wish Dad was here."

When his symptoms began to ease, I explained my experience and asked Greg how he was able to awaken me all the way from his room. He laughed and shook his head, but for another hour, the three of us sat there and explored the possibilities together. Not parents and child, but three people playing with ideas of mind and spirit. By this time in his life, through many such talks, Greg has come to understand much of his own potential. His conclusion about my dream was that it was an obvious telepathic linkage with him during his extreme pain. Sitting there listening to him hypothesize, I began to think about Nikki's nightly travels. In both circumstances, without a doubt, I had been contacted as a helping agent in a time of crisis. On the surface, this was a very practical usage of nonphysical capabilities by both parent and children. Barb even complimented me on what she said would blossom fully one day into "woman's intuition." But, below the surface, both Barb and I definitely sensed that in all such experiences with our kids, they were the teachers, and we, the students.

Reflection again on that night in Greg's room and the easy discussion of what had awakened me brings back memories of when the boys were much younger. In those early days before the development of our direct channel into alternate realities, Barb and I found a beautifully casual way of introducing the boys to their spiritual natures. At that time, Greg was nine and Fred, eleven. Somehow, during those weekends when Fred was visiting from Clearwater, the conversation invariably concerned dreams. At first, it was the old scary game of swapping nightmares, until obviously with just a little structuring from the adults, a new pattern could emerge.

It's truly incredible what you can learn from children by asking occasional questions and then sitting back, listening attentively. It's even more incredible watching that process, as it allows children to productively explore their experiences and feelings in a noncritical atmosphere. That particular communications technique, when applied to the boys' dreams, worked exceedingly well. It didn't take long for them to remember old dreams, and eventually, to develop a greater recall capacity. Bit by bit, Fred and Greg reintroduced themselves to their own inner aspects.

Greg surprised himself one morning by detailing a very complex dream: He had seen that place before. The rushing river, the plants and the high rocks were so familiar to him. The only difference was the pyramid sitting in the midst of all that nature. Never having seen this object before, he investigated and found strange writing on its face. This dream was so vivid and the writing so clear, that he reproduced on paper the same unusual symbols. Holding the paper in his hands, he told us, "In the dream, I knew what this meant but now I can't remember." With a quizzical look, he was off to school. But, a few weeks later, he shared his wonder at a very interesting, coincidental event. "We had this movie today in social studies," he started, "and it, well, it was about the Grand Canyon. I'd never seen it before. I just don't believe it, but parts of the movie were exactly like my dream: the water, the plants, rocks, everything except the pyramid. How can that happen?"

Greg's readiness was evident, and by discussing such dreams, we gently opened the possibilities for him. Now, he was ready for the idea that sleep may be his connection to other worlds, as well as a link to his subconscious. Now, he was ready to consider elementary symbolic dream interpretation, precognition and past life recall. Cautiously, during this and many other such times, we would sprinkle those conversations with answers from our own reading, our experiences and the Writings.

Although our time with Fred was always limited to occasional weekend visits, the sharing of dreams sparked within him one particular memory. His own words can best tell the story:

"You know, I've had this dream a million times, but I've never remembered it during the day until now. Brother, it's so dull. Every time it starts, I say, 'Oh no, here we go again.' I mean, it's dumb. I just seem to float on the ceiling in my room. It is borrrring!! Hour after hour, I just float up there, watching myself sleep in the bed below. Isn't that crazy?"

Again, readiness. Each dream for both boys seemed to have its unique characteristics that lead, as always, in a very casual way to possible explanations including those of a more spiritual nature. In this particular case, the dream was such a textbook description of an out-of-body experience, that all of us spent over an hour comparing those times in sleep when we could remember flying, jumping, or floating.

Our explanations, as casual as they were, definitely stayed with the boys. Each succeeding dream event would show that they had been listening and were fascinated by the possibilities. During each new discussion, there would be just a few more questions, showing the edges of curiosity. When the subject of telepathy came up, their eyes sparkled. They, too, had known what someone was about to say and both boys had seen their own mothers' uncanny abilities to know where they were, or when they were on the way home. For over a year, every time the boys got together, they tested their abilities, and ours, in mind-to-mind communication, by trying to transmit or receive mentally, colors, shapes or numbers. The results were never analyzed for conclusive proof of telepathy's existence, but the fun and the exciting thoughts of expanding one's self opened other pathways for further learning.

And so it went, even into those first months when Barb and I plunged headlong into the development of our trance communications. The boys knew we were into something, but just what, they couldn't be sure. For that matter, during the first year of the Writings, we weren't really sure either, so why get them involved? Our responses to their questions were vague references to some sort of experimentation with psychic communication, but little more. How could we explain what we didn't yet understand? It would have been unfair, and confusion could have ruined what we felt was an excellent beginning.

Then the events of one evening jolted Barb and me into rethinking our position. As Greg sat facing us during a discussion in the family room, he kept blinking his eyes and turning his head ever so slightly. Curious behavior patterns are the hallmark of the early teens, but it continued for a period of minutes. Finally, Barb asked, "What are you doing?" Greg hesitatingly explained that, in front of each of our faces, he was seeing other faces shift and change. It frightened him a little, and his blinking was an attempt to rid himself of the unwanted experience.

Our discussions on dreams and telepathy had come far enough for us to assure Greg that whatever was happening was a natural phenomena, not to be feared. Sleepily, he nodded with a yawn and said, "O.K., but I don't want to see any more." Later in the week, we asked about Greg's visions in one of our scheduled Writing sessions. From this very brief exchange, we were able to grasp a simple, but revealing explanation, that we found quite useful in helping Greg when it happened again:

Q: *Tell us about Greg seeing other faces in front of ours the other night.*

A: "Your son has struck out upon his own course of phenomena. Within his needs is a surfacing aspect which is serving him well. This has been to develop an awareness which will open his own door to future teachings here. You are helping him to see his own reflection as he has a purpose here, as do you."

It was to take well over a year from our initial contact with that identity called Ollie, before Barb and I sensed a readiness to approach the boys with our psychic explorations. Greg's visions, the boys' maturity and openness finally combined with our own developing sense of competence in what we were doing. Greg was twelve, and Fred, fourteen. Their adolescent education was about to take a new turn; Barb and I began to plan an in-depth orientation regarding our beliefs and experiences.

True, it was a carefully staged affair, but it had to be. Weeks ahead of time, Barb and I plotted precise strategies that would insure a smooth, stimulating evening for those two young men without any pressures or apprehensions. From our own casual attitudes, to the exact topics and listening techniques, we planned the atmosphere of presentation. This was probably to be the first and last encounter of exactly that nature, so it had to be as near perfect as possible. If we had laid our foundation properly in the years before, and if this activity went as we hoped, the boys' interest, openness and perhaps even their personal experiences might be substantially increased. If we miscalculated in some way, it was doubtful that we would have a second chance.

The long weekend with Fred came quickly, too quickly. A slight feeling of uncertainty laced its way in and out of all the preparation and positive anticipation. But, as soon as we asked the boys, on the spur of the moment, if they would like to learn more about our psychic experiences, their immediate enthusiastic response melted any hesitation on our part. The timing was right, and this was going to be fun. We could all feel it in the air.

As soon as Nicole was tucked in bed, we called the boys to join us around the coffee table in the living room. Barb had prepared the snacks that often went with our relaxed family discussions in the evening by candlelight. When everyone was comfortable, from my position seated on the floor, I began to outline most of the events that appear in the first four chapters of this book. The boys were spellbound for awhile, as Barb and I shared the presentation, but before long, the questions began. Not only questions, but their beliefs, nonbeliefs, experiences and dreams not yet divulged poured into the conversation. From ghosts to mediumship, we covered the waterfront. Time slipped by at an incredible rate as the round table discussion bounced back and forth like an adult seminar. Only when someone realized that it was 3 A.M., did Barb and I return to the parental role, ordering a halt to the continued introduction of new thoughts that could have gone on all night.

It was glorious! It worked! From then on, it became standard during the weekly family night barbecue to share any new experiences, dreams or ideas on the psychic. It might last five minutes or an hour, but such talks have become an integral part of family togetherness. And, as might have been expected, the boys were intrigued with the messages flowing from Barb's trance linkage. After playing bits and pieces of tape recordings of Sandy Gibson and Mae Ward for them, the boys implored us to allow them to participate in our writing sessions from time to time. Barb wasn't sure about that kind of involvement and neither was I. She had never done a session with anyone but me, and besides, how would the messages affect the boys if directed at them individually?

By the time of Fred's next visit, after that first big discussion, Barb and I hammered out a decision allowing the boys to occasionally attend writing sessions. This final determination was based on a series of assumptions. First of all, if we kept the boys out of that experience, this could well destroy the rapport so carefully nurtured over time. Second, our source was now a proven and trusted friend. What if the boys could actually benefit from the messages? Third, the material was often complex, necessitating adult interpretation. We could then filter anything that might be questionable. Fourth, as active young people, those guys wouldn't be wanting to sit for too many hours of droning trance utterances, followed by our involved translation of the material. Fifth, Barb was finally beginning to feel comfortable with thoughts of delivering sessions with Fred and Greg present.

That eventual transition to involvement of the boys in our sessions was smooth and comfortable. Barb had no trouble moving easily into trance. With rapt attention, occasional questions, and a desire to understand, the boys proved their abilities to deal with what went on, as well as with their need to be a part of it. The logic of our decision to include the boys has been confirmed over the years, even to the point of their asking for a synopsis of anything pertaining to them, without having to actually participate. They now view our sessions and the trance information as very interesting, sometimes useful, sometimes boring and by no means gospel.

The first joint trance session served multiple purposes. On the surface, it was an introduction for the boys into what we considered a very useful method of gaining information from a nonphysical source. But, additionally, that session, and others, provided Fred and Greg with first-hand experiences in meditation and the manipulation of imagination for constructive purposes. To accomplish this, just before the session began, we introduced them to our preparatory stages for trance communications that over the years have evolved into the following:

Stage 1

Sit back, relax and close your eyes. Think of a white light cleaning out all of the thoughts in your mind.

Stage 2

Now, think about the Wekiva River where we go swimming and canoeing. See how clear the water is? We are all in a canoe heading downstream. The river is the roadway to where we are going. Help us paddle the canoe. Look around. It's a beautiful day and so quiet. The cypress trees drip the Spanish moss overhead, and the water birds feed on the shore.

Stage 3

We stop the canoe to swim for just a few minutes. It's a shallow, crystal clear pool, glittering in the sunlight. We get out and start to swim, but as we do, we turn into bright balls of light. As balls of light, we can skip across and under the water, and even fly through the trees. We have many such abilities that we never before imagined. But, now it's time to return to our physical selves and continue paddling down the river.

Stage 4

Look, just ahead! A lovely, grassy piece of land juts into the river. On it sits a huge, beautiful house. This is our psychic house. We dock our canoe, walk up the path to the front door and enter. It's warm and cozy inside. There are lots of windows that overlook the river. Shafts of sunlight come through some of those windows and shine on a wall containing many, many books set into a bookcase. In the middle of the house, so that it can be seen from every room, is a giant, glowing, tropical fish tank. It starts at the floor and goes up through the ceiling into infinity. Beautiful fish look at you through the glass; big bubbles percolate upward, and with the bubbles rise other boiling masses of white, smooth material much like that in a lava light.

Stage 5

There are many comfortable chairs around. Here, let's pull some together in front of the books. The books are full of all the knowledge that exists. Take any one you wish. There are also other people in the house visiting. See who they are. If you want to talk with any of them, go ahead.

Stage 6

Now, let's all just walk through the glass of the fish tank and swim with the coiling bouncing bubbles.

It's always at this point that Barb begins the actual trance communications, as the rest of us separate ourselves from the psychic construct. There seems to be a power in our joint preparation in this way that then propels Barb into an altered state as the rest of us watch and listen. To the boys, we simply say that, to our way of thinking, they are assisting us in establishing contact.

The concept of reincarnation and the occasional references to

Children—Colleagues in Awareness

previous lifetimes in the Writings stirred the boys' interest more than anything else. We weren't certain how useful that kind of information was, but we had to admit that it could be fascinating. Once in a while, the descriptions of a past life would include personality traits similar to ones we were exhibiting in this present life. With the boys, we would then pose questions that boiled down to something like, "O.K., if previous lifetimes existed, and if those traits are still present, what does that tell you?"

From some of those early sessions, came these excerpts about such former existences:

To Greg, November 27, 1980

"Your reminiscences of this past will become as useful as you may permit it to be, my child. Your wisdom, Greg, will increase with these messages as their influence will remain tenfold, as your mind experiences these present promotions. On your days of past lives, you were, at times, a resentful character."

To Greg, December 30, 1980

"This young man was a 'soul catcher.' He taught others how to internalize their thoughts, thus removing any demons that lay dormant in their souls. His people came from all around to watch his tricks portrayed. They came and they listened and believed. He, therefore, became a wealthy miser. He died a poor man in that life, however, after spending his money in a wave of bad luck."

To Fred, December 29, 1980

"Answers to your questions are multitudinous, Fred. They involve a multidimensional series of incarnate lives.

"You were a still maker who proposed to promote desire into lives of people who otherwise created nothing but superstitions. Their lives were drained, so your purpose was to blend a sense of your desires with their inadequacies."

About Nicole, December 29, 1980

(Delivered at our request with the boys present. To be shared with Nicole at the proper time.)

"She was a pleasant child before, but this has now created an obstacle for her growth, as she was a deliberate child, also as now, and grew into a self-serving person. Her life was eternally miserable, but her choice was made many years before. This inevitability came into existence for her soul's purpose. You (Barb) were eventually a child of hers."

To both Greg and Fred, December, 1980

"You are now awakening to the possibilities of your parents' ideals. They are fused by my thoughts, not alone, but in conjunction with their past incarnate responses. You are flowing well with our thoughts as you newly adjoin this process. However, be cautious not to abide within yourselves, but do in turn reach outward toward these passages for your own individual benefit. Prior to this knowledgeable session, you were joined by our multitude of spiritual entities who gave their utmost attention (to this session)."

To Doug and Barb with Greg present, May 3, 1981

(In response to the question, Why were Nicole and Greg born together into this life?)

"Their opportunities are given from an implanted seed, far beyond their entry to your present environment. Following each other was a way to defuse the cooperative neglect that they once formed with each other in a previous existence.

"Your (Doug and Barb's) purpose with them now is twofold. One is to act as a tongue depressor between these two. Your willingness to resurface their own ideas through arbitration was discussed as a gentle opportunity for recoiling their attributes. As a second opportunity, you (Doug and Barb) also learn as parents, a control of methods given from deeply within, instead of your present day peers, who react unjustly through their open pores of surface communications."

Greg's interest in psychic communications picked up considerably when he was advised during a writing session, that he would meet a young lady who could well have a definite effect on his life. Intrigued, he kept his eyes peeled for weeks, despite our caution that "if" this came about, it could be years until it actually happened. Eventually, his enthusiasm cooled, until he stumbled upon a cute, little blonde during a family vacation in Venice, Florida. The relationship was to exist with varying stability over the next year, as Greg continually shook his head at the accuracy of the prediction. The ups and downs of this long distance romance often prompted him to ask the Writings about his connection with the young lady. From his questions, came subtle answers that gave hint to the continued instability, based upon the need for joint learning interactions left over from a previous lifetime.

The Writings, in this particular case, gave Barb and me a chance to logically discuss a touchy subject with our teenage son. Using the Writings almost as a disinterested third party, Greg was actually able to begin looking at his emotional involvement more clearly. Together, we analyzed the information flowing from our source. Casually, Barb and I added our own thoughts and observations to these discussions. Amazingly, an easy interaction between teenager and parents developed about a very private and difficult issue. We often wondered if this would have come about without the aid of the unseen source of the Writings.

Greg's constructive contact with this alternate reality was to show itself again soon. The story unfolded rapidly one evening, as it obviously weighed heavily on his mind. He had been sitting with a group of friends and acquaintances, when he noticed a girl fingering a razor blade. Her friends appeared upset, and Greg asked her what she was doing. Calmly, she told him that if he made a move, she would slash her wrist and kill herself. Before Greg could back off, she slowly made small incisions in her wrist, allowing the blood to trickle down her arm. When the group tried to alert a nearby adult, the bleeding girl bolted. Eventually, the authorities found her, apparently with only minor lacerations, for within days, she was back with her friends.

Luckily, the event was not as traumatic as it could have been, but Greg was obviously disturbed. Barb and I talked it over with him at length, but the depth of his need surfaced when he wondered if he could participate in a writing session. He wanted to find out why someone his age would do such a thing. Looking at the teenage suicide statistics, we shared his distress. On an early Tuesday evening, the three of us merged into one probing mind:

Q: *Why did this girl slash her wrist?*
A: "Her spiritual complaint was similar to that of her physical one. Her ideals are higher than her body is able to accept at this time of life. As a tool of passion, she decided to tear apart her spirit's re-entry into this life, as a challenge for her own growth, thus weakening the growth of (a specified relative). If she continues this track, she will seek destruction again. Should her spirit be torn from this body, her life's end of violence will certainly dispose of this destructive atmosphere in her (a specified relative) life.

"The atmosphere of fear has ruled, for her childhood is marred by hostility and resentment of her life. Having anger as a method to control a body will not suffice the spiritual methods of control, for this individual is thriving on suppression of ideals, thus allowing her atmosphere to remain unchanged."

The discussion and analysis that followed this message seemed to satisfy Greg, somewhat. He experienced a shocking life event and was able to put it into a clearer, although still uncomfortable perspective. To see the intensity of distress drain from his face made the development of our trance communications worth the effort, if only to see this one positive result.

Both Fred and Greg were soon to reach another, unexpected stage in their development. As a family, we decided to cap the waning days of my career in the school system with a giant backyard picnic. It was timed to coincide with the ripening of Zellwood's delicious sweet corn and was quickly dubbed, "The Corn Party." With Fred planning to visit us during that time, he would be able to join family and friends in ravaging crates of plump Harvest Queen.

Guests began arriving in the late afternoon, when the June sun was less fierce. The welcome sight of our blue canoe full of ice, beer, and soda and baskets of fresh white corn, brought smiles to friends perspiring in the humid air. It loomed like an oasis. Soon, the throng of kids and adults filled the open spaces in our jungle-like backyard. When the huge iron pot started to boil on the barbecue, the first of many ears of corn began to cook. The dining room table groaned under the increasing weight of multiple platters of salads, meats and casseroles. One thing is always certain, at the Dillons' everybody eats.

The food and drink flowed well into the evening, until everyone was stuffed to capacity. The crowd thinned eventually, to those few who just wanted to enjoy the flickering torches and the cooler evening air. In the midst of this relaxation came our good friend Millie Stephens and her husband, Bruce. The boys were delighted. They hadn't had a chance yet to talk with Millie about their developing interest in the psychic, but their chance had finally arrived.

After allowing Millie to finish her meal, the boys moved to seats next to her at the large, circular picnic table. With Bruce involved in an animated conversation elsewhere, she and the boys had their opportunity. Barb and I sat back, watching the alert attention the boys gave Millie, as she explained various aspects of psychic perception and spiritual contact. A nearby candle framed the three faces, as if to connect them beyond the words being spoken. Now, it was time for the boys to merge their own experiences and our guidance with an exceptionally perceptive individual. Smiling at each other in the sparse light, Barb and I relaxed and listened.

The teenage years are often a stage when young people concentrate on themselves and shy away from adult instruction. But here, on their own, two young men actively pursued an understanding of existence. Their abilities to exchange ideas and to carefully listen were amazing as well as gratifying. The boys absorbed everything and kept coming back for more.

Toward the end of the conversation, Greg began to tell Millie about an impressive dream he had about a month before that night. In mid-sentence, she stopped him. His mouth fell open, as she proceeded to "tell him" about each dream event, in sequence. Then, Millie told him parts of the dream he hadn't remembered. His eyes widened. Her words fit. Those things were part of the dream, and recognized only after Millie's description.

Looking at us incredulously, Greg glanced at the torch flames dancing in the night. Now it was Greg's turn to stop Millie in mid-sentence. "Do you see that?" he asked nervously. "Yes, I do," Millie replied, simply. What they were referring to, nobody knew.

With Greg still staring out into the yard, I finally asked, "Ah, excuse me, but what's going on?" Greg's response was calm but full of self-doubting wonderment. "Dad, out behind that torch," he said pointing, "It's . . . well, I see something. It's like the body of a person but with rounded arms and legs. I can see through it." We all peered through the gloom, seeing nothing, all except for Millie, who said, "Greg, you're seeing into the world of spiritual essence. I can see the same figure. This experience is simply meant to reinforce the messages sent to you in your dreams."

Reminding us of her responsibilities at home, Millie broke the silence that followed. She and Bruce bid us farewell, followed soon after by Mom and the few remaining guests. Nikki was in bed and the boys retreated to Greg's room. Sitting alone on the porch, Barb and I silently watched the sputtering torches. With crickets occasionally clicking among the darkened plants, the sense that another step had been taken permeated the night air. Within that experience with Millie, two teenagers had been indelibly impressed, and two parents confirmed their commitment to the development of their children's innate abilities.

Throughout those times of learning for the boys, Nicole's education was taking other avenues. Our exploratory dream discussions with Greg and Fred started when they were in the nine- to eleven-year-old age bracket, quite different from Nicole's much younger years. No matter what ancient wisdom lived within that "old soul," to us, she was still a very little girl.

When Nicole's communication skills really started to blossom at age four, the timing seemed right to begin a developmental program, but of what sort? Four-year-olds are not known for their ability to relate, in depth, to things psychic or spiritual, so what do you do? Then, somewhere in my memory, Millie's words stirred the primitive ingredients of an answer into a firm concept. "Doug, have you ever thought of being a writer? You will be a writer one day. You will write children's books." Of course! What a perfect solution. Nicole loves books. If only I could weave some of our basic understanding into stories . . .

Mustering a very raw talent, I launched an effort to design picture books that would capture both the attention of our little one, and instill within her a living awareness of her own multidimensional being. Using typing paper and colored pencils over a two-year period, three little books were born. In all of their simplicity, Nicole has been delighted with them and with the fact that they were made just for her.

Reading along with her, Barb and I have had many opportunities to enlarge on the books' basic concepts, and to answer questions. It has worked exceptionally well. What a pleasure it has been to see conscious understanding build through the natural medium of a child's entertainment.

Each book has a separate message, but all three provide that springboard for creative and imaginative growth. The following descriptions briefly show the essence of this material so that you can better see what our reading sessions might encompass:

THE DREAMING POOL

Through what could be interpreted as either a dream or an out-of-body experience, a little girl finds herself in tune with a deeper reality than is usually apparent. Her secret place in the woods takes on a brilliance of being, as she is instructed by the living consciousness of nature's inhabitants.

FROG FINGERS

Remembering our terribly inadequate attempts to help the boys comprehend my father's death, FROG FINGERS was created so that when Nicole eventually faced similar circumstances, she would be able to weather the storm.

Through the story of a little boy and the death of his friend, the frog, Nicole has come to understand that death exists as only a transition point in the "circle of life."

THE RAINING TIME

By mentally becoming a raindrop, during the boredom of a stormy day, a little girl merges with nature's cyclical water processes. As a part of the environment, she then views the world from the depths of a pond, the edge of a waterfall, and the fury of thunder and lightning.

Nicole now projects herself, joyfully, into a summer shower or a violent thunderstorm, relishing her own powers of imagination, identification and understanding.

From the love of THE DREAMING POOL at age four, to the joy of THE RAINING TIME at age six, Nicole's acceptance of her spiritual existence and her boundless potential is rapidly increasing. From those little books, we have been able to expand her natural awareness and to gently approach even complex ideas such as reincarnation. Now, she giggles impishly when we say that her little spirit was on the bed last night, and in her happy chatter, she occasionally makes vague references to her "other lifetimes." Through her own dream construct called, "Nikki's Place," she can be guided easily out of the aftermath of nightmares, and, recently, FROG FINGERS eased the sadness of death.

Nicole knows that we do something called, "The Writings," but she has no idea of what trance communication is all about. Comprehension of such things will come much later, as it did for the boys. All along, our intentions have been to lay our base with Nicole, nurture it for a few years, putting off direct linkages with alternate realities for a long time. Such things have no place in the life of a little one, or so we thought. One thing we hadn't considered in our planning, though, was the possibility that Nicole might develop her own connections, regardless of our wishes. When it happened, Barb and I had to roll with the punch.

Nicole's nursery school always sent her home at the end of the week, laden with worksheets, drawings and paintings recently completed. Sitting down with her, Barb and I would review each article, accompanied by Nicole's precise explanations. Her unrestrained enthusiasm, coupled with beaming pride, could cut through the cares of even the most difficult day in our adult existence.

A painted picture sat on top of her sprawled stack of material, one Friday, awaiting our attention. Picking it up, she pointed out the details of her art work, showing her nursery school's playground in use. There they were, the swings, slides and other climbing equipment, along with figures representing Nicole and children of all sizes. Explaining each item, as usual, she somehow skipped the two huge, brown blobs hovering over one portion of the scene. Pointing this out, we asked her what they were. Rather annoyed and with a downward glance, she said, "Oh, those are just my ghosts." Barb and I exchanged glances that said, "Oh, oh. How do we handle this one?"

Deciding to inquire about the nature of these "ghosts," Barb asked, "Is this for Halloween?" Silently shaking her head no, we realized something was happening that Nicole didn't necessarily want to discuss. Cautiously probing further, we gingerly extracted an explanation, that these "ghosts" were always visible to her, hovering in the same spot on the playground. Nobody else could see them because they were her friends only. They talked to her, were sometimes scary, but usually nice. She simply would not go beyond that explanation. What was said by her "friends" evidently wasn't for our ears. Pushing her further would have been fruitless and perhaps damaging, so we backed off. Intrigued by this situation, however, we asked about Nicole's ghosts in a Writing session and received this response:

"Her ghosts are my friends, too. They are seeing her as a possessive child who yearns to weed out the destructive nature from her spirit. Her friends are there to perceive her at will. This, therefore, becomes a game by which she can imagine and fill her purpose also. Should her mental escape provide any uncertainty with friends, she will always maintain a justified balance.

"Shouldering her ghosts is only a playtime adventure, she will pull their merits into her own selfishness and determine their platonic benefits. Nicole has advantages over other children, as she has painted an image which gives her pleasure, as well as peaceful manifestations. Her willingness to observe these entities has already increased her own awareness and promised a most lucrative future exercise that will maintain her abilities beyond the present age.

"Her mental images were already impressed through her mind by others, whose call of a 'ghost' was that of a holiday nature (Halloween). That sense of comfort then placed itself within her reach of mobilization and provided an avenue of response for her methods.

"This has not been a well manifested entity and will not live long in her mind's memory."

This information gave us a great deal of insight. According to our interpretation of what was said, Nicole herself was directing a personality restructuring plus an expansion of consciousness and psychic abilities. Through visualizations of actual entities from other realities, she was able to manipulate those visions through her imagination. It was the combination of a playful game and an actual process of growth. The only reason for the scariness of her vision was to provide a logical base for acceptance, because everyone else thinks that "ghosts" *should* be scary.

Two particular passages in these Writings caught our attention: (1) "(It) will not live long in her mind's memory"; (2) "She will always maintain a justified balance." Although our philosophy of accepting the potential validity of childhood visions was very strong, these assurances certainly helped. Instead of worrying this situation to death, we decided to just let it ride to see what would happen.

Since that event over a year and a half ago, Nicole has never mentioned her playground ghosts. Her personality has continued to develop beautifully, and she seems even happier and better adjusted than before. Several minutes ago, she came into the room as I was writing the previous paragraph. Casually, I asked her if she remembered drawing ghosts in a picture at her old nursery school. Blankly, she stared at me and shook her head no.

Shortly after Nicole's playground ghost encounter, she startled Barb with a question that was difficult to understand. "Mom, how do Indians turn into people?" Indians turning into people? What? Barb asked her to explain what she meant, but in frustration, Nicole kept repeating the words in nearly the same combination. Trying to probe into the source of the question, Barb got absolutely nowhere. With her little hands on her hips, Nicole stood there and asked again, "Sometimes Indians turn into people, why?" Mumbling something about the evolution of man, Barb decided to put this one off until later.

Unable to add any dazzling clarity to Barb's talk with Nicole, I quickly deferred to our Writings. Admitting defeat in the physical world, Barb agreed to see if our source could be of any help:

Q: *Tell us about Nicole's question regarding Indians turning into people.*

A: "Her yearning for truth stems from a previous life. To know all, was critically important. Her life, then, became a channel of intrigue, as it performed through a network of past remembrances. Your feelings of tiredness when she awakens, have become a sensory option that you chose to remember as an aftermath of conferences with her, through her sleep period. This period has rejuvenated her thoughts on that plane, thus instilling a partial memory lapse.

"When she awakens, her body becomes a pendulum in time. It progresses as it remains in this way. It actually finds a need to recall a past experience of faith, where an Indian healer became a part of her existence. She contrived ways to help a sick group of people to wade through her teachings of health.

"Her religious sectors admired her abilities to comprehend life on other planes. Her values were instilled as a person of faith. It was through this life's faith, that her purpose became directed toward a more valued historical approach. As you recall her conversations, look into this aspect. Her change does promote fear, although the subconscious mind will not allow the total truth to be carried. So, eliminating a portion, thus brings incomprehensive facts, left open for piecing together. As a child, she will restore much that otherwise might be lost to an adult. At her sixth year, she will recall another life experience. To withdraw from it would show her a lack of wisdom. She will place it upon your ears as a cautious token of her own past problems. Heed her remembrance as it will clearly indicate a lesson for you both."

Somehow, the arrows of learning seem to consistently point to Barb and me. For us, there has been no such thing as a one-way street of instruction and guidance from parents to children only. Standing back and observing, the family seems to exist as a circular unit of psychic exchange, in some other spiritual dimension, just beneath the surface of consciousness. On that level, there is apparently an equality of experience and understanding that transcends what we see as physical maturity. From that perspective, there are no parents and children, only entities, interconnected through some sort of choice, bound together in a pact of mutual learning via physical existence. Then, the unique phenomena actually experienced by children are ways to encourage new learnings for the adults, and to serve as personal reminders to the children themselves of their own greater depths of being.

In actuality, what Barb and I have created, with our children as partners, is nothing more than an open vehicle for our family's self-discovery. In the admission that we don't have ready answers to many of our children's questions, dreams, or visions, we are really saying to them, "O.K., let's grow together. You've probably got as many answers as we do, so, help us find them." True, it's a delicate parental balancing act, trying to give guidance while being a learner at the same time. But, for us, it works, and the process feels as if it mirrors an even more valid form of reality existing beyond daily events.

As I think about children and their psychic potential, I find it fascinating that they, as well as many grown-ups, love superheroes. The Supermen, the Batmen, the Wonder Women, the Hulks, and the whole array of characters with capacities way beyond the normal, haunt comic books and Saturday morning television. The child psychiatrist will point out rightfully that these powerful beings are adored by children, because children themselves have so little power. The child psychiatrist will also point out rightfully that a child's desire to immerse himself in super hero adventures is a natural and healthy outlet for creative imagination. But, let me take these ideas one step further. A child's fascination with superheroes is also a joyous, laughing recognition of self and the ultimate, knowledgeable power that exists within his own true spiritual nature.

I delight in the super hero's potential for helping children recognize who they really are. For Barb and me, the words, ". . . she is already a highly developed soul," stitch themselves into every soaring childhood fantasy.

9

Death Experiences Viewed Differently

BARB'S GRANDFATHER was nearing his one hundred-and-eighth year. Presents and cards didn't have much meaning for him, as his mental abilities and attention span were decreasing noticeably. What do you do for a gentleman of that age and condition on his birthday? With Barb's nature, she had to contribute something, but nothing seemed appropriate. Nothing that is, until the *Today Show,* on NBC, sparked an idea. Willard Scott, the show's weatherman, always took note of birthdays being celebrated by America's older set. Maybe recognition on national television could be her gift this year.

Only two weeks remained before the Old Doctor's birthday on the 31st of January, but gamely, Barb fired off a letter to Willard in care of NBC. After allowing several days for delivery, we moved breakfast in front of the television set to monitor the implementation of her gift. With flying colors, Mr. Scott came through just a few short days before January 31. Using the background material Barb included in her letter, he smilingly told the entire country all about the amazing Dr. Tolbert Hill from Athens, Illinois. As the telecast moved into the nation's weather, I looked at Barb. With the moisture of love and satisfaction gathering in her eyes, she said, "Well, he probably didn't hear it, but I feel so much better that I could at least share him with other people even if it was just for a minute."

Mom and Barb were at the opera when the phone call came from my father-in-law. Unknown to us during the *Today Show*'s salute the day before, Barb's grandfather had been taken to the hospital, seriously ill. The Old Doctor hadn't survived this final bout with the world, and it would be up to me to break the sad news.

Waiting for Barb's return that evening, I wondered at the chances against her one night at the opera in nine years coming on the same evening as the call from her father. It evidently was meant for me to be the one to tell her. Death of a loved one over the age of 100 is something continuously expected, but what about the shock of final loss? What about Barb's acceptance? How would she handle it?

It was late when she returned. With tongue-in-cheek, I kidded her about the historic event of mother and daughter-in-law painting the town red while poor Daddy rode herd on the "younguns." Feigning apologies for her transgressions, Barb slid into bed. My nervously inspired jokes continued so that I wouldn't have to jump directly into the bad news. Eventually, under the cover of darkness, I gingerly explained the nature of the call from Illinois.

Barb's initial reaction was a combination of stunned rejection and concern for what her father might be enduring. But, somehow, my words didn't really seem to penetrate. She just lay there for a while in quiet confusion. Slowly, the logic of the Old Doctor's age and failing health merged with her knowledge of the spiritual purpose of existence: He had accomplished whatever he was meant to do on this earth; he had led a long and satisfying life; he had been recognized nationally; he had been of great service to mankind. Period.

The silence hung heavily in the air after Barb's quick pronouncements, until I detected stifled sobs. Emotion was surpassing reason. Barb's trip to Illinois had established a closeness to her grandfather that now released itself in a jagged sense of grief. In the short time of her stay in Athens, the Old Doctor had become a friend, no, somehow a part of her. Instead of a grand understanding of the universe, Barb could now only see a moment on her grandfather's porch, when together, they shared the simple beauty of lilacs gently waving in the soft warmth of an Illinois springtime.

The emotion was intense, heartfelt and short-lived. Within an hour, Barb's acceptance was nearing completion, but feelings of guilt peppered her thoughts. Almost with a sense of shame, she seemed to be saying that our extensive probing into the nature of existence should have made her immune to grief. "If I really believe in what the Writings say," she began, "then there shouldn't be any sadness. But look at me, crying and shaking. I thought I was getting a pretty good handle on death, but now . . .? What can I say, it still hurts."

On she went for a while longer, literally talking herself in circles. Back and forth she bounced, between the seemingly opposite poles of spiritual understanding and the reality of her pain. My objectivity was easy. It was her pain, not mine. As an observer, the answer was clear, but in that clarity of vision, I began to understand much about myself. "Barb," I pleaded, "no matter how much you understand, you're still human, with human emotions. Death is a loss, and it'll always hurt. Maybe all we can hope for is that as our knowledge increases, the pain will be lessened." The sense of reasonableness in my argument captured her attention and drew a, "Hmm, maybe. I'll think about it." Her "maybe" turned into a, "Yeah, you're right," a few days later.

That conversation was to take place as our "time of troubles" really began to accelerate. The next seven months were to be extremely difficult, and more than once, Barb would remind me of my objective observations the night of her grandfather's death. Especially during those painful days of defeat in the business world, Barb would gently say, "Doug, you're only human with human emotions." To which I would respond, "Yeah, right. I think I've heard that astute, dispassionate observation somewhere before."

The death of Barb's grandfather brought an instant recollection of the first trance communications predicting such an event. The discrepancy was that it happened two and a half years after the forecast. Now, anyone could reasonably predict the passing of a man his age, within a few years. Maybe, subconsciously, Barb had done just that. But, then again, Millie warned us to expect such distortion and to "wait and see." Our problem with "wait and see" was that within the original Writings were also hints of other deaths in the family. An uneasiness crept over us during the next two weeks, but daily survival needs pushed such feelings into the background. Financially, we were barely staying afloat, as my business venture dipped drastically to the tune of America's unstable economy.

It had been a morning full of headaches at the office. My grand dream of establishing a thriving business in seminar sales was teetering precariously. The marketing of training programs and tapes was showing only a minimal return, while creditors still expected full payment. If, as the Writings continually stressed, a part of me had purposely chosen these circumstances, my selection mechanisms needed a lot of oiling. It seemed to me that I could learn just as much with a little less stress.

The phone on my desk blinked with incoming calls that incessantly interrupted my conversation with one of our sales people. Again, in mid sentence, the intercom buzzed and Jean said, "It's your wife." Rubbing my forehead in exasperation, I calmly reminded myself that Barb rarely called unless it was important. Line One stopped its winking as I punched the button. Barb's voice was tense. A little hesitancy punctuated the strain I was sensing in her conversation. Something was wrong.

Finally, it came out. "Doug, your mom has been trying to call you, but all of the lines have been busy. Doug . . ." she wavered, "I . . . your brother, Wally, died this morning. You'd better call your mom."

Bill, our salesman, had been patiently waiting. As he excused himself when the gravity of the phone call became apparent, I sat in the utter confusion of conflicting emotions. Then all at once I thought, "Oh, my God. It really has begun. The Writings were on target." At the same time, I dialed Mom's phone number. Her voice was shaky but she seemed to be under control. "I'll be there in thirty minutes, just hold on," I soothed, trying to help her maintain that stability. The business would just have to wait.

Mom and I sat in the Florida Room of her home, talking for hours. Long before that afternoon, both of us were forced by Wally's many recent slips into near fatal illnesses, to accept the inevitability of his impending death. Aggravated by increasingly severe epileptic seizures, Wally's deteriorating physical condition left little doubt that his life could come to a close at any moment. When that end finally came, the intensity of Mom's grief had already spent itself.

Carefully, we explored each other's thoughts about Wally and the meaning of his existence. Painful memories occasionally stabbed Mom's consciousness, as she recalled the thirty-seven years since the day of his birth during World War II. The sadness in her eyes revealed the anguish that must have struck when the doctors first explained Wally's hopelessly retarded condition. A slight quiver of her chin accentuated the depth of emotion lying beneath her story of how she and my grandmother literally kept my brother alive, by round-the-clock care, during the first six months of his life.

Never developing beyond the mixed capacities of an infant and toddler, Walter W. Dillon, Jr. was forever enclosed in a shell, impossible to crack by family or medical science. Test after test, over the years, simply confirmed the original diagnosis of severe brain damage due to a lack of oxygen at birth. There was nothing anyone could do and the medical community consistently advised institutionalization.

My parents agonized over what was best for Wally and the family. How, they wondered, could they ever begin to give him the constant care needed under the relentlessly changeable conditions and demands of military life? In the mounting tension of questions without answers, Mom's parents stepped forward, insisting that Wally live with them. To their way of thinking, institutionalization was out of the question and the quiet permanence of their home in New York was a perfect compromise. In the absence of a better solution, Mom and Dad agreed.

My grandparents cared for Wally for twenty years, first in their home in New York, then later at the old farmhouse nestled in the hills of Connecticut. I can remember my childhood visits with them as happy, laughing times, with everyone sharing Wally's care in a natural flow of combined responsibility. But, as a youngster, I still sensed a sorrow underlying the adult responses, as I asked why my brother wouldn't ever get any better.

In those earlier days, before Wally's awareness began to dim dramatically, he would shake with delight at the sight of my parents, after several months of separation. In his exuberance, he would cling tightly to them both, even knocking Mom down accidentally, as he got older and larger. Within those reunions was always the bittersweet combination of obvious, candid love and never-ending heartache.

When Granddad Coords, Mom's father, died in 1963, Wally was institutionalized. Unable to handle him physically, my grandmother accepted arrangements to have my brother enter the state-operated training school at Southbury, Connecticut. The rest of his life would be spent there, in the excellent care of some very dedicated people. During his time at Southbury, Wally was always glad to see visitors, whoever they were. But, he then would just as happily roll his wheelchair back into his room, enclosing himself again in the mystery of his deepening affliction.

As Mom and I exchanged such memories, I recalled the sounds of Wally's late night epileptic seizures during those days of visiting in my grandparents' home. Either Dad or my grandfather would be with him until the convulsions passed. In the darkness, I often lay there, touched by the union of suffering and compassion. Thinking about this as Mom and I talked, I wondered about purpose and how it related to Wally's linkage with various family members. Interlocking connections were beginning to form in my mind. Mom's comment finally gave voice to a part of what I was feeling. "You know, Doug, my father often told me that he felt his only true purpose on earth was to care for Wally. Maybe that explains why my parents were so insistent on taking Wally into their home."

In talking about such things, I could still see in Mom's glance, the pain that ached and gnawed for so many years. She believed in the immortality of the soul and reincarnation, but the anguish of Wally's thirty-seven years of existence maintained its hold on her being. Beneath her genuine gladness that Wally was finally at peace, lay a mother's rejection of her child's lifetime of helplessness.

What had the Writings said about Wally? Bits and pieces of that session floated across my mind:

> ". . . The spirit is in full cooperation in his physical manifestations . . ."
>
> "He is about to become a fully potential being . . ."
>
> "He is serving the purpose for his soul to become a higher being."

Since Barb and I had shared that information with Mom many months before, I reminded her of its contents. Nodding, Mom's anguish seemed to modify as we explored Wally's purpose of this physical existence. Back and forth we shared the effect his life had had on so many people. As we examined the possible lessons all of us might have learned through linkages with him, the magnitude of one helpless being's influence on the world began to mount. In that magnitude of influence, a web-like pattern of intentional connections emerged, dissipating much of the sadness we were feeling. Mom was more at ease and I . . . well, for the first time, I could feel the solidity of the understandings to which Barb and I had been exposed, through our Writings and experiences. In those few moments, that web-like pattern of connections surrounding Wally's life cast itself in some unknown concrete of my perception.

By the end of that day, I had spoken with Wally's doctor at the Southbury Training School's hospital and with the funeral director, only to find that February burials in hilly, rural Connecticut were quite impossible. Mom definitely wanted Wally buried beside my grandfather in the Warren, Connecticut town cemetery, but ground couldn't be broken until April. What a damnable thing. Mom would have to wait for two months before burying her son. That kind of situation, she just didn't need, but there was no choice. Deciding upon cremation, we reluctantly gave the funeral director instructions to hold the remains until the family arrived in the spring.

The next big hurdle was my grandmother. How would Wally's death affect her? How would she react to his interment next to my grandfather in the spring instead of right away? After all, she and my grandfather cared for Wally for so many years; he was more like a son than a grandson. At the age of eighty-three, her health was not good, and we feared that the news might aggravate her existing physical ailments. Luckily, she was visiting Deane and Taddie, her son and daughter-in-law, at their condominium in New Smyrna Beach, Florida. That gave Mom time to make her own adjustments before approaching her mother. Much to our relief, the breaking of the news to Grandmother Coords went reasonably well, with no apparent adverse effects.

Within a few days of Wally's death, my full concentration returned to the business. With a notification in hand that a federal tax audit of the company was to be conducted in March, I absent-mindedly responded to the intercom. Again, Jean said, "It's your wife." In the split second before connecting with Barb, I could feel my thoughts congeal into "Oh, no, not again." Quietly, Barb said, "Your grandmother has been taken to the hospital. She had some sort of attack at the condo. They've taken her by ambulance to Fish Memorial in New Smyrna. Your Mom was pretty upset when I talked with her; upset enough to want me to contact you."

A quick call to my mother confirmed her agitated state of mind and the few sketchy details of what had happened. Mom's intentions were to drive to the coast and then let us know what was going on, but those I immediately vetoed. On my way out the door, I notified my ever-enduring business partner that, again, another emergency needed my attention.

Mom was ready when I arrived. In no time we traversed a large part of Interstate 4 heading for exit 56 to New Smyrna. Small talk failed miserably on this trip. Mom's knuckles occasionally whitened as she squeezed my hand in a combination of fear and anxiety. Muriel Dillon was a very strong person, but she had just lost a son, and Dad's death six years before was still a phantom lurking somewhere in her mind. If my grandmother were to die, could she bear it? If my grandmother were to die, had Barb and I learned enough to effectively grapple with that situation in all of its complexities? Returning the squeeze of Mom's hand, an inhalation of breath caught momentarily in my throat, giving me cause to recognize my own fears and anxieties.

Exasperatingly, the parking lot at the hospital was filled to capacity. Round and round we circled until an opening appeared. Rushing to the front desk, we bought only frustration when no record existed of a Mina Coords having been admitted. Finally, one of the more experienced desk volunteers suggested that we check the Emergency Room. Perhaps she was still being examined. Hurrying through the corridors leading to the back of the building, we eventually stumbled upon my aunt and uncle worriedly sitting in a corner of the Emergency Room.

After hasty greetings, we found that Deane and Taddie had been

Death Experiences Viewed Differently 139

waiting for some time with no word on my grandmother's condition. The inane prattle of a television quiz show literally broke around us from a perch high above our seats. Several patients in bathrobes blandly absorbed the program's content, since they obviously had little else to do. The meaningless words and constant noise competing with our quest for information, set all of our nerves on edge.

Nana Bird. That was my nickname for Grandmother Coords. Its origin came from the days of Lyndon Johnson's reign in the White House. Stealing the term "Bird" from Lady Bird Johnson, I simply added it to my childhood endearment, "Nana." As thoughts of this name's beginnings seeped into my consciousness, orderlies wheeled a patient towards a room down the hall. Nana Bird was being sucked past us by medical efficiency, and I absolutely did not recognize her.

Without her glasses and dentures, the pain-constricted individual moving toward the opposite end of the Emergency Room looked like no one I had ever known. But, Mom and Taddie recognized her immediately. With permission from the nurse on duty, Mom and Taddie quickly disappeared, to find Nana Bird and to give her what reassurances they could. When they returned though, I could tell by Mom's look, that things weren't going well. Taking me by the hand, she said, "Come see her with me."

As we approached Nana Bird's bed, her breathing was labored and her glazed eyes incessantly moved from side to side in apprehension. With Mom holding one of her hands and me holding the other, Nana Bird's slurred speech revealed only one distinct sentence. "I love you." Fighting back our tears, we replied to her pitiful communication by saying, "It's all right. Everything will be fine. We love you too." But, everything wasn't fine. Nana Bird had all the indications of having had a stroke. Our presence seemed to agitate her further, so Mom and I finally broke away. Within the next hour, Nana Bird was finally tucked into a comfortable room on the third floor.

So far, we had seen no doctor. When Mom questioned the nurses, they thought he had gone back to his office. I couldn't believe it. Four distraught relatives waiting for a diagnosis and the doctor goes back to his office without seeing them? On the main floor, I found a telephone and looked up the man's name. His receptionist put me through to him rapidly when I caustically explained our circumstances. Without apology of any kind, he stated that Nana Bird's stroke was most likely correctable with the medication he was giving her. Stroke! Damn! So that was it as we suspected.

The elevator whined its way back to the third floor. In a corner of the Sun Room, I explained to Mom, Deane and Taddie what the doctor had said. The information about such a dreaded illness, despite the medical prognosis, settled over us all like a chilling fog.

Nana Bird lay quietly now, eyes shut, a slight tremor in one arm showing beneath the covers. An intravenous feeding tube wound its way from high above the bed, down toward the more stable arm. At least she seemed to be comfortable. For the next several hours, nothing changed. We convinced Deane and Taddie to take a break for some rest and food, but Taddie was soon back, lending whatever support she could. Since I had guests awaiting me at home, as well as a business to help run the next day, Mom finally convinced me to head back to Orlando. She would stay with Deane and Taddie at the condo, monitoring Nana Bird's condition. If I were really needed, she would call. Nodding my agreement, I hugged her and headed home.

Barb's step-brother, Mike, and his wife, Donna, were visiting from California in the midst of this chaos. We had planned to take them to dinner that evening, but I needed to stay near the phone, in case Nana Bird's condition worsened. I insisted they go without me, but they rebelled. Instead, they visited one of our favorite restaurants, Casa Gallardo, bringing back delicious Mexican dishes. It was a bubbling, happy meal, with the kids joining the silliness of the adults. The change of pace from the tenseness of the hospital was a welcome relief, and I silently thanked all the participants in our crazy feast. Later, Barb and I would talk in depth about Nana Bird's illness, but, just then, enjoyment and life prevailed.

Mike and Donna Holstrom rapidly changed from unknown quantities into fast friends. Through a remarriage late in life, Barb's father provided her with a brand new step-brother, whom she had not met until he and his wife arrived at our home just before Nana Bird was taken to the hospital. We found them to be very easy-going people, close to our own ages. They were fascinated with the psychic, read Seth books avidly, and were greatly surprised to find us in the process of writing this book. Beyond that, the four of us felt an inexplicable rapport that resulted in Barb's feeling so comfortable, that she agreed to their request to participate in a Writing session.

The ease with which Barb delivered material in that session amazed us both, because this was the first time that she had permitted observers other than myself and the boys. The information flowed beautifully. It explained past life connections which created our instant rapport, and gave Mike and Donna accurate and reassuring data about some very personal circumstances. It was an enjoyable episode in our

Death Experiences Viewed Differently

lives and a most meaningful one to Barb, as she moved onward into the eventual sharing of her communications with other people.

During the few short days of Mike and Donna's visit, Nana Bird's condition did not improve, and she edged into longer periods of unconsciousness. On the morning of our guests' departure, Mom's morning phone call gave a definite sense of uncertainty that we hadn't detected before. As soon as Mike and Donna left, Barb and I decided to deposit the kids with friends so that we could get to the hospital and stay for however long we might be needed. On the way out the door, Barb grabbed a pile of fairly recent trance records, and we aimed the old Chevy towards New Smyrna.

Thumbing through the Writings while I drove, Barb came across notations preceding three separate trance sessions. They were records of visual perceptions encountered by both of us on the imaginary river and the psychic house. At the time, the meanings were obscure, but with the two recent deaths and Nana Bird's illness, they were forming a more sensible pattern. In these visions, both Barb and I were continually seeing waving arms and welcoming hands. They appeared up and down the river and in the house. We had never before observed such things, and we wondered at the time, as to their significance. In the house, many, many people milled about, apparently expecting guests. Appearing in the crowd, were my father and Grandfather Coords, Nana Bird's husband.

Since the series of deaths and tragedies predicted by our earlier Writings included Nana Bird, we couldn't help but fear for her. This was even more painfully evident when Barb reminded me of a writing session only months before. Pulling that record from her stack of material, she said, "Remember after Nana Bird's illness last fall, we asked the Writings about her?" I remembered. The information was definitely negative in the physical sense. We had therefore decided at the time, not to share it with Mom or Nana Bird. Including Barb's visions interspersed through this Writing session, here is what that record shows:

Sunday, October 18, 1981

Q: *Any comments on Nana Bird's recent illness?*

A: "She (Nana Bird) has become another form; a spectrum of many who desire their life's ending to slow down."

(Here, Barb could see a round crystal with a multitude of separate facets. Each facet was a brilliant light, and each was apparently a selected lifetime, chosen ahead of time by the all-encompassing soul—the total crystalline structure.)

"Should her physical falling increase to a point of immeasurable repair, your mother (Doug) will seek to then repair any of her own fears attached to the ultimate descent of her mother, through this physical life's period."

(Then, Barb could see Nana Bird falling between one and four times, as she had in Connecticut, with one fall to be a big one. This would be a time of decision and fear for my mother according to that same impression.)

"Her (Nana Bird's) wishes to become a strong personality are not going to be granted in this life. However, due to the lack of control that she has now shown throughout this period, her subsequent life will be of grave potential filled with power, thus releasing her need for it."

(In the next vision, Barb saw a "future" life for Nana Bird as a man in Shakespearean England. We thought it rather curious that a future life might actually occur in the physical past.)

"Her (Nana Bird's) access to these thoughts are difficult for her present perception, as she nears the end of a confusing life's period. Her willingness to perceive is less of a challenging effort anymore. Yet, however, her original desires of a strong and willful connection with our purpose are pleasantly there in her brain's intent for survival."

(At this point, Barb could see Nana Bird with a light, lacy film all around her. It was a pleasurable and comfortable sensation for Nana Bird, but flimsy in its permanence. Apparently, some part of her was connected to the spiritual world, but deeper penetration than that wasn't wanted.)

"Her soul has a yearning to be free from her bodily commitments at this point. This restraint from pressures allows her bodily mind the attention for which she seeks. Her ploys are now being answered. To her, attention will bring many who therefore need to acquire a use for their own direction of pathways, thereby entwining with her calls for recognition."

(In the accompanying vision, Barb saw thin lines emanating from Nana Bird to others standing nearby. These were purpose lines intertwining in a planned fashion that pleased Nana Bird.)

"Should her soul reunite with its now active physical position, shortly, you (Doug and Barb) will take a full position of belief in her acquisition of purposeful death, thereby totally surrounding your mother's (Doug) opposition of fears."

(The final vision showed our belief system being a strong net of purpose lines supporting my mother. Her fears were being absorbed in us.)

Parts of this information fit the current circumstance perfectly. Nana Bird's illness resulted in a few more falls after October of 1981. Perhaps this collapse was the "big one" Barb saw during the session. As the distance to the hospital shortened, the remaining span of Nana Bird's life seemed to diminish with it.

Mom was visibly relieved to see us. Her mother's condition was worsening. Breathing in hollow, exaggerated gasps beneath an oxygen mask, Nana Bird remained unconscious. The illness had taken its toll. Weight loss was painfully obvious. Her eyes and cheeks had sunken noticeably, and her hands looked so frightfully delicate. In her usual courageous way, Mom smiled and listed the few positive medical indications that existed. But, Barb and I knew without a doubt, that Nana Bird simply couldn't hold on to life much longer. I was sure Mom felt the same, but it wasn't yet time to admit to the world that her mother was dying.

Hour after hour, the sound of oxygen bubbling through water competed with the constant rasp of Nana Bird's breath. Every two hours during the long night, nurses entered the room to shift her position and monitor vital signs. Periodically, one of us would sit by Nana Bird's side, hold her hand, talk to her, and caress her forehead. The probability was that she could sense nothing. But, just on the chance that some part of her could be comforted, we continued our attempts to help, if only in very small ways.

Well after midnight, Mom, Barb and I took a slow walk through the hospital corridors. The late night quiet, resting gently on the highly polished floors, was a welcome relief from the agony each of us felt with every breath Nana Bird took. Only our own soft footsteps or those of an occasional nurse disturbed the peacefulness. By the end of that night, we would know every small stain on those floors, every imperfection in the ceiling, and the details of each painting that hung on the walls.

The nurses had seen it before. The death-watch was nothing new to them. Although hardened by exposure to sickness and death, compassion still filtered through their assigned tasks in the form of small kindnesses. No one spoke of death; yet, but when Barb slipped out to question one of the nurses, the inevitable was confirmed by the answer, "It will only be a matter of hours."

While Barb was gone, I sat back in my chair, and Mom closed her eyes to steal a semblance of rest. Strong coffee sat heavily on my stomach and the constancy of Nana Bird's struggling breath kept sleep at a distance. Her body shook slightly, and the exhalations condensed momentarily on the inside of the clear plastic oxygen mask. It was a pitiful scene and painful to view. For all that I thought I understood about life and the spirit, it still hurt to watch someone I loved suffer. "We're still human with human emotions." Then the real meaning of what I had said to Barb about her reactions to the Old Doctor's death became increasingly clear.

As I looked at Nana Bird lying there, a dreamy awareness made me recognize that I wasn't detecting any aura or emanation coming from her whatsoever. Not that I was very skilled in sensing such things, but my limited experience over the past couple of years made me wonder why there seemed to be such an emptiness around my grandmother. So many times, Barb and I had observed mists, lights and splashes of color around and between people. These visions seemed to occur during times of relaxation or periods of great emotional intensity.

One instance stood out in my mind, particularly because it happened during my days as a school administrator. Jane, our computer operator, wasn't concealing her anger over someone's foul-up, and she was ably venting that displeasure in the doorway to my office. All at once, at the height of her agitation, red balls of light seemed to shoot outward from her head. It was as if the anger was molding itself into a visual disruption of the atmosphere.

My thoughts returned to Nana Bird, and suddenly I realized that the emptiness around her seemed to have deepened, if that was possible. Without warning, the full clarity of the situation dropped into my lap. Nana Bird wasn't there, or at least her spiritual essence was "missing." No aura, no emanations, no vitality of being at all. It was as if Nana Bird's body lay there in a vacuum. Her physical being functioned, but "she" wasn't there. How oddly, yet obviously clear. Barb later offered the same feelings to me in almost the exact language of my thoughts. For both of us, Nana Bird's death was a reality, many hours before her physical body ceased to function.

Official checks of Nana Bird's vital signs showed her blood pressure diminishing hour by hour. It was then that we told Mom of Barb's conversation with the nurse. Final confirmation of impending death affected her only to the point of increased nervousness. Hoping to cushion the inevitable just a little, Barb and I brought out the Writings from months before that explained Nana Bird's death. Mom heard the words and our explanations, but at that instant, she was a little girl trying

Death Experiences Viewed Differently 145

bravely to face her mommy's disintegrating existence. No belief system or understanding could alter the course of what must happen, and the child within was becoming very afraid.

Sitting there, again, in silence, I marveled at the difference between this night and the night when Dad died. Granted, the types of relationships involved weren't the same, but in Barb's glance, I sensed the fullness of our expanded awareness. Nana Bird was not dying because of some arbitrary quirk of nature, she was dying because it was her intention to do so. Everything we had learned pointed to this concept, and it almost stood beside Nana Bird's bed in the solidness with which we granted its full reality. This was life and death balancing themselves through one being's multiple purposes, in multiple realities. As hurtful as it seemed in its outward appearances, that event had an ultimate goodness of intent Barb and I never dreamed of while Dad lay dying years before.

Spiritual purpose aside, I couldn't shake the need to do something more for Nana Bird. True, Barb and I sensed only emptiness around where her body lay, but I felt we were needed in some way that I couldn't quite grasp. As Barb and I sat on either side of Nana Bird, Mom rose, saying she wanted to take another walk, but by herself this time. As soon as she was out of the room, it hit me. "Barb," I whispered intently, "let's take Nana Bird down our river to the psychic house just as we do before a writing session. Somehow, by doing that, I think we can help her make the transition to the next reality." The words came so quickly, that I startled myself. Responding with a pleased nod, Barb closed her eyes. Almost immediately, we were both on the river in our thoughts. Most of what we each experienced in the five minutes of Mom's absence was so similar that the following account is offered as a combined narrative:

The clear waters of the Wekiva River sprang immediately to mind with all the warmth of previous trips, whether physical or spiritual. We entered our canoe and steadied it for Nana Bird but she refused, saying, "See how sick I am? How can I even move? Besides, you don't want an old fuddy-duddy like me around." After much cajoling, she finally tried to walk, finding to her delight that it was possible. Once comfortably in the canoe, we explained that she was in a spiritual body, not a physical one. Quickly going on, we then told her that we were there to help her into the next world. Surprisingly, she accepted all of this without question.

The trip down the river was calm and pleasant. Shortly, we reached the house, tying up at the dock. As we helped Nana Bird out of the canoe, she faltered at the thought of going up the slight hill, until reminded that she could do anything in her spiritual body. Opening the door to the house, Doug shouted, "Is anybody home?" With that, a multitude of people flooded the hallway embracing Nana Bird and welcoming her. In the group stood my Grandfather Coords, my father, and Barb's grandfather. Then, most poignantly of all, Wally stepped out from behind the crowd, walked up, kissed Nana Bird and spoke with an intelligence he never possessed in life.

Eventually, the gathering thinned, until it was gone completely. Only Barb, Nana Bird and I were left. A nearby rocking chair caught Nana Bird's eye. Tiredness seemed to overcome her as she sat in the chair and began to rock back and forth, as any ailing grandmother should do. Apparently, she couldn't divorce herself too quickly from her illnesses. Trying again to get her to recognize her spiritual body, Barb and I helped her up so that she could walk to the fish tank. Hobbling just a bit, she approached the tank, finally under her own power. As her head tilted upward to look through the glass, she was instantly transformed into a beautiful little girl, eight or nine years old. Turning her head for just a moment, she flashed a lovely, youthful smile in our direction.

The sight was incredible. It was as if Nana Bird had reverted to the child she had once been, and was again delightfully sensing the joys of childhood. With fingertips and nose pressing against the glass, the brilliant white light from the fish tank reflected against her face, hands and torso. The almost glaring brilliance of that reflected light, shining from the child/grandmother created a reality beyond any experienced previously in our psychic house. It was as if this were Nana Bird's moment of rebirth and we were privileged to be a part of it.

Somehow, Barb and I felt impelled to assist Nana Bird at this point. Grasping the child gently by her arms, Barb and I pulled her easily through the glass of the fish tank into the fullness of light. Together, the three of us swirled, merging in a joyous combination with the bubbles and aquatic life. Circling and spiraling at unimaginable speeds, we shot upward into infinities freshly created by our own beings.

Mom returned from her lonely walk at the precise moment of our ascent into the fish tank. Instantly, our eyes opened as her steps neared the door. Briefly, we mentioned to her what a beautiful and positive experience had just occurred. This sharing seemed to help her a little, but, as dawn pierced the early morning fog outside, the next blood pressure check showed a continuing decline. On it went for another hour or more, until we finally convinced Mom to grab a quick bite at the snack bar. We all needed energy and caffeine.

Our appetites were far from hefty, but the food and coffee brought a welcome boost. Noticing that a small gift shop adjoined the snack bar, I recommended that one of the stuffed animals sitting on the far counter would make a useful and fitting last gift from Nana Bird to Nicole. As we agreed on the mother kangaroo with a baby in its pouch, a call requesting that Mrs. Dillon return to the third floor interrupted our conversation. I hadn't paid for breakfast yet, so I urged Mom and Barb to start upstairs without me.

I fidgeted with the package containing the kangaroos as the elevator groaned its way upward. Knowing that Mom and Barb were probably already on the third floor, the seconds seemed to expand in a heaviness of time. It was much like swimming toward the surface of a lake from twenty feet below, without a breath. It looked as if that elevator would go on forever. But, once the doors popped open, I relaxed and headed around the corner. Too late. With Barb's arm around her, Mom emerged from Nana Bird's room totally shattered. As nurses scurried behind her, Mom looked up at me and moaned, "Oh, Doug! She's gone. My mother is dead. Oh, Doug!"

For an instant, time now simply stood still. From my perspective, Mom's grief froze, revealing the childperson who couldn't accept the loss of a parent. Within that grief could be seen the agonies of other deaths not yet salved by the passage of days or years. The sparkle of tears in Barb's eyes disclosed her own mixture of loss, sympathy and dread of hospitals, stretching back long before our marriage.

In a second, time resumed its normal course. All I could do was embrace both Mom and Barb, trying, I suppose, to drain the overflow of their feelings. When nurses indicated the Sun Room wasn't occupied, Barb volunteered to take Mom there if I wanted to be alone with Nana Bird one more time. Nodding my assent, I watched them slowly walk down the hall.

It was something I had to do. Open caskets at funerals appall me, but I had to face this death and my own feelings. The room was so quiet. When I entered, nurses slipped out, closing the door behind them. No more bubbling oxygen. No more painful breathing. The oxygen mask was gone now, and Nana Bird's pale, gaunt features lay before me in the utter stillness. My eyes stung, and the human sadness of seeing a life's end, struck me a gentle, glancing blow. But, Barb and I had really said our goodbyes, in those early morning hours, when a lovely child pressed her nose and fingers against the brilliance of a fish tank. I smiled with the beauty of that picture, for it had within it a ring of truth, far surpassing the physical death before me. Silently, my thoughts trailed after that child, as she joyfully spiraled upward with the bubbling water.

That afternoon was spent at Deane and Taddie's condo, sharing our grief, making necessary arrangements, and having a much needed drink. The long, emotion-laden hours at the hospital had drained us completely. Exhausted, we finally left New Smyrna, attempting to get home before nightfall. Collapsing into the kindness of sleep, Mom rested soundly in the back seat of the car, as Barb and I quietly talked away the miles.

With Greg's involvement in our trance communications and its developing philosophy, he took the news of Nana Bird's death very well. The contrast to his silence and tears, when my father died, was gratifying. Nicole, however, was another matter. The tender age of five is a very difficult time to lose a loved one, and Nana Bird was very important to her.

Fighting the numbness from lack of sleep, Barb and I took Nicole into our bedroom and closed the door. With the three of us sitting on the queen-sized bed, I tip-toed into an explanation of Nana Bird's death. Using my homespun picture book, FROG FINGERS, I asked Nicole to recount the story and its lessons. This she did beautifully, showing her understanding that "the circle of life" includes death as a transition into another existence. Then, delicately inserting Nana Bird's illness into the conversation, I explained how Nana Bird, like the frog in the story, needed to journey into different adventures.

With her mouth drooping slightly and tears forming in her big brown eyes, the impact of Nana Bird's death began to penetrate. FROG FINGERS was a help, but the immediate hurt and sadness wasn't to be avoided, nor should it have been. To ease the pain slightly, I brought out the kangaroos purchased at the hospital, and told a little white lie. A lie in one sense, maybe, but it held a greater actuality that gave Nicole a good deal of comfort. "Nikki, before Nana Bird died, she wanted to make sure that you had these sweet little friends so that you wouldn't be too lonesome without her." With a crushing hug of the stuffed creatures and a brave smile, we could see that she wasn't going to be overwhelmed by sorrow. Later, at bedtime, I would read FROG FINGERS with her, as the kangaroos peeked at the pages from beneath her covers.

Mom's initial shock at the loss of her mother shifted to an agitated period of adjustment. As in the situation with Wally, the frozen ground in Connecticut prevented Nana Bird's burial until spring. The prospects of waiting two months for a double funeral put us all on edge, but especially for Mom, the turmoil mounted day by day. Although we could only sweat it out with her, Barb and I wondered if something more tangible would help Mom during that interminable waiting. What if we could find a physical object that would divert her focus, even ever so slightly. Would it be possible to find an object uniquely symbolic of spiritual being, expanded awareness, and hope for the future? It seemed a tall order but surely, we felt, something would come to mind.

The answer came in two parts a week after Nana Bird's death. First, we were reminded of Barb's distinct vision of Nana Bird's soul, during a writing session months before, as a many-faceted crystal sphere. This merged with other references in writing sessions, over the years, that mentioned "facets" of the soul. What seemed to evolve was a concept of a crystaline soul structure, where each facet was a separate entity, apparently projecting itself outward into life as an individual human existence, seeking knowledge and understanding. Simple in its visual impact, Barb and I began to sense the formation of a very tangible idea.

The second part of the answer came directly from Barb's stepbrother and his wife. During their visit, they had told us about the beautiful cut crystal ball, given by them as a gift to Mike's mother. According to their description, if properly placed, sunlight would reflect through the crystal in a myriad of colors, shining on everything within the room. Crystal! Projections outward! Of course! The same gift for Mom would be perfect. The symbolism of our visions, trance communications and combined knowledge could be encased in one compact, tangible piece of the physical world.

Pleased with our discovery, Barb and I planned a trip to the Far Horizon's gift shop, in nearby Winter Park, to look over their excellent selection of such crystals. But, before that discussion came to an end, Greg emerged from a closed door project he had been working on in his room. His recent interest in creating artistic designs, this time produced something of startling similarity to our conversation. Greg's sheet of paper contained the angular edges and flat surfaces of an irregularly shaped crystal, showing shafts of light emanating from its facets. Greg's own deep resources had given him the same answer to our quandary about a gift for Mom, that only moments before we were discussing.

Mom's reception of the gift and its meaning was a heartfelt acceptance and appreciation. Holding the crystal in her hand, something seemed to click in her mind. Excusing herself, she left the room, only to return a minute later with a small crystal bowl in her other hand. This she sat on an end table, bathed in sunlight. Then setting the crystal globe partially into the opening of the bowl, Mom explained that it had been Nana Bird's. As the many faceted sphere sparkled in the late afternoon sun, rainbow colors danced around the room, and the match of the two crystal objects spoke volumes of unplanned meaning.

During the two months before the double funeral in Connecticut, Barb and I squeezed several writing sessions into our hectic days. Interestingly enough, we could see Nana Bird waiting for us each time, as we took our preliminary trip down the imaginary river to the psychic house. Although somewhat happy in her new existence, we kept feeling that Nana Bird's full acceptance of death was not yet complete. Continually, we would see her revert to the arthritic walk of her recent physical life, and at times, she seemed to view herself still physically wasting away.

Through these encounters and occasional dreams, Barb and I could feel the reality of Nana Bird's presence. To us, she existed in our minds, just as if we were all communicating across the dinner table. In that sense of actual linkage, we deliberately recalled her physical death and the vision of the child in front of the fish tank. Consistently, we challenged Nana Bird to forget the pains and attachments that might be holding her back.

As the weeks toward the funeral narrowed, Barb repeatedly saw during writing sessions, a younger, healthier, smiling Nana Bird, who was always working with a smaller, shriveled old woman. Nana Bird explained to Barb that the other woman was actually herself, or at least a part of herself. It was that part, she said, that was as yet unable to release its grasp on the physical world. Nana Bird seemed to be saying that she was working with the older, shriveled woman, to make her understand where true reality lay. With each passing week of these visions, Barb saw that other, smaller individual shrink in size, until just before the funeral, when she was reduced to nothing. It was almost as if the funeral would be the final point of Nana Bird's adaptation to her new existence.

Mom was also sensing something that she explained as an "uneasiness" about Nana Bird, as if my grandmother were not truly at rest. With that opening, we shared our visions as a confirmation of her feelings. Later, a friend of Mom's related similar impressions regarding the reality of Nana Bird's spiritual condition.

The actual trance communications at this time held a new and interesting twist. As we tried to help Nana Bird, the source of our Writings spoke directly to her, as if letting us in on a spiritual counseling session. Then, speaking directly to us, the source provided information

Death Experiences Viewed Differently 151

relating to Nana Bird and our attempts to be of assistance. Divided between those two categories, the following quotes came during the two months before the funeral in April of 1982:

To Nana Bird

"Soon, you will drop the repetitiveness of angles revolving around the fear which you now sustain. Overwhelming attitudes of peace will flaunt themselves in front of you, until you desire to withhold the fear and release the joy of your afterlife surroundings. Be peaceful, and calm yourself, as each entity of spirit comes as a forthright obligation of the soul.

"Should you regain the will to live again as a daily servant towards life's remisses, you will become a speciality through the past incarnation. This was told to you as a purpose for future adjustment. I will lend my support to your being, so please aware yourself of this."

To Us

"Your effectiveness in helping this woman through this period of remorse will come as a wafer between life and death, for her own soul's recovery here. Bond yourselves as a pillar of strength for her to lean on. Should she sense a way to recover through her own period of instant death, she will remember that, until her soul was watching, her body was weak and anticipating a fall from life.

"Encourage her now to be pleased with herself, as a purer entity than before. Her promise to maintain a willful direction will take place, but only through a time period which allows certain acceptable challenges. But, the final separation will take place. This period of wisdom comes through the soul's yearning for self-preservation. Its own acknowledgement precedes any angles of release from within the body's spirit. Her adjustment period is not lost to a dwindling effort of surprise, but does sustain the uncommon need for reliving a partial existence of a past lifetime. She will search into a realm of past lives, discovering at the pace intended.

"I will help you to guide yourselves through this need for compassion toward another being (Nana Bird). Her soul strayed afar from its purpose of compassionate self-realism. Only partly does she feel that perception and is aware only through life's clingings.

"I accentuate to you that, through her body, was she aware of a past presence here with us. I enveloped her soul's cries as she portrayed a lost being in part. Your (Doug) hope to initiate recovery for this being was granted on a minute scale of receptivity through her acceptance of death. She will always allow a generous portion of time between these acceptances, as each soul has its own trial period of acceptance, and this is hers.

"Here, she will take a proud step for her soul and incorporate herself with you for the further, future teachings of life's other side to be shown through your work, eventually. Find a way to remit the material of past presences to her in your thoughts. Then through this, she will seek her recovery here."

A few short days before the trip to Connecticut and the funeral, Barb and I decided that Nicole needed to understand what was going to occur. Mixing the lure of an airplane ride to the possibly snowy north with the details of what would take place at the funeral, we tried our best to maintain a balanced and realistic outlook. Nicole absorbed it all, with equal measures of enthusiasm and solemnity. But, detecting a lingering sadness at the loss of her Nana Bird, I hugged her, explaining how in dreams, Mom and Dad could see how happy Nana Bird was becoming in her "new life." Though still wishing that her greatgrandmother were still with her, Nicole easily accepted Nana Bird's "dream" existence. To Nicole, dreams had a validity all their own, and now, she, too, could visit her Nana Bird if she wanted to.

Heavy thunderstorms gushed their way across central Florida on the day of our departure for Connecticut, but nothing could dampen Nikki and Greg's excitement about flying. After the short flight and an overnight stay in Hartford, we all piled into the rented car. Mom acted as navigator, getting us through the confusion of early morning traffic and well on the road towards Warren. The drive was a joy, especially for Greg and Nicole. Snow still hid in shadowed pockets along the road, and the barren pre-spring countryside provided seasonal contrasts not available to our Florida children. Barb had never been to this part of New England, and my last visit had been ten years before. Almost as if trying to fortify ourselves against the near future, the entire family immersed itself in pointing out the uniqueness of New England in mid-April.

Nana Bird's home had been vacant for many months, so the pantry needed replenishing. A quick stop to gather provisions at a grocery store in the little town of Bantam gave Nicole a chance to make snowballs from a drift of plowed snow left from a storm the week before.

It wouldn't be at all easy for Mom to enter that house, but the bustling excitement of kids, groceries and suitcases would help to soften the impact. Built in the 1700s, the house was restored by my grandparents in the 1950s, with my parents contributing untold hours to its continued maintenance over the years. There, Mom was to face the many living memories of her parents, her grandparents, her son and her husband.

Soon, the ancient stone wall came into view, as we rounded the crest of Townhill Road. There was the house, standing as if in a lonely vigil, aching for life to again fill its quiet rooms. Peeking hesitantly into the cool air were a few of the spring flowers that Nana Bird always tended with such care. Both Barb and I shuddered as we thought of the thousands of other reminders in the house that would make those days just before and after the funeral a psychological pressure cooker for Mom. As the old door swung open, we entered not just a house, but a week of emotion-filled hours that tumbled over each other in a conflicting cascade of sadness and quiet understanding.

The day of the funeral was breezy, but mild. The Warren Congregational Church stood stark white against the blue sky. As Nana Bird's friends and neighbors entered the church, many family members gathered near the entrance. While greeting each other with forced smiles, the funeral director interrupted. A mix-up in communications had left us without the pallbearers that were to have been provided by the funeral home. It had been agreed that such an assignment was an unnecessarily emotional task to request of family or friends. But, at that point, my cousin Schuy, several family friends and myself were selected. Knowing how I hated such things, Barb took my arm in a motion of understanding, as we followed the rest of the family through the front door of the church, and down the aisle toward the reserved pews.

The organist was playing "How Great Thou Art," as Mom had requested. The music and the old church brought back memories of Sunday morning sermons and my involvement in the young people's group during the summers of my teenage years. Friendships and laughter from those days glided with me as we edged into our seats.

Nana Bird's casket and the container holding Wally's ashes sat before us, awash in a sea of beautiful flowers. As the organ music subsided, Reverend Reeves began the short service by smiling at the congregation in his kindly way. His words softly captured the essence of the two people being memorialized. But, Barb and I had acknowledged Nana Bird's movement into another existence so long before that this event seemed to be merely the final punctuation at the end of a lengthy and complex story. As Mom shivered slightly, we recognized the agony she must be going through.

With the minister's words filling the otherwise silent church, a part of my consciousness drifted into an altered perspective. The scene before me took on an unusual clarity and brilliance. The colors of the flowers were somehow more perfect, and the individuality of people and objects was unified in some inexplicable way. Slowly, my attention was drawn upward to the balcony. For an unknown reason, my gaze centered on a corner of the balcony, just above Nana Bird's casket. It was as if someone were there, but that upper part of the church was empty. My feeling intensified, and as it did, the minister's voice sounded much farther away.

Closing my eyes for a few seconds, I could still see the church and its interior as it had appeared an instant before. The minister's voice droned on, and everything was the same in my mental vision, except that Nana Bird sat in the corner of the balcony. With that now familiar sense of time almost standing still, I could see her as clearly as if she were just another mourner, come to pay her respects. Chin in hand, Nana Bird's elbow rested on the dark railing. Her white hair was perfectly coiffed. She wore a light-colored, flowered dress I had seen many times, topped with a white sweater. Her glasses twinkled in the sunlight, and a slightly bemused smile crossed her face, as she watched the proceedings of her own funeral. As the minister's remarks drew to a close, my eyes opened to find the balcony as empty as it had been seconds before.

The oak casket was heavy, but we were able to maneuver it awkwardly into the hearse after everyone else had left the church. Family and friends waited in the procession of cars across the street for our arrival at the head of the line. With funeral director and pallbearers included, the hearse slowly moved down the street, drawing the string of vehicles with it into a coiling, segmented snake of shining metal.

The service on the windy hillside was a simple one. Mom trembled, as Barb and I each held one of her arms. Greg stared impassively ahead, while Nicole curiously stooped to pick up a rock, precisely at the "ashes to ashes" part of the minister's address.

One figure stood alone, away from the cluster of people around the grave site. Leah's tears were for Wally. Her extraordinary devotion to him during his years at Southbury Training School went far beyond duty and standard institutional responsibility. She had grown to love him as much as any of the family had, demonstrating an intense linkage that she was at a loss to explain. Through her presence, we once again realized the incredible complexity of purpose expressed through the halting life of one retarded individual.

Later, everyone gathered at the old farmhouse to share food, drink, and thoughts of better days coming.

Once the funeral was over, Barb and I no longer sensed Nana Bird's attachment to our physical reality. For a while, Mom felt Nana Bird's connection to the farmhouse, but this, too, diminished in time. What stood out in my mind, though, was that distinct image of Nana Bird in the church balcony. Soon after our return to Florida, we ap-

Death Experiences Viewed Differently 155

proached the source of our Writings, and the following exchange took place:

Q: *Would you please explain Doug's inward vision of Nana Bird at the church?*

A: "While your apparitions are not always self-evident, they are actually around your beings constantly.

"This vision's accuracy was immensely important for your re-creation of this spirit's (Nana Bird's) abilities, to reconstruct her own visual presence. Your worth was tied to the ability of sequelizing these events. Acting as a part for your reconnections, this spirit was then able to show herself to you, as an entity refined only through your visions.

"Becoming aware of her own death was not an apparent event to you totally, until her apparition was sighted in the midst of others' mourning. While you (Doug) were active as a catapult for her thoughts, you were seen by her to recognize the *fact* of her presence. This was reassuring to her. Be aware of this.

"You will flourish through this period, yet your suffering will become increasingly difficult. Being strong in this work will shelter your future sadnesses, so bond yourselves with this material, again facilitating a way to meld us all together.

"Love yourselves as I do."

10

Startling Dream Events

"KEEP A CAREFUL RECORD of your family dreams." That early Ouija board message first alerted Barb and me to the importance of dreaming and has since led to the realization that portions of our dreams are very specific modes of communication between realities. Unfortunately, over the years, our attempts at keeping dream journals haven't been as successful as we might have hoped. With the struggle of simply trying to get fully awake in the morning and the press of daily activities, those little bits and pieces of nocturnal wanderings seem to get lost in the shuffle. Only the more intense and coherent of our dreams tend to push their way past the crush of life's events, lasting long enough for recording or for a quick discussion at breakfast.

We've already shared some of those more lasting and meaningful dreams in past chapters, with others to come later in the book. The purpose now is not to discuss a variety of dreams at random, but to pursue a specific developmental series of occurrences that resulted in the title of this book becoming *An Explosion of Being—An American Family's Journey into the Psychic*.

Barb's trance state is a form of communication with another reality that allows a transmission of words and concepts into our lives. That method of conveying information works well for her, but as for me, I can't seem to function in that role. Oh, I'll engage in some "stream of consciousness" writing, and just let the words sweep along as they will. It opens my imagination and stimulates a creative writing ability, but I don't yet feel comfortable with a more direct, waking linkage to other realities. I'm usually too busy critiquing my own psychological make-up to avail myself of that possibility. Besides, with Barb, information is generated beautifully. Why take the time and effort to develop my talents with such a ready connection at our fingertips?

Little did I realize that during all of those refusals to work on my own conscious linkage, a unique communication route had been under construction in my sleep state even before Barb's ability began unfolding. Looking back five years, I now can see the beginnings of that connection as I review my dream journal.

On the twenty-seventh of September, 1977, I awoke in the middle of the night, almost capturing all of a very colorful and active dream. As I edged back into sleep, suddenly, I was facing what appeared to be the muted colors of several very symmetrical, molecular-type structures. Each looked much like the patterns visible through a child's kaleidoscope. The contrast to the previous dream's color and fast-paced action was surprising, especially since there was no movement or sound of any kind. Still close to consciousness, I woke myself, vaguely sensing that something important was happening. But, tiredness won out. As the last drops of awareness faded back into sleep, the kaleidoscope images flickered briefly into view.

This phenomena recurred randomly during other nights over the next several years. Each time, the encounter began in the dream state, flowing over, eventually, into a waking consciousness. This repetitious event never varied and was consistently monotonous. But, the continual reappearance and visual clarity of those images seemed to be forming a comfort based on familiarity. No, it was more than that. It was almost as if I had always known the meaning of those structures and was slowly uncovering that knowledge, layer by layer.

In May of 1980, Nicole was still young enough to take afternoon naps. One rainy Sunday, as a dutiful father, I stretched out with her to insure drowsiness. Soon, according to Barb anyway, I was snoring while Nicole happily played with her stuffed animals. In that short span of slumber, I again encountered those familiar geometric shapes. This occurrence, in itself, isn't noteworthy except for its direct connection to a later, more important event.

What happened during the early morning hours after I went to sleep that same night was so forceful, I had to get out of bed and enter that experience in my dream journal:

May 26, 1980 2:50 A.M.

"Got to sleep about midnight. Extensive dreaming. In one particular dream, Nikki was calling me. She needed help or assistance of some kind. Soon, she ran to me and threw her arms around my neck.

"At this point, I awakened. I could hear thunder and raindrops beginning to fall on the plants outside the window. Realized that our storm from the evening before was returning. Didn't open my eyes, but when I was about to, a voice in my mind said, 'Just relax and enjoy the storm in a different way.' Immediately, my body calmed with an unusual thoroughness. I, or the essence of me, was almost detached from that relaxed flesh. My mind then became filled with visions of beautiful patterns of color. These patterns would ebb and flow, brighten and change. How wonderful! I was maintaining full consciousness and prolonging a view of something that I had seen only in snatches during previous dream conditions (the geometrical, molecular structures).

"The color patterns then changed to a magnificent panorama of textured greens, containing minute particles of varied color. Vibrations seemingly emanated from each particle. The whole mass appeared to shift and rotate. The depth of this sight began to fluctuate as I sensed that now, I was seeing the 'true' sense of color, and perhaps the core of the children's book I was writing for Nicole.

"Suddenly, my mind was partially filled with a finely textured white light. It gave me a feeling of warmth and expanded my internal perceptions to a much greater degree. I had the distinct sensation of some sort of intelligence trying to contact me. Chills ran up and down my body as I then responded by reaching out for more communication through my mind.

"The patterns of color returned, but there was a noticeable difference. They were tighter, almost spherical in shape, with much finer color hues. The words came to me, 'You must begin to fully understand these things if you are to grow and progress.' With that statement, the spheres of patterned texture actually pulsated outward toward me and seemed to penetrate my being with the understanding.

"My consciousness of the thunder returned. As a gentle, long rumble bounced in the distance, thoughts of the children's books for Nicole sprang to mind. Then, I truly understood this pulsating communication I was experiencing was related to all of the books Barb and I would ever write.

"I opened my eyes and looked at the clock. 2:15 A.M. Lightning was flashing through the window. I thought of Nikki. Before going to bed, she opened her curtains to watch the storm. She made me promise to keep the curtains in our room open for us to do the same. I wondered if she, in some way, had helped to awaken me with the original dream so that I would have this experience and see the lightning as well. For some reason, seemingly apart from my consciousness, I sent her this mental message, "I saw the lightning as you wanted, and I do remember the old days." Old days? What the hell was that and where did it come from? When Nicole and I took a nap yesterday afternoon, I had seen the patterns of color. Was there a communication between Nikki and me at that time as well? Was there some sort of reincarnational link between us?

"It's been over a half hour since I've been up. The compulsion to record this material and imprint it on my conscious mind is incredible. I still have chills."

Sharing those notes with Barb the next day reminded me of the brilliant clarity of that experience, but beyond the recorded words was a depth of feeling that I found very difficult to describe. Something penetrated my being during those early morning hours in a way that I could sense but not explain. It was almost a physical realization captured within my cells, but unable to translate itself to the world. Direct contact was the one inescapable conclusion that kept filtering out of my feelings, but contact with what, or whom? The geometric forms and those vibrant colors felt so alive. When they swirled towards me, I was literally engulfed by physical sensation, non-verbal communication, love and warmth.

Neither Barb nor I was able to precisely define the nature of my contact. It did seem to be a natural outgrowth of our other communication with alternate realities, however, so we left it at that. For the next couple of years, I would awaken during the night from time to time to see the now familiar visions, then drift back to sleep in the midst of a very comforting, but indistinct exchange. It tended to become a random ritual, bringing with it, each time, a very peaceful sense of ease.

It was late evening on the 17th of March, 1982, one month before the funeral for Nana Bird and Wally, when Barb and I were finally able to steal enough time for a writing session. The outcome proved interesting and seemed to be preparing us for something yet to happen:

Wednesday, March 17, 1982

"Be prepared to inspect an even higher element of surprise from me. Your visions are accentuated and need to perform with accuracy. Therefore, be acceptable of your thoughts as they will become your visions of truth. Be accepting that I am your guidance here, as your selves have ordained me to this position. Be sure to accept the graciousness of self, as you will understand more of our ultimate values through this lesson of self's creativity.

"Becoming apparent in your reality is not always an easy challenge for us. To recreate a visual experience, one must surmise that he or she is accountable for each error of misrepresentation. This alters the ego and therefore becomes a mirror image of one's self's possessive structures. Being kind to one's self and delivering more readily acceptable ways do not always coincide.

"There is an energy which has a force beyond your present control and power. It seeks to guide your wisdom and strength. Become acknowledged in our realms as one who seeks to dissolve all fears of visual perceptions. Again, accelerate your need to become perceptive of these ways as a transmitter for deeper understanding of prior purpose. You will seek to enjoy a many-faceted avenue during this period of visions. We are actually visible to you as reminders when you are able to forfeit any other outstanding achievements of thoughts or possessions that hinder your ways.

"Varieties of visions are merely ways to deliver potent perceptions. The information that is guided through this awareness will gain you much knowledge as a couple whose understanding of others has great depth of perception. Avail yourselves of the problems that others will have receiving your transcripts, as they will reach toward unending self-passions, annoying themselves with their own vindications and efforts. Remember, 'to seek is to find.' You will both find. Growing together, you will form a new relationship with others who accept your work as a golden thread of peace and tranquility."

Then during a writing session on the evening of April 10, 1982:

"You are about to begin a new venture for yourselves. Try to lubricate your thoughts. I operate here on the promise that you will surmise my intentions, thereby unleasing secrets of time and immortalizing our thoughts from within each entity whose net purpose is planted already.

"You are both becoming a peak of spiritual unity. This foregoes any self-righteousness, allowing purposeful strength to become your guide for future welfare. Be, however, allowing of yourselves, for only through this allowance will you seek the destruction of old ideas that may torment you. Be quietly observant in yourselves, actually obtaining the right way for your beings to reconnect and accept this guidance as a truth for your learning. Positioning yourselves toward awareness will undoubtedly be a help to draw your senses into further kinship with each other."

After another paragraph of different information had been delivered, Barb opened her eyes and stopped the session. "I can't go on that way," she said. "I'm getting so dizzy that I'm afraid." Dizziness or not, the material was flowing perfectly. My distinct impression was that of seeing Barb at the threshold of a higher level of communications, but fighting the physical sensations that went with it. After explaining my thoughts to her, she acknowledged the possibility and agreed that our source might help us to better understand what was happening. Within a few minutes of closing her eyes, Barb indicated her readiness, and I posed the question:

Q: *Why is Barb having such feelings of dizziness?*
A: "Acting as a perceiver of thoughts, she will sense when actual thoroughness of consciousness is taking place. This will help to lead beyond the already mentioned acceptance of pacing yourselves. Your willingness (Doug) to act as a guide to help her through this period will provide the assurance that she will solder herself to your work, thus rechanneling herself in order to program a different source of information. She will physically advance herself into a state that works intently for her personal advantage.

"Alter your (both Doug and Barb) awareness only to that point which alters your understanding. Be'calm and accept these changes as they will alert your beings to higher influences than your own. Formalize a pattern that accepts these ideas as actual vibronic states. They will seat your beings into positions of openness and acceptability. Be light, and awareness will come as easily as you will it to.

"I will not dwell on this, for it will occur many times as have the changes that are now part of your permanent nature. While you are steadfast in your perceptions, your spiritual side has many others, and as the physical relates only to what is comfortable for him, it may adjust accordingly to whatever his spirit may deem necessary for readvancement. I will wait your promise to accept yourselves becoming a part of this reality. You are friends. Accept me as such. *Your will be done.*"

This last quote was almost like the ending of a prayer, but with an interesting twist. "Your will be done." The statement in context of the total message struck us as being strangely correct. Concisely, the words encapsulated fullness of philosophy that had been coming through over the years, and it felt very comfortable. Evidently, we were being directed toward new experiences, but the choice was clearly, always ours. All we could say was, "Amen, and don't forget it!"

Independent decision making aside, we were definitely curious. In two writing sessions almost a month apart, specific indications had been given that something was afoot, but what? We were always ready to probe further into alternate realities but just what changes lay in store, neither of us could say. All we could do was acknowledge a readiness to proceed and wait. It didn't take long. At 2:45 A.M. in the early morning of April 12, I bounced out of bed to record the following experience:

Monday, April 22, 1982. 2:45 A.M.

"What an incredible experience! For the past half hour or more, I've been undergoing a very vivid semi-dream state. It began at some point when I awoke, lying on my side, facing Barb. I had been awakened by what I heard and felt to be a tremendous explosion. It was as if something had actually detonated over the house, like a huge firework.

"As I lay there, everything was agonizingly quiet. Barb was still sleeping peacefully. No lightning. No fire. No retreating thunder. No children running to us in fear. No neighbors clamoring outside in amazement. Lying there with a distinctly physical feeling that indeed something had blown up, I began to wonder if I was the only one who had heard it. Impossible!

"Finally convincing myself that it must have been a dream, I turned over and went back to sleep. Dreams floated over me. An old friend and I were looking at a car that needed painting. Someone patted the car in question, and we agreed on when it was to be delivered. With my hand on the friend's shoulder, we left through a darkened hallway. How mundane it seemed.

"At this point, I awakened again. I could have sworn that a bug was crawling on me as consciousness returned. Groggily, I pushed the covers aside. One leg was pulled up as I lay on my side, but somehow, I just didn't have the energy to move any further. The arm that pushed the covers aside lay across my leg in what normally would have been a most uncomfortable position. But, my body felt heavy, tired and very relaxed. In contrast, my mind was highly alert.

"Realization then struck that no bug was crawling on me, and there actually had been no explosion in the physical sense. Suddenly, my left ear began to ring furiously, and I understood without knowing how that all of these things were psychic impressions made into physical constructs to capture my attention. Recognizing the goodness of what was occurring, I closed my eyes and began what seemed like a totally natural, but never before experienced, inward journey. Early in this state, an impression came over me that what I was to experience might be likened to a very controlled and safe LSD trip. What was so scary and dangerous for the LSD user was not to be scary or dangerous for me, because I understood what was happening, and I was in total control.

"Most of the perception, visually, during those moments, did not consist of sight in the usual sense; concepts, feelings and impressions were mixed with words and sights in an initially tangled jumble. Feelings and views abounded but not in the usual physical sense. The 'scenes' consisted of great flowing and pulsating patterns as well as colorful granular structures, much more massive and alive than anything I had ever experienced before. I seemed to feel these things as much as see them. In effect, I became part of them. I was even consciously able to flow into and around my 'visions,' enter them at will, and perceive them from different angles. This depth of view/feelings, at times, was overwhelming.

"All of these events were completely conscious. As they were occurring, I was thoroughly aware of what normally was a very awkward physical position in bed. I knew that my body was safe. At one point, Barb even turned toward me in the midst of my experience.

"Again, the thoughts came to me that this experience was under my control. It was to be a learning event and one that would continue for extended time periods. It was impressed upon me, in a very clear manner, that this type of thing would happen on many nights, for many, many years, perhaps for the rest of my life. Seemingly apart from my consciousness, the statement flooded my being with the words, 'Now it begins.'

"Slowly, I started to realize that the 'explosion' heard just minutes before had actually occurred inside of me. It was some sort of 'explosion of being.' Somehow, this all related to our psychic work, the Writings, etc. At that point, I conceived my own being to be in 'explosive interaction.' That original burst of sound and feeling, in essence, became me, and I, it. Unbelievably, I then literally felt myself become a brilliant, expanding firework. Fully, I could sense every particle of my being gloriously and joyously explode and enlarge, sending pieces of myself into every part of existence. *I could feel it!* I could feel myself, not as a distinct being, a body, or a separate entity, but, instead, I was existing happily as multitudinous amounts of bursting consciousness. The sensation was so unlike life as we think of it. How incredible to simultaneously *feel* myself in multiple, separate, expanding showers of my own being. I thought that perhaps this was how God felt when He showered himself to create the reality that we know.

"It was then that I had a distinct need to find our 'psychic house.' I had to see the flow of that infinite fish tank. I also had to see Nana Bird, but why, I couldn't say. Instantly, I stood within the house, awed by its absolutely sparkling clarity. In front of me, the beautiful fish tank bubbled, percolating its way upward. Nana Bird stood in front of the tank, but her image was blurred, in contrast to everything around her. Gradually, the image began to come into focus, and as I had seen in the hospital the night of her death, Nana Bird again was a beautiful little girl, looking into the brilliance of the tank.

"Turning slowly, she looked at me and smiled. Then the changes began. In a blinding series of flashes, her face changed into other faces at an incredible speed. Some of those faces I seemed to recognize, but many, I did not. It wasn't a fearful experience in any way. Somehow it seemed to be a very natural event. Once again, as a beautiful child, Nana Bird returned her gaze to the fish tank. But, as the movement was completed, her head became what I had seen earlier; swirling, pulsating patterns of granular colors of incredible depth. It was as if all of the physical that we know blended into what was the true essence of her being. The sight filled me with warmth, recognition and thankfulness that consciously I was beginning to understand.

"In one sweeping motion, both the child and I then flowed into the radiance of the fish tank. Immediately, I merged with the swells and bubbles, expanding ever upward. Again, as in my 'self explosion as a firework' experience, I became the joyous, separate existences of this bubbling material. Part of my being was thrusting constantly upward and outward, and yet, I could look down and 'feel' the parts of myself that were being 'recreated' at the bottom.

"Gradually, my focus turned from the fish tank to my own body lying in bed beside Barb. The strange thing was that part of my consciousness had never left. During all of the perceptions and events in the 'psychic house,' I could feel that part of me still in bed. When the fullness of my consciousness returned, I focused on Barb. Somehow, I thought that she might join me in my experiences. In less than a second, she physically moved closer to me. Pulling the covers around her, she mumbled some indistinguishable words and stayed asleep. Had I contacted her? Within the asking of that question, I was seeing back into that 'other reality.' Flowing towards me with pulsations of its beautiful, granular form, was one of my 'living' molecular structures. Familiarity and love caused my physical body to smile, for I knew this being was Barb's spiritual essence. She was with me in the totality of the experience.

"Physically smiling again, I focused on my body, realizing for the first time how absolutely in control I was. I knew that I could open my eyes, physically move and not disturb the 'other reality.' To test this, I decided to recognize finally the very awkward physical position I had been in for some time. 'Decided?' Evidently, it was up to me to feel or not feel. How strange! As my eyes opened, everything in the dullness of the late night gloom was perfectly normal. I turned over and stretched. Stiff and chilly, I pulled the covers around my chin.

"The next decision was to return to the 'other reality.' Instantly, it was done. Again, the flowing, throbbing structures bubbled with their granular intricacies. Watching those forms somehow made me think of out-of-body experiences and within the thought came the flash of understanding: 'Out-of-body experiences are nothing more than pulling the physical inside-out.' What? The concept made obvious sense to a deeper part of me, but the calculating logic of my surface consciousness wondered how I could comprehend such an obscure bunch of words.

' As if to clarify the concept, another thought pierced the confusion and explained, 'The spiritual is simply the underside of the physical. The two are actually interchangeable.' Realization: I had always known this but the depth of knowledge had previously been far beyond what my conscious mind could accept. Then words seemingly apart from me said, 'This is not the time to sense what is considered by many to be an out-of-body experience. These occurrences are definitely valid but not for you, Doug, right now. Out-of-body experiences are childlike and linked directly to the physical world and to physical understanding. You know better! It is your responsibility to work on a comprehension of the true underside of the physical being that you now have seen as a flowing, pulsating substance. Out-of-body experiences are merely an in-between state, or a playtime, compared to the truer reality you are sensing.'

"I opened my eyes again. My body was rigid but under control. Could I sleep? Should I continue with the experience? No, I had to write it all down, capture as much as possible before it was forgotten. It's still clear as a bell. Why do I feel it's so vital to write this down in such detail?

"It's now 4:11 A.M. I've been writing and thinking for quite a while now. When I got up, I had to look outside to see if it was cloudy. The physical sensation of that original rousing explosion still tingled in my being. Maybe a distant flash of lightning would indicate a recently passed storm. Perhaps that could explain the explosion. I smiled at my need to try and explain the recent event in physically acceptable terms. Bright moonlight drenched everything except the ink black shadows of the trees as I stepped onto the back porch. Dark sky speckled with glinting stars arched quietly over neighboring yards. A very light mist hung in the air all around but no clouds or lightning. But, then again, I knew there wouldn't be any.

"How wonderfully, beautifully incredible, all of it. I wish I could transport everyone in the world into my feelings, understandings and experiences. I ache to transmit it somehow, not just on paper, but in the full, glorious, multiple explosion of my being."

Later, I would find it almost impossible to elaborate upon those early morning notes. Trying to explain it further to Barb was frustrating because I wanted so for her to feel what I had felt. The intensity of the event had wound its way deeply into my being, but it just seemed to hum gently at some sub-verbal level.

The frantic pace of the two weeks following my experience left precious few moments for analysis. With the double funeral in Connecticut looming on the horizon, and problems with the business increasing day by day, we were barely able to hold onto our roller coaster lives, no less investigate a psychic dream event. It would only be in late April, after the funeral, that we would begin to look at my late night occurrence. During a writing session on the 25th of April, this exchange took place:

Q: *Do you have any comments on Doug's extended waking dream?*

A: "Your vivid body, Doug, was acting as a unit of exposure for your reminiscing to be completely physical. As a unit of time, you were exposed to a degree of solidarity that broke this time into many sections.

"Your abilities to perceive this reality are increasingly intense. As your perceptions accelerate, your wisdom will flourish easily with comfort. Ascertain the various lessons that resulted in this chapter of your life. It was actually a penetration into a deeper state of being for operative powers to be withheld, but observed. Your nature must also observe creative abilities within the spiritual levels.

"The accent of the explosive scenes was intended to behold actual vibratory states that you are fully responsive to. Finalizing your crystalized thoughts, you were able to perceive the underside of every vibration that encircled your wisdom of many past lives. As a guide from other areas of time, you are now more peaceful within yourself, but be pleasured in knowing that through these experiences, you will start to relive other adjustments that have been made here before.

"Isolation will not always recreate this portion for you. However, a part of other existences will come into your lives and slowly respond to your demands. Become increasingly aware of these pasts and act upon them. While opening an image of yourself, Doug, you were acting as the spark within each creative being; your own challenge, therefore, being answered from within yourself. The reality of which you spoke was an actuality. This was then placed before you again, to help you relive the actual experiences that are a commonality on this plane."

The "explosion of being" incident, as we now call it, was for me an extremely personal culmination of contact with an unseen existence. In a way, I still feel very much a part of that experience. It's as if it were continuing somehow, laying foundations for further perceptions and merging with Barb's trance communication to form a comprehensive pattern of understanding. For both of us, the "explosion of being" event has become so symbolic of our increasingly expanded awareness that no other title for this book could have been more appropriate.

11

Reflections

THE CUT CRYSTAL BALL shimmered in the candlelight at the end of a gracefully curving metal rod, which in turn was attached to a small wooden base. It was Doug's Mother's Day gift to me, matching the one I had given him for his birthday. It seemed so very appropriate to have it sitting on the redwood picnic table during this particular weekly family night barbecue. It was the first time since Nana Bird's death that Fred had been able to spend a weekend.

After tucking Nicole into bed, I rejoined Doug and the boys on the patio. This was our time, as always, to sit back, relax, and engage in quiet candlelit conversation. It's during such moments that the casual sharing of interesting dreams or unusual coincidences always emerge. My placement of the crystal was intentional, because I knew Doug wanted to tell Fred about Nana Bird's death and to explain our developing philosophy of the soul's crystalline structure. But before Doug was able to approach those subjects, Fred became fascinated with the crystal, detaching it from the hook and peering at the candle through the multiple facets.

Conversation ceased, as Fred held the crystal in front of one eye, then the other, with exclamations of, "Wow!" and "Look at that!" Soon, Greg was vying for a peek and before long, all of us were passing it back and forth. Fred was right. Looking at the candle through the crystal produced beautiful colors and an abundance of multiple visions. When the crystal was finally returned to its stand, Doug explained its meaning to Fred and how our understanding had grown out of Nana Bird's death. Recognizing that his intense attraction to the sparkling little globe had come well in advance of Doug's explanation, Fred shook his head in wonder.

Like a warm spring breeze, the thought of Fred with the crystal glistening in front of his eye, continues to pleasantly brush over Doug and me from time to time. The lasting mental picture of that event, for us, will always symbolize the individual's search for himself, which can result in a delightful and dazzling discovery of the true nature of his own greater being. It was also as if Fred were reenacting, within a few minutes, the essence of our own psychic journey over the years, following the death of Doug's father.

Life has taken on so many different meanings since those agonizing hours when we watched Walt's physical being diminish, hour by hour at Orlando's Naval Hospital. Now, Doug and I view his death and the occurrences surrounding that event, as the sparks that ignited our insatiable desire to comprehend the enigmas of existence.

Since that time, life, for us, has developed a mirror-like quality, which seems to reflect patterns and purposes emanating from our crystaline souls. We view physical existence, in itself, as a psychic event, constantly suggestive of a much deeper validity. Even beyond that depth, we see a primary source of being that some may refer to as God. Perhaps, God's reality lies in the totality of all the crystalline soul structures, somehow giving birth to a timeless, spiritual existence, but leaving the creation of physical worlds and the planning of material experience to those multi-faceted entities glistening their way through infinity. The earth, as viewed by the soul structures, might then be seen as a circular pattern of past and future human history, into which they permit the introduction of their facets through what we call reincarnational existences.

Doug and I have finally concluded that we must be two personality projections radiating from the same soul. In effect, the greater portions of our beings are probably two individual facets of that larger entity, using this life as some sort of cosmic schoolhouse. Each of the other facets of our soul is also a separate, unique personality. However, because the soul exists in a reality that doesn't recognize the limitations of time and space, those other facets may be projecting into other time periods, past or future, or into different realities entirely. From the soul's perspective, existence must look like a continuous Now, with earthly history from beginning to end a simultaneous, living theatre of potential participation.

Again, from the soul's perspective, each personality facet probably appears to blink on and off as it periodically reincarnates itself into the physical world. Apparently, then, each reincarnational "blink" varies as to racial distinction, sexual identification, physical characteristics, geographical location, living conditions, social atmosphere and placement in physical time, so that the soul's growth ultimately benefits. My next lifetime, according to this process, could be that of a Chinese foot soldier during the T'ang Dynasty of 627 A.D.

As more or less twin facets, Doug and I feel that we have selected many incarnations together. We suspect that this joint selection of lifetime, according to this process, could be that of a Chinese foot soldier within families, religious groups, fraternal organizations, or any other combination where close ties are felt. Such choosing, most likely, even carries over into groups involved in specific events such as wars, political movements, or mass disasters. The groupings may be that of several facets of one soul, or various combinations of facets from a multitude of souls.

We have found that through the sleep state, traces of our other incarnations are, at times, recognizable. In my dreams, I can recall distinctly several instances that startled me with their sensations of absolute reality. These were no fuzzy, isolated wanderings of my mind. In each circumstance, the feeling of having physically existed within those other lifetimes was total. The clarity of vision, the physical impressions, the unique psychological frameworks, and the occasional repetition over the years have convinced me that those experiences are very natural perceptive flashes, showing the multi-dimensional aspects of my crystaline soul connection.

In one particular dream, I am observing a large, muscular black man. Watching him from a distance, I can see that he is wearing only long pants and is barefoot. Sweat streaks his body as he labors over a project. I get close enough to see his sharp, handsome features and his close-cropped, curly hair. The man is young, apparently in his early twenties. Only vaguely do I sense that this scene took place several hundred years ago.

As I study his face, it's as if I'm looking into a mirror. Suddenly, I recognize that *I am* this individual. Instantly, I become that man, losing my sense of objective observation. In that split second, I begin to see everything through his eyes. "My" large, dark hands are grasping a huge mallet of some sort, and I feel the full force of my strength as I pound something into the ground.

It's very hard labor, in that open field, but I'm certain of my ability to handle it. Sporadically, I bend over to pick something up or I shout over my shoulder to other blacks working nearby. I do my work well, but I am angry. It's a deep, subtle anger that expends some of its energy as I pound with my mallet. I am a slave, and I hate it. There are no chains, but it seems as if my whole being is shackled. Pound, pound, pound. Feel the power of my physical being as it tries vainly to crush the frustration of existence.

When I first recognize my physical oneness with this man, I'm taken aback. How can I be male and black, when I'm really white and female? The contradiction lasts only for a second, before total comfort and identification with this individual takes over. Doug and I have concluded that what's taking place here is a lesson in reincarnational stages of a soul's facet: multiple existences include lives where race and sex vary from incarnation to incarnation. The pounding in the dream may well have been a reality, but it is probably also quite symbolic that this lesson needed to be "pounded home."

With that "lesson" in mind, let me share another recurring dream:

The girl is about eighteen or nineteen years old. She is blonde and attractive, dressed beautifully in an expensive, hoop-skirted gown. The location is a southern plantation, the time shortly before the Civil War. As in the "black slave" dream, I suddenly recognize that this girl is me. Merging easily into the force of her personality, I see the world from her vantage point.

I've just recently come back from town, with its dirt streets, brick buildings and carriages bustling here and there. Everything is set for the party. My new gown is lovely and Daddy smiles at me as he comes down the staircase. He is a fairly tall man, slender, with dark hair and a moustache. In addition to his approval of me, I sense that we share a mutual warmth and devotion.

I thoroughly enjoy living in this huge house, with its white walls, chandeliers and fine furniture. In fact, I love this kind of life. How glorious to have what you want, when you want it. I have no responsibilities, no problems and a great deal of influence. And the servants! They care for my every whim!

As I think about that spoiled southern belle, I wonder what the black slave would have thought of her. I wonder if he ever dreamed of such luxurious plantation living. Looking at both of those lives together, I see some very interesting contrasts that give the picture a rather unique balance. Maybe, that's what reincarnation really is: a process of balance.

A final recurring dream of this type involves a war. It's hard for me to distinguish whether it's World War I or World War II, but it's definitely happening in the twentieth century. I observe the young man in full battle dress, as he and a group of about fifteen other soldiers run across an open space, jumping feet first into a trench. At this point, I become that young man, directly experiencing everything happening on the battlefield through him.

It's night, but there's enough light from somewhere for us to see. We've been advancing like this for quite a while. The noise is deafening. Smoke fills the air around us. I'm apprehensive, but in control of my emotions.

It's up and over another trench rim again. Small groups, like ours, are scurrying forward. We run and crouch, dodge and shoot. The rifle is heavy in my hands. There's no time to be afraid. Just keep moving and shooting. The enemy is everywhere. Men are dropping. Oh, my God, I'm hit. But, it's not too bad from what I can see. Keep moving and shooting. The noise of battle is incessant.

A rest at last. We're behind some bushes, out of the mainstream of the fighting. Some of us grab a quick smoke before we move on. Got to patch up my wound. We're waiting for something or someone.

Reincarnational flashes, such as this, besides demonstrating the multi-faceted aspects of reality, can also be instructive on one particular issue of current life. Doug and I found this out late one night, just minutes after going to bed. No sooner had he apparently drifted off to sleep, when Doug turned over to tell me about this dream:

"I was partially asleep just now. You know, that semiconsciousness right before going under completely. In that short time, I, well . . . it was as if I were actually . . . physically existing somewhere else, but conscious of being here in bed at the same time.

"I was in Russia, near the turn of the century, say, early nineteen hundreds. I could feel the bitter cold through the heavy clothing I wore. Snow covered the streets where I was standing. The day was dark, as if again, it was about to snow. The building in front of me, and those up and down the streets, appeared massive and grey in the gloom.

"My comrade lay crumpled at my feet, dead from a hail of bullets. I knelt before his body. The snow crunched beneath my knees. The firing squad was behind me. I knew that I would be executed also. Seconds later, the rifles exploded, ripping through my body, tearing my lungs apart. Strangely, there was no pain. With total serenity, I toppled over my friend to join him in death. Then, almost as an observer of the entire scene, I casually realized how the shredding of my lungs by those bullets, in that lifetime, was a direct cause of recurring asthma in my childhood, this lifetime."

Reflections

Doug and I are now beginning to see how our dreams reconnect the multiple layers of our soul facet. It's as if dreams are a place of reintegration and sharing among our many existences. The sleep state, for us, has become a very natural and automatic fusion of the being, where those artificial barriers of physical consciousness, subconsciousness and separate incarnations, cease to exist. Whether or not remembered or recognized by our conscious minds the next morning, the process continues its nightly blending, until death eventually reunites those multiple aspects into a greater totality of existence.

In our view, the refreshment of sleep doesn't result only from physical and psychological recuperation. It results also from that nightly "rebirth" into the naturalness of a spiritual reality. It's a time of recharging our psychic batteries, as we "plug in" to the source of physical life. Out-of-body experiences seem to be elementary forms of the "rebirth" into spiritual reality, and from what we have observed, they are often meant to force the conscious mind to accept its true spiritual connections.

One night, during the early days of our Writings, what at first seemed like a dream, turned into a very real event. As I lay on the bed next to Doug, I felt a lightness, as if I were a balloon being filled with helium. Slowly, I began to float upward, inch by inch, until the sensation stopped when I must have been three feet above the bed. With a surprising calm, I realized that I was in an out-of-body condition, and my eyes opened. As I turned my head to the right, there was Doug floating beside me also in an out-of-body condition. Even in the dark of night, we both seemed to be somehow illuminated. In that brightness, Doug turned his head to look at me. As we both extended our arms so that our hands were touching, I saw shining bands of blue on white emanations around our spiritual bodies. At the moment of contact, I became totally aware of our physical beings sleeping below us. Instantly, I knew beyond a doubt, that nonphysical existence was a definite reality. For me, that experience solidified my intellectual belief in life after death. Doug, however, remembered nothing of what occurred. But, some weeks later, he told me about his own unique encounter:

"I was dreaming off and on during the night. Can't recall much of what was going on, except that, occasionally, I would be looking directly into an air conditioner vent. Staring at that idiotic vent for awhile, out of sheer boredom I would then lapse into another dream. Time and again, though, back I would come to look at my friend, the vent. Finally, the absolute dullness of the scene disturbed me so much that the next time around, I focused all of my attention on what was happening. With my full consciousness peering at the vent, it was just more clearly dull. Metallic fins projected in various directions, with spaces between the fins, allowing cool air to push into the room. Common, ordinary screws held the stupid thing into the ceiling.

"Ceiling!? I wondered why the word seemed so strange. That's where the vent in our bedroom is fastened, so what? Then, as I scanned the rows of fins, it hit me. The ceiling was eight feet above the floor, and I was lying flat on my back, almost nose-to-nose with the vent. Realizing that I must be floating near the ceiling, I wondered why I hadn't figured this out before. It was so obvious!

"It was the dead of night, yet what I was viewing was perfectly clear. For a while longer, I just stared at the vent and the ceiling in fascination. The complete repetitive dullness of that scene had awakened my consciousness in such a way that I couldn't help but recognize my out-of-body condition. It was inescapable and absolute. My body was sleeping some yards away, while my consciousness, without a doubt, was perceiving the vent at close range. No logic, none of my understanding of psychological aberrations or knowledge of dream states came to mind at that moment. I was living a separation from physical life, and I knew that it was real. I'll never forget that stupid, tedious vent, because it brought me face to face with my spiritual self."

As we no longer question the multidimensional aspects of our beings, neither do Doug and I any longer question the multidimensional aspects of daily living. For us, we look at every occurrence in life, no matter how small, as part of an intricate planning process that involves the nonphysical portions of existence. What we used to call coincidences are now definitely viewed as indicators of a complex, but invisible decision making structure. The "accidents" of life, such as the minor car wreck that prevents someone from boarding an airplane that later crashes, stand like beacons of revelation, awaiting our acknowledgement. As our trance source pointed out to us long ago, "Go to your minds and recall what I have said before: There is no coincidence, and there is always a connection."

It has been a most interesting process to watch Greg as he explores for himself the nature of coincidental events. From time to time, he notices purposeful connections to what might normally be considered accidentally related happenings. When a particular series of such connections surfaced one day, within a few minutes of time, Greg was awed by the chances against what he had just experienced. It was so important to him that he brought Doug and me together to tell this story:

"O.K. you guys. You're not going to believe this. Dad, you know that phone call a while ago? Well, it was from my ex-girlfriend down in Venice. I haven't heard from her in months. When she called, I had just started to write about her in my journal. I was going to write about meeting her on the beach 'n stuff and "bang," she calls.

"Now, that's not all. After I got off the phone, I saw that I was wearing the shirt she gave me. And, listen to this. A second later, a song from the Barbra Streisand album I gave her came on the radio. Can you believe it? You guys aren't kidding about coincidences, are you?"

As in Greg's experience, the natural flow of discovering daily connections with deeper portions of reality can be intriguing, but can at times also be a little unsettling.

One of our more intriguing occurrences began when Doug came home after one of the many crisis days, during his ill-fated venture into business. His half-joking statement didn't make me laugh at all. "Well, Barb, guess what? We've got our first exorcism." What!? I was horrified. What a terrible prospect. "You're kidding, right?" I was beginning to back out of the room. "Ah, well, yes, kind of, but . . .," he stumbled. "What I mean is that one of my associates at work has been seeing this, ah, well, ghost-like vision and I, ah, well, sort of promised we'd find out what it is."

As the story unfolded, it seemed that Doug had shared the concepts of his children's books with a woman in the office. This led to a discussion of afterlife and subsequently to a discussion of *An Explosion of Being*, including the trance communications. Doug's friend was fascinated. She proceeded to tell him about a ghostly image that kept presenting itself to both her and her daughter. Their request was simply to investigate, through our trance source, the nature of the sightings. The request was simple, but its execution was not. Yes, Doug and I had seen images that might commonly be called ghosts, and, yes, our trance communications explained their appearances, but to actually investigate somebody else's haunting?

Through Doug's gentle pressure and a few days of careful consideration, I agreed to give it a try. As long as Doug's friend understood that we guaranteed nothing, and the investigation would consist only of asking questions of our source, in our own home, then I would participate.

With just Doug and me present, the writing session went perfectly, giving us a full page of information. Apparently, my nervousness left me entirely, as the words flowed of their own accord, in the usual manner. A little study showed some sort of cryptic reference to a spiritual guide that had always been with this woman. It seemed as if this continued appearance was meant to remind her of something that she needed to learn. The words had a logic about them, but we had trouble deciphering a completeness of meaning.

The next day, Doug took the typed session to work, handed it to his friend, and explained what little we understood from the messages. Almost apologetically, Doug told her that the material may have no significance for her whatever, and to feel free to discard it if what was said didn't feel right. When his presentation was done, she said, "It may not make a lot of sense to you, Doug, but to me those messages are perfectly clear." She went on to explain how, since childhood, she had seen a spiritual guide such as the one mentioned in the Writings, but she had forgotten about it in recent years. She seemed very pleased with the content of what Doug gave her, allowing us both to breathe a sigh of relief.

The matter would have ended there, except that a couple of weeks later, Doug happened to ask his friend how the ghost was faring. Her response was a startled revelation to herself. "My God, we haven't seen it since you and I discussed the messages from your trance communications. It all made so much sense, somehow, I didn't even realize that we weren't seeing it any more."

And I hadn't wanted to participate in an exorcism?

From intriguing to unsettling is a big step, but this terrifying dream of Doug's and its conclusion in the physical world showed how quickly that transition can occur:

"Dream after dream shot their ways past me in rapid fire succession. They made a blizzard of random movements, people, objects and colors. Tossing and turning, I was physically and psychologically restless. Everything moved too quickly and nothing was understandable, until the motion slowed to a comprehensible focus on a small child. It seemed as if the child were a little girl, but I wasn't certain because she, or he, was running so fast.

"In a moment, the child's desperation was all too clear. Someone was in pursuit, and the child was fleeing in panic. The scenes then changed too rapidly to follow, until, once more, the focus was on the child, but this time he, or she, was sitting in a blue pickup truck. Again, the child tried to escape, but as the door opened, a slashing knife seemed to cut completely through the small body.

"Before I had time to react, the child was staggering through the woods, finally stopping just in front of me, critically wounded. Crouching in pain, the child looked at me, turning my growing revulsion into an agonizing desire to help. Reaching down, I gathered the youngster in my arms and held it close. In absolute horror, I realized that I was literally holding the child together."

Lurching awake, I found myself trembling and in a cold sweat. Nicole must have sensed something. She had arisen, entered our room and was just standing by the bed, looking at me in the darkness. I reached out and hugged her, dissipating some of the dream's terror.

The next day, I began a scheduled business trip along Florida's East Coast. On the way towards Jacksonville, a radio report, describing a child's abduction in south Florida seemed like just another bit of the world's negativity, so I paid little attention.

"After finally arriving at my destination and settling into the Holiday Inn south of town, I went in search of a restaurant for dinner. But, again, the radio blared news of that abduction. On it went, with the final chilling news that part of the child's body had just been discovered by search teams.

"My hands began to shake. Pictures from the horrifying dream the night before flooded my mind. Instantly, I knew that the dream action of holding a child together was symbolically valid. Somehow, a part of me had spiritually stumbled into that event to help the child's consciousness repair the damage done through the pain and fear of that gruesome killing.

"Supper that night didn't settle very well. I left most of it still sitting on the plate and returned to the motel. Using the noise of television and the need to prepare for my meeting the next day, I was able to push thoughts of my dream and the child into the background. Sleep came much later, but only after wrestling with a piercing sadness and a raging anger at the injustice of physical life. I could still feel that trembling youngster in my arms.

"Incredibly, within the next couple of days, my original travel plans put me on a road passing the exact spot where the child's remains had been found."

Expanded awareness can be a double-edged sword. As Doug found out, it can indeed cut two ways. On the one hand, it can clear a path for beautiful and satisfying perceptions, but on the other hand, it can reveal information that I suspect we might otherwise prefer to hide from our conscious mind. So-called "psychic phenomena," then, are perhaps just tiny bursts of recognition, both positive and negative, reminding us of the truer reality from which our physical existence springs.

Following that logic a bit further, the dreams and trance communications that Doug and I have experienced are probably methods of reacquainting us consciously with our higher selves. The origin of this information is, most likely, none other than that crystaline soul's structure from which we are both projected into this reality. Keeping this possibility in mind might prove helpful as you move into the next chapter and your own special encounter with our source.

12

To the Reader from a Source with No Name

(This chapter was specially planned, as an opportunity for a direct communication between you and our connection into another reality. Somehow, it fit the developing pattern of our own understanding and underscores the purpose for which this book was intended. All along, our source has given us comfort and guidance. We're very happy now to extend that same personal tie to you as a new friend. Your inclusion into our private network of communications is offered openly, with hopes that you might feel just a touch of your own infinite connections.)

"YOU ARE ALSO WELCOME, as my readers. Every particle of your own being is now focused in this direction. Should you become exposed to a further advancement, your beings then will follow suit and recharge this present formation of channeled particles.

"You, as readers, will enjoy various parts of this book. They are as varied as the particles of which I just spoke. Your individual needs are consoled only through your own soul's choices. Be prepared to accept this. As each of you follows a pattern of substance throughout your own existence, your will to delve into ultra perceptions may seem a bit stronger. This has enabled your being to pull toward this material.

"The soul must reach for and be guided by a source which allows direct motivational resources to become thoroughly established. Without this motivation, your needs to become a patternized individual would short-circuit themselves. The apparitions, past life remembrances and basic psychic principles, will adjust themselves within your learning centers. When necessity finds a course of reason, this book will allow your freedom, totally.

"Being sure of one's self, during life, will promote decay of its own. By this, I instruct you to look at past experiences whose self-confidence overflowed into egoistic ways of denial, thus resulting in a lack of search. For your own purposes, therefore, be relieved to know that through a searching process, you will not become stagnant, nor will the gain that you already sense be lost. Your arrow has been directed to this book as a proportionate means to allow your soul the freedom of choice. Appreciate your own freedom. It is a precious commodity that many earth-bound entities pass away lightly.

"There is an air of certainty which prevails amongst all of you who have allowed yourselves the material of our book. Your experiences of other lives are entering a reconstructive period now, which shall enable your own inner forces to dip into a light source which will come to hold a cleared evaluative position for each of your introspections.

"I thoroughly understand that, through this reading, you will find contradictory messages which act as antagonisms within your physical brain network. Be patient, however, with yourself, as each entity has its own period of allowance. This newness, for some, will come as quickly as understanding the purpose of each one's birth. Some of you, at times, will find a system of rejection, which floats into a comatose period of your own past. Pleading with yourself to understand, where lack of strength to comprehend is not available, is perfectly acceptable. Your strengths lie there quietly, within yourselves. As you will yourselves to withdraw from any of this material, then find in it a satisfaction that peace is allowed here. Your intellect shows its wisdom through many avenues. As a protective device, your intellect will change according to your emotional structure. Evaluate this, please.

"As you promenade mentally through these pages, you are recalling a memory which will be awakened. Somehow, your understandings will be enhanced through this material. Your needs are so profuse that their crusts are not yet fully formed. But, your opening them will allow these areas to be comforted, as in your youth, you were perfectly admired by others who watched and waited on you (as the baby), giving your needs a total priority. Again, you have reached this point.

"Become aware that these needs are not yours alone. Each individual wishes to share a part of himself called fear. His beliefs are founded on much that others have forwarded through many years of others' wisdom. This wisdom is accurate only if totally believed. However, there is a lack of this total belief, as each falters throughout a daily pattern of life. Your purpose in reading this book, again, is to show that your own needs are not always filled through outer connections with past faiths.

"Nearer to the core of your own existence lies a pattern so intricate that, only through many years of webbed experiences, will you find total adjustments to this core. I will allow your personages to avail themselves to any freedom toward this goal that you choose. However, do not expect reality, then, to become a neutral ground for psychic passivity. Your viewing of such, instantaneously, would not serve a direct purpose to these inner workings of which I speak. The unification of your present environment, along with your future reading here, will flow together as quickly as you wish the rain to help your flowers grow. Your growth will pattern itself after your needs, so relax through this information.

"Your wishes, as readers, will only be fulfilled through your personal internalization of this material. Acting as a self-influencing guide, you will merge your present thoughts with a level of desire that shows further adherence to 'unusual' concepts. You are more apt to delve into a period of time that rejuvenates a youthful part of your triangular existence. This is seen as obviously as if, through a glass, you were to visualize your childhood and then, in return, look from the other side, into adulthood.

"The reality in which you now exist will always be useful to your being, as a partial, coherent slice of your total existence. Each entity must break down his or her guidelines of past formation. Your present mobility of mind is not useful if there is no openness of growth. The act of one's growth period is slowed by the choice of immobility from the mind. You are all effervescent in your ways of doing things, which arrive only in a fair result. Be careful to choose each of your own paths as directly as if a map were in front of you to position yourself. In this life as a programmed entity, you will seek an avenue.

"You shall each enjoy the fruits of being in touch with your own inner self, by working through a period of rejoicing or remorse. These highly emotional times provide introspective inklings, where one is in touch with an inner portion of himself. Your own periods of rejoicing will come at points where the unexpected shows its face, in tune with those remorseful periods. Your unexpected newness is a part of the planned reaction that you share with yourself. During these times, ideally, the conditions of which I speak are entered into a cosmic record for your beginning awareness, each lifetime. As a child, you were told by your inner being that through rechanneling these efforts, the womb of peace would remain with you always.

"There are many people who do not recognize their own sense of awareness, merely due to the fact that each has his harmony measured in other ways. Purposeful events will help those who recall this period. Your sedative process begins when each entity takes the choice of rebirth. During this time, a unified part of your own record divides itself again as a useful free placement of power, to derive more energy that will be needed to refurbish the soul.

"I will await many of you, here, to see this refurbishing take place. As each of you begins resurfacing, while awake, you are in touch with your own physical and mental needs. Emotionally, your awareness is open to anything that shows a purpose for your development. However, if that purpose does not seem to be placed directly, a rejection takes place. This, my friends, is understandable. I, too, have experienced this, many times before.

"Isolating yourself in order to follow a doctrine of another, is purposeful only if the other gives you the freedom and the choice of pursuing the intertwining needs that result throughout the emotional analysis of such a doctrine. Your needs of understanding in this area are very young, yet strong enough to show rebellion, if such deeply acquired resistance is met through another's doctrine.

"You have met your own changes while attending a mental seminar which allows your presence here today. Your beings are creating certain impulses which relate directly to their own needs. Thereby, through a vibratory state, your will has exposed itself in order to perform a 'chance' situation.

"Your understanding of these chapters relates only to your personal, individualized goals. Be careful not to add or delete any periods of purpose, for these will form by themselves through your inner guidance. In other words, an outer spiritual system is not totally critical in absorbing this spiritual information period. As you have shown us here that your wildest interpretations of life are open to discussion, you are extracting a fear from within to divulge a part to yourself.

"In reading this book, your other parts (of self) will comply through a spiritual unity, thus enabling your nest of comfort to remain on a physical level. Your needs are young now, seemingly, but will, however, be altered throughout these pages. As your teacher, I will help to show your authors here how to incorporate any lack of physical achievement with spiritual attainment. Your work will enable them to become a more developed entity themselves.

"Your being is now mortal, therefore your actions are also. As lightly as possible, dwindle not from life's changes. They are teachers for you and your own individual development. Your needs are always there. However, you shall show these needs to be exploiting themselves, at times, for your own self-recognition. Thus, through happiness, sadness and total exultation periods, you will seek to announce these periods mainly without the depth of purpose. Only shallow beginnings are being formed, as there are partitions which will begin allowing the choice that you have now begun to visualize beyond the shallowness.

"Your neatness of life will not change, as a certain expectancy period is bound to overwhelm underlying spiritual needs temporarily. However, both your physical and spiritual levels will be charmed by the solidarity of aptitude within each of you to comprehend this material, without thoroughly understanding it in a physical manner. A natural response to these words will be set for your ability to conceive your own inner projections. How this process works exactly, I will come to instruct you at a later time. Be patient, as your own inner guide has seen the structure of your individualized plan. Be cooperative with him. Your human intelligence is purposed in order to speculate on life's deepest meanings. Some will veil their discoveries, as each has various levels of intellectual acceptances. Your beings are not ready for some levels of achievement yet, but others are waiting in the wings.

"Be patient and guide yourselves wisely toward a higher goal. Too many earthly entities are enticed through their own means of physical surfacing. By this, let me pretend that, through a baby, you would see a candlelight of spirituality. This baby would uphold his own spirituality by waiving a physicalness to another, whose need was more prominent than his own. You are creating, at this point, the leverage for accepting a baby's existence as a higher individual than your prior perception. A physical being shall choose his own place of awareness for that particular length of time. If he decides to become a physical entity for long periods throughout various lifetimes, he will indeed have chosen not to stay upon this path throughout his goal here in our realm. You are now being taught a small lesson which shows that through being a physical entity, your problems and process of aging will help you grow to become a deeper, more spiritual, and wiser entity.

"Five senses are so many less than which your spirit has hoped for you to maintain. However, through the periods of lives, you will eventually begin enhancing these senses into a multitude, thus recreating in part, a then current remembrance of your entire process here in this realm. You are now allowing yourself to become physically aware of your other senses. This shall place a layer of potential within your current, everyday path for experiencing many other new existing factors. Taking pride in yourself will allow the entity its freedom to show off your other senses. This pride, however, must go deeply into your creative being. Finding a way to release an unseen portion of this material, which now seems bottled up in each of you, will help your progress to help itself more, at a more rapid pace, to a point of self recognition.

"I have, of course, my own intent for furthering your aptitude. As you see, I have willed myself to be able to permeate your veil again, from a spiritual level. Your choice was for me to show our joint progression here. This I say to you, as through your choice, we are actually helping each other. Your acceptance or denial will not alter my own entity's choice, but it will shelter your physical self for the time being.

"This comprehension device I am now using will again be explained further, at a later chapter. Your time has no limits, but should you face your own physical sense of time, you will be mostly gratified in knowing the future and past have linkages beyond any physical understanding.

"Your views are only existing to you from a current level of understanding. This is acknowledgeable from our realm, but will not continue. As each of you has a different course now, your levels are changing. See that by this knowledge, you are partaking again of an eventful period. You will someday become reborn into an era of spiritual fertility. Your strengths will become immensely empowered with their own choice.

"While not bothering with others' ideals, you will seem to flourish rapidly. Thus, your angles of thought shall remove any obstacles that had previously become deterrents to your adherence to this spiritual growth. Idolizing your counterparts (past and future lives) will not become a productive force for your beings. These counterparts are directly involved with their own beings. As their time periods eject themselves, they will want to become a more epitomized entity. However, as your own source will tell you, they will not change every angle of growth for you.

"As your rebirthing process occurs each lifetime, your periodic counterparts will remain intact. They are ahead in certain ways, yet your replacement of their negative growth periods are equally important for the total function of each soul's existence. Nurturing all of these pasts will become a most acceptable way of working with your soul. Become familiar with this lesson.

"As due to you, your basic knowledge of this realm has intensified already, through an adjusting period of sleep. This information has been given more credence. Your own abilities to seek a higher spiritual level will come as quickly as you progress through any of the physically negative roadblocks. Actually, physically visualizing your growth may be different, however.

"These preliminary steps may be taken as a guide for further development:

1. *Listen to your own inner chords of strength.* They will be mostly directed in the pattern by which you maintain your development.
2. *Be sure that your involvement with anything spiritual has no negative setbacks.* If your areas of strength become so affected by any spiritual wisdom, then temporarily withdraw, as it will not benefit your present path.
3. *As a lesson to this world, you will be a teacher also.* Rejecting this point is not valid, so be willing to trade your thoughts through your counterparts. Each soul will give its own current direction, according to the absorption level.
4. *Ask yourself to maintain a high need of understanding.* Through a higher developing question system, you will seek to annoy your

mind for internal answers. Be aware that these answers are within you and expect their wisdom to help your spiritual understanding of yourself.

"Through these steps, you will decipher the areas of importance for your maintenance. The avenues are open constantly for your own surfacing. At times, you will work through doubts of loneliness and wariness from others. Your abilities are each so profound that, without advancing physically, you are always advancing anyway, on a level that your understanding now lacks. Become attuned to your own development as a way of helping others, also. Then they will thrive through this connection with you.

"As your children become more windows of light for you, be a good listener. Be attentive, as their minds are attentive to you. The nurturing of family guidance is always a beautiful lesson for others to perceive. However, as this nurturing dwindles, your constancy in spiritual understanding has to encompass a working relationship with each side. If your understandings are free of negative insight, your trust levels within each member will be enhanced. With truth, these vibrations will be felt through each child, as you will feel theirs also.

"A connection device, here again, should be mentioned. Your internal ways of promoting unity are always unlimited. The physical lessons provide a withholding period in order to chance yourself upon various thresholds of negativity. These thresholds will act as retainers in some cases. The agonies that many people go through are again linked within this inner connection of thoughtful existence. Your indulgence of others within your realm is a critical acclaim for your soul's habitation of that realm.

"Be patient with yourself, as this attribute is one which will require a long endurance record. Your patience is accelerated only through love, as love is the prime motivator for the entirety of all structure within all souls. Your patience is thus being linked to your love as a part of that entirety. In order for progression to occur, patience must play a part. Each lifetime incorporates many circumstances that will require such patience. The learning process, by which you are presently accustomed, has been crystalizing since your birth. At that time, your entity began swirling with a weakness of physical form, but at the same time, was overwhelming its spiritual parts of the actuality of another conception.

"Your inability to cohabit both planes is indeed an inaccurate perception. At birth, your spiritual body is a part of your physical one. However you place the importance of this division does not matter, ultimately. Your entity begins at a level that has become self-adjusting. Your birth was akin to the variety of soul perceptions that may remain throughout its existence. Your present life will always have a sustaining effect on the soul, but will not drive its power continually. Therefore, be reluctant to advise yourself of the permanence of each flaw that develops within your present period.

"As you alternate the ego with the spirit, your remembrance of other times during physical life will come to pass. Other realities also will begin intermingling through your eyes of acceptance. If your rejection of this seems appropriate, that is all right, now. However, you will again anoint your own thinking, purposely replacing it with another pathway at a later time.

"You are not only a dual personality, but also actually many, many more. As you see, your abilities to find other placements in each realm have no ends, therefore, the connection of these abilities with each other. Your points of learning are at these connections. As your beginnings here have taken on a new meaning for you, be aware that this choice was yours, not ours, entirely. Isolating yourself from these principles will only help to preserve another angle of yourself, which may unravel in a later course of time. After your physical death, you will begin to see a mirror of earthly images, recreating a particle of your entire being. Each of these images will teach you to be freer with your thoughts, thereby learning from each experience.

"As you each begin to welcome yourselves into this lifetime, you will see a truer pattern for your existence there. Your needs will seem somewhat smaller in the way of material items, as they will not be at the end of your goal structure any longer. Fortunately, your present system of incurring debts does have its alternating realities also. By this, your reality that is seen primarily extensively through material needs and sacrifices will mature in itself, through the testing that will take place within your being.

"You connection with these authors (of *An Explosion of Being*) is not only limited to your reading this book. Actually, its limitations go far beyond your current understanding of any fenced area. You will be seen by these people (the authors) in other realities to have permanent ties with them, even through 'minute' ways. A challengeable effort of your souls has been linked to a previous existence when each of you was straining for further knowledge. This knowledge now comes as a source of easy access. This has become a primary reason for your interacting. Your logical, spiritual progression has intertwined with the need for further development through a physical means. With the actual reading of this material, you each will therefore be in connection with the authors of this book. Your daily connection is irrelevant as to their physical premises, but you shall maintain an awareness that will be sensed by some who have finally come into contact with them physically. At this point, there will be an immediate rejuvenation of a lost purpose for both sides of your beings (physical and spiritual).

"The interconnection of your beings is also locked with another mass of people who are watching your eventualities take place under the current level of opposition to this material. There will be some of you who do not wish to await the presence of any further understanding. However, as your negation takes place, your viewing of the spiritual connections remains a fact.

"You, as readers, are enjoyable to the authors not only for your participation in reading and purchasing this book, but also through the teachings that are becoming a part of your lives. They have actual interest for each of you who obtains any absolute messages through this material. You will learn to decipher, which may help you most quickly, and they will, in turn, give to your needs.

"Your abilities to further develop your creative awareness are lingering on the sidelines of a theatre. They're always in touch with you through your finer particulars of memory, but may only be released when your current needs are evaluated. Being kind to yourself will help the release of these abilities, as through the finer moments of your lives, you will seek a higher development period. These abilities, then, will be released for you.

"Calmness of thought will help to provide the adequate base for your desires to become outstanding; therefore, your threshold of hope is taken to a higher point of reality. Your peak of existence shall be admired *through your soul's wisdom to appreciate life.* This path that was chosen by your inner needs of sanctification will once again be released. Your development here has been astonishing. If you could possibly view the complexities which are involved, your memory stimuli would be confounded. The spiritual objectives are much like the physical ones; only you are responsible for their completion. Your dullness of interpretation comes from a lack of wisdom within your present being to decipher these partitions of realities.

"Before your present life, you were seen to be a myriad of images beyond a total evaluative soul process. The complete withdrawal from this structure became necessary for your physical life to begin. You, however, do have the ability to partake of a searching process that will probe into the reasons for being. This perhaps will help you to relax further within yourself. As you have found many avenues of light, you will show that light toward purposeful memories, shedding it on all possibilities of growth. As your development then increases during this period, you will need much less than you have before, in your material senses.

"The employment of wealth does not necessarily defeat your avenues of self-discovery. However, should your goals not be enhanced through actual introspection, you may fail your own self-image at times. Become a minute particle of life within a million structures of other lives. Only then, will you see a full pattern of development. Your period of contentment was over when your birth took place. Your lives were changed abruptly as each one's decisive abilities were once again put to the test. As a sheer form of this placement, your soul's advantages then became many. While adjusting to this life, you were each given special instructions through your own beings in order to relate totally to your earthly existence. As your soul then became enchanted with another one of its spectrums, your will became stronger.

"To manipulate another with the knowledge of this soul process may not be a fruitful gesture on your part. The many aspects stemming from your relationships with others, however, naturally will help all who are involved, thus recreating a necessary grouping within the soul structures. Your families are nearer to life than death now, as you see them to be. However, their subscription to life must end temporarily as will yours, in time. Should you breathe heavily from this statement, do not show apprehension. Your dreams will be flourishing on each realm here, as within your present lifestyle.

"Formulate your own acceptabilities, but within these, also formulate the possibility of acceptance from another source than your own physical self. The sources of which I speak may be multiple for each of you. They are not in question. They are available only to you. Your own truest source is your self-guideline stemming throughout the various realities from your point of existence to another, weaving through layers upon layers of alternate existences. Becoming aware of this will shelter only yourself, but there is no need to ignore the position of others.

"Your advantages are many. Throughout the expansion of your own development, you will cease to dwell upon negativity at points that, before, were dwelled upon. Your need to flounder within indecisive periods will also become lessened. The wisdom is pulled by grains that then collectively portray a newer path for physical acceptance. Your realm does not play its every moment as a specific purpose.

"As your physical enjoyments, pleasures and negativities perform an operation of thought, you will see that I am relating to your physical world in the nearness that parts of you relate to mine. Do not become ashamed of your physical self for any reason that is comprehensible. Your paths are alternated between positive and negative. Therefore, your many learning periods will be advanced.

"Belief in yourself has the ultimate importance that you will ever use during your lifetime. Here you will find the basis of all immediate needs met. Your avenues of belief will diversify from this base point, as you alter each others' beliefs. Your will to delve into a higher realm of receptivity is due to the forming of your ultimate beliefs in the purpose of individualized existence.

"Finite ways are inevitable means to show your own purpose. They will screen out any formal uselessness that has been transmitted through previous existences on that planet. Each planet has its own source of resistance to outside influence. Yours, particularly, is sheltered through the mass needs for encompassment. The belief, again, that you see in others will, at times, dwindle, but the remaining strength of your ultimate conviction will never change. Areas of this belief which are divided will seed themselves into a portion of your being which has smartly played out the necessary plans for your guidance system. Being quick to act upon this actuality will help to preserve a later influence of self-denial.

"Factual curbing of any self-denials will form a leverage, thus permitting your entity to filter the idiocies of life, which then cause such denial. Love yourself, as each being has a total characteristic of love beyond that which romantically ties one another's physicalness to each other's needs. The importance of this particular message has a depth of meaning that I must again repeat. Belief in yourself is totally encompassing. It will permeate into other areas of your soul not now recognizable by you.

"Love is another area which you will sense from birth as an entity. Throughout your lifetimes, the needs of self-acquiring love will be met by others who sense the need of rekindling a private part of your existence before the present one. Your bonds of man and woman are eventually changed into a total conceptual agreement in this realm that denies physical, sexual differences. Your aims are now created to find one another's satisfactions through physical attachments. You may show another a part of your soul, which otherwise stays protected. Love, therefore, becomes an expansion of your own awareness. Truly to yourself, it teaches one that he must re-enter openness, unprotected by falsities, thereby exploring the depths of personal, spiritual and physical existence.

"Be calm and adjusting to your own love. Each entity's respect from himself will grow and thus be fed by another who shares his needs, thus recreating the same procedure for that individual. Finalizing your self-beliefs on love and its ultimate impact will someday become clearer to your entities, because of due lack of consideration toward others in your realm. This love maintains itself, usually, at a temporary level.

"Your responsive qualities are pre-purposed to surface quickly. From childhood, you see the needs of love being met not only through yourselves, but also through others. Your children will stem from a unit of immeasurable love. This is not the physical conception of which I now speak. It belongs to the soul. Your development since birth has been partially a memory-linked connection through the aspect of soul love.

"Forced love does not exist. It is fruitless. Physical agreements of sharing physical needs are not measured through love. They are again temporary. Your own needs that find beauty in a fulfillment will reach the depth of another individual. Perhaps your part will lessen, but the other has still gained much from the initial experience containing love.

"We are each a part of one another's existences. This complexity forms a multitude of questions within your beings. This is understandable. Your letters to those in religious positions many times question this partial concept. I will try now to clarify your need of understanding these connections.

"As each entity forms its own existence, it completes a cycle which needs only lubrication. This lubrication shows itself as a way to remain intact within one's self. The area of exposure is then sent outwardly to gain a connection with the next part of your encompassing soul. Your religion shows this as old testimonials from individuals who have sought to relive the aspiring memorabilia of soul integration.

"The light between each of you now remains as a constant flame. Your beliefs are founded upon a premise of pre-planned purpose for reconnection with others who have formed this ability. Be attainable as a source for other people to rely on, as their changes will be supported through yours.

"Your development is actually not as different as you may now perceive it to be. You are again intertwined with each reality. Therefore, your levels of current physical expectations are met beyond your present awareness, through areas unseen. Your development may become a primary source of interest for you, but as I see it, the majority of you will read to enhance your enlightenment only to a point of interaction of daily events, providing basic linkages. This is already forming as you have read the material presented here. Showing yourself the mirror of timelessness will result in the outward challenge of facing the self within yourself.

"Your present belief that, only within a system of known realities are physical definitions provided, is seemingly incongruent to your ways here. You see, the areas of developmental patterns are infinite, thereby creating a life force within each spectrum that produces power for interchangeable sources. These sources then become a linkage to each part of mankind's development as persons. Each of you is linked within your developmental pattern to another part of your soul; that, then, has many other various linkages.

"As you bind yourself to these thoughts, remember that, only through your own development power, will each of you discernably grow. As your growth here permits an unmistaken identity, your growth there will also provide the same boundaries. Your willingness to be free from any physical boundaries is acceptable. However, your flow of concept must naturally be provided by you, in a context of which you are now, or have been, preparing.

"Your permanent delivery within yourself will come partially from this resistance. So, as you turn your visual contact to a point within your spirit's mind, be placed in an ultimate group of realities whose present source is now yours. You have then achieved a higher point of learning by which you will adapt more readily.

"You will develop quietly, as those who restrain their inner teachings become a quieter source of inner knowledge, simply because their strengths need not be exposed to others, entirely. As a result of this personal solitude, your image will be lessened as the ego shrinks. Becoming indulgent in this practice will help your inner senses grow also. A stream of consciousness will provide the areas that are open to you at a rapid level. If you choose to further accept their presence as this takes place, your present physical surroundings may take on another look.

"Be interchangeable with yourself. By this, I mean that adaptation to your inner source is always needed as a prerequisite for higher learning. Your physical errors are a developmental stage in themselves. As each of you will find many floating through your life's years, *learn from them and accept them as a position of strength*. Therefore, these will remain intact for further reference and usage, by and for, the soul.

"Once you have established a pattern of these errors, become adaptable again to the repetition of your ways. Each pattern has a purpose. Perhaps the 'negative' areas of life are seen to be arranged incongruently. Your newness of recognition of this may not be as those of others, you know. Accept things you do not know. While obtaining the personal data within yourself, your friends will be learning from you.

"Isolation is not necessary for growth. Those who take on this belief must limit their progress to a finite point of development. If the soul's choice is to be free itself, within a being, then a multitude of paths are assigned by the soul. Your beings are accelerated through these paths at the wonderment of other souls who obtain a prominence within themselves, but at a varied level. Their needs may be sufficient for their present purpose as yours may be. Now, should they be altered in order to accommodate your circumstantial awareness, then, guiding yourself to these alternatives will be of utmost importance for you.

"The physical world must not be placed as a vanishing point from your minds. This also is seemingly destructive, as each must relate to his present surroundings. Your surroundings now were placed by your soul when a choice was necessary. Therefore, your impatience with the physical at times need not be relinquished because of the spiritual knowledge that some people feel they are privy to. They require extreme self-indulgence in that area. Your physical existence, in effect, is actually part of the entire concept.

"Your needs as people are limitless. This I understand. The poverty, sickness and lack of self attainment are only a few of the neglected ways being provided throughout your lives. The physical realm is not always a pleasant place to be. However, your needs are there. Do not suffer unwisely, as you will learn much through each period of sadness. Your needs, again, are important to you, and this is part of your present existence. If you choose to dwell upon negative forms of life, then perhaps you will also choose to dwell within a bubble. You will then not see much growth. Every being has its own level of growth and will provide for it as each lifetime sees necessary. The choices of which I have spoken, again, may not be necessary for you as an individual, but as a majority, you will see that next level of growth just beyond your reach. Go toward it and flourish within your physical lives."

13

Our Purposeful Linkage with You

THE SHARING OF OUR JOURNEY into expanded awareness is nearly complete. We've done our best to condense seven years of exploration into a comprehensible unit, and to include some very special moments in our lives. During the writing of these chapters, we have felt an increasing affinity for you, the reader, as an individual. We are very private people, but, for us, the daily development of this book was like sitting down with a close friend to discuss old times. Each reader seems even closer now, as if we had all completed an adventure together, hand in hand.

An Explosion of Being was never meant to be a "How To" book. Its specific purpose was, and still is to offer you a confirmation of your own vast psychic heritage, through our experiences. Within our discoveries, we hope that you recognize the absolutely total expansiveness of your own being. That same explosive potential exists within you, just as surely as it exists within us.

But, whether or not you should try to develop your own natural perceptive abilities beyond their present condition is a question only you can answer. It may or may not be purposeful to do so. We have, however, included an appendix and a bibliography at the end of the book to give you further assistance if needed.

As you know by now, we view life events not as products of "chance," but as the outcome of multi-dimensional selection. We see this selective planning process happening in daily consciousness, at night during sleep, and between reincarnational existences. Within that framework, we believe that before you ever heard of this book, a portion of your multi-faceted being designed a plan whereby you would encounter our experiences. In itself, we see your reading of *An Explosion of Being* as a psychic event awaiting your recognition.

We feel that you've been in contact with us about this book and its contents long before publication. That occasional spark of familiarity or compatibility you might have felt while reading this material is certainly not coincidental, nor is it adequately explainable in standard terms. It is a process of remembering. It is the tapping of your own timeless banks of wisdom, and the re-establishment of a connection long forgotten.

To us, *An Explosion of Being* is not an isolated production of the Dillon family. Its origins can be found within you as well as within us. We regard this book as the final product of a mass intent, cooperatively planned and executed through a multi-dimensional effort. We see ourselves and our readers together, jointly determining on a spiritual level that this publication would be developed as a method of re-acquainting our conscious selves with the depth of an infinite and never ending existence. To us, you are actually a co-creator of this book, and as such, we embrace you as a colleague.

Welcome yourself to your own unique "explosion of being," for that was the unspoken intention of your multi-faceted self when you chose to read these pages.

Appendix:

Revitalizing Your Natural Psychic Heritage

THIS FINAL APPENDAGE to *An Explosion of Being* is included as a series of helpful hints, if it is your purpose to further uncover those innate understandings, abilities, and connections that have always been yours. As a part of a beautiful multifaceted reality, you have already determined to what extent your psychic awareness will probably be expanded in this physical life. We are simply providing that basic framework from which you may, or may not, begin to meet those pre-established developmental needs. It is not our intention to provide in-depth instruction within these final pages. Instead, you will find only handholds, offering gentle support as you carve your individual path of self-discovery on the face of an infinite crystaline structure. Remember, you are your own best teacher.

The topics in this appendix are arranged in the form of an interlocking network of steps and stages, leading you logically from the elementary to the more complex. This network was created as we thought back over our years of searching and asked what guidance would have assisted us most in our own development. From that very personal vantage point, we offer you the following thoughts:

1. A Psychic Notebook

If it is your intent to pursue a path of personal exploration into the nature of existence, we then strongly recommend that you establish a simple record keeping system. A spiral notebook does the job very nicely. In it, record by date, every dream, event, perception, coincidence or communication that could possibly indicate your linkage with your own truer reality. This exercise will do four things: first, it will force you to begin evaluating all sorts of life circumstances; second, it will promote the possibility of further occurrences; third, it eventually may show patterns of information and events that you never would have suspected without such careful day by day attention; fourth, this record may some day provide a historical account useful to others within or outside your own family. In our case, our notebooks evolved into *An Explosion of Being*.

If you don't like to write, it can seem difficult to maintain such information, but its importance can't be overlooked. With a little effort, tiny segments of time can be found, and shorthand methods of entry can be devised to minimize the burden. If you follow the steps in this appendix, use the notebook as a storehouse for the results.

2. Ask Yourself Why You Are Alive At This Moment

It's a simple question and you may say, "Oh, come on, now." As simple as it sounds, an answer forged quietly, honestly, and fully, will show you the edges of your current belief system. We suggest you write your answer in the Psychic Notebook, because the act of transferring such thoughts to paper will force an increased clarity.

If your answer is, "I don't know," or "Mom and Pop wanted kids," fine, write it down. Once you have your answer in all its complexity or brevity, file it away for three months, six months or a year. At the end of that time, bring out this same question and your answer and try again. The difference between the two answers, or several answers, over longer periods of time could show some interesting changes.

3. Why Did You Read This Book?

Was it out of curiosity? Did someone recommend it? Were you looking for specific kinds of information? Were you hoping to find some answers to questions sensed, but not formulated? Look at your own definition of what your conscious purpose was, because it sets the stage for the potential usefulness of this appendix.

4. About the Psychic or the Spiritual, I Believe That . . .

Coupled with your answer as to why you are alive, take another page in your notebook and complete the statement above. Whether

Appendix: Revitalizing Your Natural Psychic Heritage

you use one line or three pages is not important. This exercise will help to solidify your current outlook. Also, this repeated over a period of months or years can show some very startling changes.

You might find some enlightening information about yourself if you also respond to the companion question, "About the Psychic or the Spiritual, *I Wish I Could Believe that* . . ."

5. A Support System

It's very tough going it alone if you seriously intend to explore your relationship to your multifaceted existence. Without someone to talk to and share with, you can begin to feel quite isolated. This is especially true if your closest daily associates criticize or poke fun at your thoughts or experiences. Therefore, whatever you do, find a friend or a group having similar interests. It may take time, but take it from two who continually multiply their enthusiasm and experiences by constant caring interaction. It works!

You will find a support system a must if you wish to pursue your own direct communication with alternate realities. In this way, also, you may increase the power of contact potential, while decreasing the possibility of discouragement.

6. Psychic and Spiritual Literature

There has been and will continue to be an abundance of written material explaining various "insights" about man's true nature. Some of it will benefit you greatly, some of it will confuse you, and some of it will try to enslave your mind. We suggest only that you read as widely as possible, eventually concentrating on that information which: a. satisfies the intellect but also feels right in some inexpressible way; and b. allows you the greatest freedom of choice and expression possible. You must feel good intuitively about the guidance you are receiving, and *you* must be the one in control.

Our bibliography has some excellent works that, to us, reasonably fit both these criteria. We offer it to you only as our backward glance at information that has been helpful to us.

7. Courses and Seminars

As with the literature in this field, we suggest that you get as wide an exposure as you can to the great variety of thought. The structure in these educational settings can vary from intellectual objectivity, to zealous promotion of one particular belief system. If ideas opposite to yours are offered, use them to clarify your own belief system. But, if you feel that a belief is forced upon you or that your thoughts are ridiculed, get away as fast as you can. Conversely if you suddenly feel that a particular presentation is *the* flaming key to the universe, step back, slow down and give it a little time. Jumping on an attractive bandwagon too quickly doesn't give much leeway for the sensible weighing of information.

8. Guidance from Intermediaries

In addition to books and courses, there are, within society, people who either view themselves or are viewed by others as the middlemen between you and the world of the psychic or the spirit. Their knowledge, abilities and intentions are often of reasonable quality, and their counsel can prove very helpful. Most of us on this earth need assistance from others who apparently know more than we do. Our only observation here is basically a repeat of what has been said before: absorb what seems to be useful, but if pressure is applied for you to change what you feel is right, or if messages are transmitted from spiritual sources that might part you from your bank account, step away.

9. Looking into Your Own Past

Everyone has had things happen in his or her life that are indicators of a personal connection to a larger essence of being. You are no exception, and if you haven't already discovered this, relax, look backward from this moment, all the way to your childhood and see what can be found. A vivid dream, a feeling that you've been somewhere before, a feeling about someone that proved correct, a vision you never shared with anyone, a coincidence beyond belief, or the knowledge of what someone was about to say are just a few of the possible memories that could emerge. Write them down in your notebook as they come to mind and leave some room, as others might surface after a period of time.

10. A Treasury of Experiences from Family and Friends

After looking at your own life experiences, think about stories that you may have heard from other people. Many family histories contain tales of strange happenings, and a little probing will often uncover much more than you suspect. If you have children at home or older relatives living with you, a wealth of information might be available just through attentive listening. What you will accomplish by this sort of inquiry is a close range verification that life contains many such very real episodes.

Appendix: Revitalizing Your Natural Psychic Heritage 199

11. Dreams

Everybody dreams but not everybody remembers them. The sleep state is your direct linkage to the spiritual world, and you can capitalize on that linkage if you so desire. In the very limited space of this appendix, we can only touch the surface of how to do this, but the following concise list should be of help:

A. When you wake up in the morning, wait before arising and think about any dreams you might have had. If even bits and pieces filter through, get up and enter that information in your notebook. If you are pushed by time, use whatever cryptic scrawl or abbreviations you wish, but write it down.

B. If you don't remember dreams very well or you wish to remember more than you usually do, give yourself the repeated suggestion, just before going to sleep, that you *will* increase your dream recall.

C. If a very vivid dream awakens you, get up and record whatever you can remember, otherwise it could well be lost the next morning. If you're too groggy to write, use a tape recorder.

D. Through setting your alarm clock sometime in the middle of the night, you may be able to interrupt a dream artificially and remember its contents.

E. When recording dreams, see if you can remember these kinds of things:

1. Are you actually participating, watching yourself, watching others?
2. Who else is involved? Are they living or dead? Are they known to you?
3. Where does the dream take place? Note the physical surroundings such as buildings, landscape and objects. Is it within the present time period as you know it, or some other historical period?
4. Are you yourself or someone else?
5. What events occur within the dream?
6. What is said?
7. What kind of emotions are you feeling during the dream?
8. Are there any particular sounds or smells that you can recall?

F. After each dream or each week of dreams, examine what the meanings might be. All dreams, in our opinion, have a layered set of meanings, and all are valid within certain contexts. Many valuable books have been written about dream interpretation, but they often cast dreams in symbolic concrete that may not always be fully correct or thoroughly useful.

What we are saying is that you and only you are the best interpreter of your dreams.

12. Time Out, Meditation, Prayer

Somewhere within your day, find small chunks of time to close out the physical world. It may be the five minutes before the kids get up in the morning, during a coffeebreak at work, or in the stillness before sleep, but if you intend to enhance your linkage with levels of existence or consciousness beyond your own, this step is essential. Here is your chance to turn down the volume of this world and tune into another.

An elementary step, yes, but it can help to relieve physical stress, establish a comfortable rapport between your multidimensional facets, and open direct channels to an infinite and highly complex intelligence. No one method is best. Search the literature, take a course, experiment, but most of all, create that which gives you a feeling of peace, safety and identity with all existence.

13. Imagination

After dreams, your next direct linkage into alternate realities is imagination. The playful, creative part of you that sometimes slips into "daydreams" is actually another point of departure into the next level of consciousness. With your physical awareness in control, this is where you can exchange information, ideas and possibilities with your multifaceted self. Through the careful nurturing and positive management of imagination, you can exert a powerful influence on the structuring of your reality, as well as help to unfold your other natural psychic talents. If, on the other hand, you give up conscious control, live great portions of your life within imagination, or concentrate on negativity, then you will be heading for trouble.

Take note of what you see or do within your imagination. This is a very private exploration and you need not share it with anyone, but the process will begin to show patterns of personal emphasis. While many times you are playing with interesting probabilities, on occasion, you actually may be seeing into or creating your future. If the prospects you see are bright, happy, and useful to all concerned, then give those thoughts additional imaginative concentration on a daily basis. If some of the prospects that you see are dark, unhappy, or hurtful to yourself or others, then flood your imagination with one of your more positive "day dreams."

14. Daily Events

Within each day, week or month, many events will show themselves as indicators of your spiritually determined purpose for being in this life. When spliced together, these indicators weave patterns of your multifaceted learning needs, often showing how your patterns connect with the purposeful experience lines of other people. From the ups, downs, hassles and ecstasies, you will begin to observe an incredibly complex and interdependent organism.

15. Coincidences

In your viewing of daily events, take special note of those things people classify as "coincidences." They are some of the more easily discernible of your inner patterns that will show you an existing structure which may have otherwise been dismissed. When a "coincidence" occurs, make a rough guess as to the odds against that particular combination of events and then double those odds for any other "coincidence" linking itself with the first one.

16. Life Pattern Analysis

While continually looking at the happenings in your own life, look at those of some other people close to you. As they fight their own battles for existence, you might find it interesting to calmly picture their ultimate purposes, learning patterns, and "coincidences" that they might not be able to comprehend in the heat of daily survival. It's always easier to view the other guy's problems objectively, and through that dispassionate analysis, you just might learn something about yourself.

17. Sensing Other People's Thoughts and Needs

Don't force it, but gently become aware of those times when you "just knew" something about another person, that you could not possibly have known through any physical means. It may be the "coincidental" knowledge that a ringing telephone has a certain relative or friend on the other end. It may be that "motherly" sensitivity that awakens you in the night to attend a sick child. It may be that instantaneous awareness of what someone is about to say, seconds before it is said. In daily living, many such events happen, but we often pass them off, much to the discredit of their origin. Keep as careful a record as you can of these events, and by so doing, you will reinforce the possibility of more such things occurring.

18. Auras, Lights and Colors

People and objects emanate the multidimensional aspects of their truer reality. Especially surrounding people, the emanations can be seen as distinct from physical reality, and may appear as bursts of light, patches of color, bands of light or color, misty clouds or heat wave type disruptions.

In our experience, these sightings usually come at times of high relaxation, sleepiness or times of intense emotion. Psychological readiness and a philosophical acceptance seem generally to determine our accessibility to these perceptions. We suggest that a daily imagination exercise be conducted where you visualize yourself as able to see these things.

19. Misty Images and Ghosts

Communication between the physical world and other aspects of reality are commonplace occurrences, but it usually happens beyond conscious awareness. If this type of visual event occurs, it does so because, on some level of consciousness, you and "someone else" planned it for a specific purpose. The contact may be with an entity that has never taken part in physical existence; it may be with the spiritual essence of a physically deceased person or it could be a portion of the spiritual essence of someone living, including yourself.

We cannot suggest ways to develop or enhance this ability, nor are we certain that it should be developed. However, the recording of any such events in your notebook might eventually show them to be a part of a pattern that, as yet, you may not fully understand.

20. Out-of-Body Experiences

Out-of-body experiences are most likely the initial stages of an emergence into alternate realities during sleep. Again, as with other

Appendix: Revitalizing Your Natural Psychic Heritage

portions of your spiritual heritage, those occurrences are normal events happening nightly, but rarely remembered by the conscious mind.

In the preliminary conscious stages, a rigidity of body and a near paralysis can cause slight panic. It is much easier to say than to do, but, if you find yourself in this condition, try to relax and flow with the experience. Fighting it causes that panic, but then again, perhaps the panic causes you to remember the experience.

Experiences, such as this, may not be of use to everyone equally. It may or may not be to your greater purpose to recall that kind of event. But, giving yourself specific suggestions just before sleep such as, "I will become conscious during any out-of-body experiences tonight," may, after a period of time, have the desired result. Then use those few precious moments after waking in the morning to recall any such night time adventures and record them in your notebook. To reinforce your belief that a conscious memory of an out-of-body experience is possible, use your imagination at any available time during the day to *visualize* such a thing happening.

21. Preparation for Receipt of Direct Communications

Have you decided that you definitely want to establish conscious contact with alternate levels of reality? If so, here are some points that you should consider before starting:

A. Remember that your subconscious is a part of your multidimensional reality. It is most likely that the subconscious is the linking force with higher levels of existence and therein lies a problem. Rightfully so, your initial direct contact might well be your subconscious, but don't mistake it for the essence of higher wisdom.

B. Be honest with yourself. If your emotional life is in any kind of severe turmoil, that is not the time to try initiating direct contact. The result could be greater upset, garbled messages, and a sabotaging of what could become very rewarding and useful at a time of more stability. During emotional turmoil, your contact is likely to be limited to a subconscious that is being bombarded with negativity and that may be what you receive as a message. Negativity.

C. Be honest, again. Why do you want to establish contact? If in any way it is to prove your superiority above others or to prove a particular point of view, you're heading for trouble. Your subconscious will obligingly create whatever you wish, but it will not be real in any sense of the word, and in the end, you will have nothing.

D. Walk before you run. If you haven't already kept track of your dreams, developed a comfortable "time out" linkage, and experimented with imagination as a co-creator of reality, do so before attempting direct contact. The solid base of those steps will ultimately save much time and be of immeasurable assistance in establishing a clear and valid communication.

E. Perhaps you have a particular object or sound that immediately makes you think of things spiritual or psychic. For us, it's our cut crystal spheres. For you, it might be a Bible, a picture, a particular piece of music, or a certain woodcarving. If you have any such object, use it as an initial "mental trigger" to establish a preliminary mind set before going to the next stage.

F. Use whatever meditation or prayer sequence that you employ daily and then . . .

G. . . . clear your conscious mind by closing your eyes and imagining a pure, white light flowing over and through your entire being. Think of the source of this light as God, Infinite Intelligence, or your own crystalline soul. See the light, feel its warmth and goodness. This process will tend to keep the subconscious in its place and will indeed assist you in establishing a clear channel.

H. Make use of psychic constructs. Create a specific place within your imagination and use it as the meeting ground for contact. Work on the specifics of this place well before you try communicating. Give it as much life and realistic detail as possible, so that you can actually visualize yourself within that circumstance. We have our river and the psychic house. You may develop a seaside retreat, a palace in Europe, or perhaps a particular setting in nature. The more care you take in building this place in your mind, the more solid the middleground you will create between realities.

I. Call for contact. Once you have followed the previous steps, in sequence, make a statement something like, "I'm ready," or "I wish to make contact," or "Is anyone there?" You determine what you want to say and whether or not you want to say it mentally, or out loud. But, whatever you do, you must reach out forcibly with your mind.

22. Initial Direct Contact

Once the preparatory sequence is complete, and the call for contact has been made, just relax and let your mind float a little. What do you see? What do you feel? Stop there if this is your first attempt at direct communication. Bring yourself back to full consciousness and write down anything that occurred. You may find that this is an adequate method of contact by itself, with a wealth of information. If so, continue with it and don't bother with other methods. If, on the other hand, you become afraid in any way, bring yourself back to full consciousness and stop trying to communicate. If your desire is strong enough, try again at other times, but you may find your subconscious is actually interfering, or it simply may not be your ultimate purpose to establish conscious linkages with alternate realities.

23. Evaluation of Direct Contact

Above all, if what you see or receive through any method of contact is negative, profane, hurtful to others or highly directive, stop doing it. Either you are in touch with an unsettled part of your own subconscious, or you have stumbled into the sphere of a much lesser developed entity. *You have the control, so use it.* Try again another day, but next time, follow your preparatory sequence very carefully with special attention to the "white light" process. In addition, throw in some specific directive of your own such as, "Subconscious, stay out of this," or, "I will converse only with higher level entities."

Now, if through whatever direct method you choose or develop on your own, reasonable or even beautiful visions or messages appear, just let it flow. Use your psychic notebook later to record what transpires and study it at your leisure. Look also at other entries in your notebook. Are there any correlations? Study what you receive, but don't give a great deal of credence to it, initially. Only over a period of time will you be able to sense its validity and wisdom. Take no direct action on information that flows until time and analysis have occurred.

Here for your consideration are some additional criteria that might be useful as you consider your messages:

    A. Do you get a sense of caring and a concern for you as an individual?

B. Are you advised to work towards a greater understanding of your truer nature?
C. Is caution advised in accepting everything that flows through the direct communication?
D. Is information given that can be verified in the physical world?
E. Are useful insights offered regarding your particular purposes for coming into this world?
F. Are care and concern shown for those around you?
G. Are useful insights offered regarding others close to you, including their purposes for existence and your purposeful relationships with them?
H. Do you receive reminders of your personal responsibility to those around you?
I. Are you given insights regarding life after death or life before death?
J. Are you given insights into the nature of the soul?
K. Are explanations given about events within your life or events happening in the world?
L. Do you receive information that explains the purposes for the earth's existence, physical life in general or the spiritual nature of material life?
M. Do you feel love emanating from what you receive, or is love discussed as a vital life ingredient?
N. Above all, are your life and thought processes enriched through the direct contact?

If a reasonable combination of these criteria doesn't exist within the communications, you may still be in contact with your subconscious or a lesser developed entity. Therefore, we advise you to ignore the information at least for the time being. If you set these criteria as a conscious goal, however, you probably will find your level of contact elevated and its validity enhanced.

24. A Word about Predictions

Extreme caution is necessary here. If you are in touch with your subconscious or a lower level entity, you are likely to get all kinds of wild predictions, including those possibilities you most desire or fear. You might simply be having something repeated to you that you either want to hear or would like most to avoid. The caution comes particularly if action is demanded by your source, ordering you to radically change things in your life. Just remember this: a good source of direct contact is a helping agent and not a dictator. If it is a valid and useful source, it will "demand" nothing.

Even when you are reasonably satisfied as to the quality of contact that has been established, take all predictions and their time frames with a few grains of salt. The view of physical life by alternate facets of existence can have distortions and symbolic meanings that must be looked at carefully. It often depends on the level of development of your source as to how refined and accurate this information may be, in physical terms. Your source may see your "probable" actions planned before birth, but not see the next "probable" path that you finally decide upon some night in the sleep state. Your source may indicate that great wealth is in store, but that could mean a wealth of knowledge. Your source may indicate impending disaster or good fortune "soon," but, as in our case, it may happen three years later.

25. Ouija boards

As in all methods of direct contact, follow the steps outlined in Preparation for Receipt of Direct Communication and the criteria for Evaluation of Direct Contact found previously in this appendix.

The Ouija is a simple device and can be found in most toy stores. It can be a valid but slow method of communication regardless of the fact that many people view it as a game. It works, because the psychic power of two individuals is unified, linking with alternate realities through subconscious muscle control of the pointer. It is sometimes a feared device, because the light mood in which Ouijas often are approached can result in the flow of subconscious or lower level entity communications.

Record keeping and the deciphering of messages takes time. The easiest method is to have three people involved so that one individual can write each letter as it is indicated while the other two manipulate the pointer. Whatever you do, don't rely on your memory; it just doesn't work. If only two of you are working the board, remember two or three letters, then stop and record these in your psychic notebook and go on. After several lines of letters have been delivered, search out words, divide them with slash marks and add logical punctuation. If they make sense, continue. If not, try again some other time but give it a fair chance.

26. Stream of Consciousness Writing

Sit down in a quiet place with pen and paper. Go through the preparation sequence for direct communication. Then, without any conscious structuring of a topic or theme, write whatever words flow into your mind. Just relax and let it flow for a page or two. Then stop, take a little time to carefully read what has been written. You might be amazed. Use your evaluative criteria and see how this material fares.

This method, if it meets a reasonable number of criteria for Evaluation of Direct Contact, provides excellent initial linkage with perhaps just the next higher level of your own being. It often will give you great insights into your self, providing you with a solid framework upon which you can grow into the deeper levels of contact, if you so desire.

27. Automatic Writing

In this method, again, sit in a quiet place with pen and paper. Implement the preparation sequence. As opposed to "Stream of Consciousness" writing, however, completely clear your mind and don't allow words into your consciousness. With pen in hand, rest it on the paper against a flat surface and say to yourself, "I will allow communications to flow through my hand, apart from my conscious mind." Then wait. The pen *may* eventually move, seemingly of its own free will, producing lines, scratches, a scrawl, letters, words, sentences or pictures. As with the Ouija board, your subconscious is controlling the movement of your hand through involuntary muscle contractions, but upon evaluation you *may* find that the primary connection came from a much higher level.

The method of deciphering this information is similar to the one you use with the Ouija, but the added complexity of the unfamiliar handwriting that might emerge may take a little getting used to.

28. Verbalizing Messages

If you have had reasonable success with one or more of the other methods of contact, then a verbalization of contact by you is a possibility. Proceed, as usual, through your preparation sequence, but stop within whatever psychic construct you use as a meeting ground. Here, your call for contact will stay centered, and you will say something like, "I'm ready for words or concepts to flow through me verbally." While making this call, keep in mind your successes with other methods. You

Appendix: Revitalizing Your Natural Psychic Heritage

may see words or feel impressions or sense ideas. Whatever happens, unless it's frightening in some way, try to verbalize it. Just let it flow of its own accord and worry about the contents later.

Here is where a partner can be of immense value as a support, a booster of your own psychic power, and as a recorder. If this isn't possible, at least have a tape recorder running, so that the messages aren't lost. Unless you have unusual recall abilities, you will forget a great deal of what comes through. In the beginning, keep your sessions short, say five or ten minutes, expanding those limits only after positively evaluating your source and its effect on you. As we were told through such early communications of our own, "Choose your source as carefully as your mate."

If this method seems to work well for you, and you wish to continue it, we suggest strongly that if you don't have a partner in this exploration, get one. If you so desire, it is possible for this verbalization to naturally blend into a trance communication where your awareness is dimmed. Under these circumstances, time can have little meaning, and you may remember almost nothing of what transpires. Here is where the definite security, guidance and even instant evaluation of a partner can prove absolutely necessary.

In the development of trance communications, the variety of levels of contact and styles of delivery can have wide ranges. The main thing is that you and your partner proceed only when you feel at ease and evaluation results appear satisfactory. If *any* part of what you are doing doesn't feel right for *any* reason, slow down, back up, or stop entirely. Look at what's happening and only continue at a comfortable pace. Keep in mind though that movement from one level of trance communication to another may be uncomfortable simply because you are learning to utilize newer and better modes of psychic bonding with your source.

29. Unique Development of Your Own

What we have shared with you in this appendix is our own view of how you *might* uncover personal linkages with your natural psychic heritage. Admittedly, what we have written is based almost totally upon our own experiences. This has the advantage of our first hand observation and the disadvantage of our isolated perspective. Please, form your own mosaic of development from what we offer and what others offer, but leave large spaces for you to color in with your unique ideas and methods. Through your sources and experiences, you will find paths of expansion that are truly yours. Then stand back and look at a beautiful and unduplicated creation, for it exists nowhere else but within you.

30. A Word About Children

If you have children and wish to help them discover their own psychic/spiritual natures, these points are suggested *only as a starter* for whatever your own special approach will be:

A. Instruction is only as good as the knowledge and experience of the teacher. Seek the solidity of your own understandings before you try guiding your children very far.

B. Develop your communications skill with specific emphasis on listening. The book PARENT EFFECTIVENESS TRAINING, by Dr. Thomas Gordon, gives excellent help in this area, with actual classes available through Dr. Gordon's organization.

    If a truly open and easy communication structure doesn't really exist in your family, start building it now. Without it, you're finished before you begin. Through effective communication, you build trust and through trust, you establish an atmosphere of sharing and a willingness to be taught.

    Think of the old railroad crossing sign that says "Stop, Look, Listen." In working with your children keep that sign foremost in your mind. As adults, we are often too busy with our own thoughts to *really* slow down enough, or to keep quiet long enough to see what's happening with our kids. It's a standard adult affliction that we'll probably never fully conquer, but the more of it we control, the more learning will take place.

C. Pace your efforts accordingly to the ages, needs and maturity of your children. Pushing too much, too soon, will only sabotage what you are trying to do. Think in terms of years and a slow, sporadic development.

D. Use your children's experiences as they arise. Work with the dreams and visions of childhood as major departure points, encouraging your children to tell you all about the particular event. If the experience seems too negative or if there is an obvious reluctance to talk, back off.

E. Remember one thing. Your children will be teaching you during all the time you *think* you are teaching them.

Bibliography

Bach, Richard. *Illusions.* New York: Delacorte, 1977.

_____. *Jonathan Livingston Seagull.* New York: MacMillan, 1970.

Bradley, Dorothy and Bradley, Robert. *Psychic Phenomena.* New York: Warner, 1969.

Buscaglia, Leo. *The Fall of Freddie the Leaf: A Story of Life for All Ages.* Thorofare: Charles B. Slack, 1982.

Capra, Fritjof. *The Tao of Physics.* New York: Bantam, 1977.

Crookall, Robert. *During Sleep.* Secaucus: University Books, 1974.

Denning, Melita and Phillips, Osborne. *The Llewellyn Practical Guide to Astral Projection.* St. Paul: Llewellyn, 1979.

Fuller, John. *The Ghost of Flight 401.* New York: Berkley, 1978.

Gibson, Sandra. *Beyond the Body.* New York: Tower, 1976.

_____. *Beyond the Mind.* New York: Tower, 1981.

Gordon, Thomas. *P.E.T.: Parent Effectiveness Training.* New York: Peter H. Wyden, 1970.

Greenhouse, Herbert. *The Astral Journey.* New York: Avon, 1974.

Karcher, Janet and Hutchinson, John. *This Way to Cassadaga.* Deltona: John Hutchinson Productions, 1980.

Koestler, Arthur. *The Roots of Coincidence.* New York: Random House, 1972.

Kübler-Ross, Elisabeth. *Death: The Final Stage of Growth.* Englewood Cliffs: Prentice-Hall, 1975.

Montgomery, Ruth. *Born to Heal.* New York: Popular Library, 1976.

_____. *The World Before.* New York: Coward, McCAnn and Geoghegan, 1976.

Moody, Raymond. *Life After Life.* New York: Bantam, 1976.

_____. *Reflections on Life After Life.* New York: Bantam/Mockingbird, 1977.

Muldoon, Sylvan and Carrington, Hereward. *The Projections of the Astral Body.* New York: Weiser, 1970.

Osis, Karlis and Haraldsson, Erlendur. *At The Hour of Death.* New York: Avon, 1977.

Ostrander, Sheila and Shroeder, Lynn. *Psychic Discoveries Behind the Iron Curtain.* Englewood Cliffs: Prentice-Hall, 1970.

Pike, James. *The Other Side.* New York: Dell, 1968.

Powell, Arthur E. *The Astral Body and Other Astral Phenomena.* Wheaton: Theosophical Publishing House, 1978.

Roberts, Jane. *Adventures in Consciousness.* Englewood Cliffs: Prentice-Hall, 1975.

———. *Dialogues of the Soul and Immortal Self in Time.* Englewood Cliffs: Prentice-Hall, 1975.

———. *Psychic Politics.* Englewood Cliffs: Prentice-Hall, 1976.

———. *Seth Speaks.* Englewood Cliffs: Prentice-Hall, 1972.

———. *The Education of Oversoul #7.* Englewood Cliffs: Prentice-Hall, 1973.

———. *The Individual and the Nature of Mass Events.* Englewood Cliffs: Prentice-Hall, 1981.

———. *The Nature of Personal Reality.* Englewood Cliffs: Prentice-Hall, 1974.

———. *The Nature of the Psyche.* Englewood Cliffs: Prentice-Hall, 1979.

———. *The Coming of Seth.* New York: Pocket Books, 1976.

———. *The Seth Material.* Englewood Cliffs: Prentice-Hall, 1970.

———. *The Unknown Reality.* Vol. I. Englewood Cliffs: Prentice-Hall, 1977.

———. *The Unknown Reality.* Vol. II. Englewood Cliffs: Prentice-Hall, 1979.

Regush, Nicholas. *The Human Aura.* New York: Berkley, 1974.

Spraggett, Allen. *Authur Ford: The Man Who Talked with the Dead.* New York: New American Library, 1973.

Stearn, Jess. *A Matter of Immortality.* New York: New American Library, 1976.

———. *Edgar Cayce: The Sleeping Prophet.* New York: Doubleday, 1967.

Steiger, Brad. *You Will Live Again.* New York: Dell, 1978.

Sugrue, Thomas. *The Story of Edgar Cayce: There Is a River.* New York: Dell, 1967.

Sutphen, Dick. *You Were Born Again to Be Together.* New York: Pocket Books, 1976.

Tart, Charles. *PSI: Scientific Studies of the Psychic Realm.* New York: E.P. Dutton, 1977.

Taylor, Ruth. *Witness from Beyond.* New York: Hawthorn, 1975.

Wambach, Helen. *Life Before Life.* New York: Bantam, 1979.

———. *Reliving Past Lives.* New York: Harper & Row, 1978.

Watkins, Susan. *Conversations with Seth.* Vol. I. Englewood Cliffs: Prentice-Hall, 1980.

_____. *Conversations with Seth*. Vol. II. Englewood Cliffs: Prentice-Hall, 1981.

Weisman, Alan. *We Immortals*. Phoenix: Valley of the Sun, 1977.

White, Stewart. *The Betty Book*. New York: E. P. Dutton, 1937.

_____. *The Unobstructed Universe*. New York: E.P. Dutton, 1940.

Wright, Theon. *The Open Door: A Case History of Automatic Writing*. New York: John Day, 1970.

Young, Samuel. *Psychic Children*. New York: Pocket Books, 1977.

Index

A

Abilities, psychic, 90, 107, 109, 128
Acceptance, 90, 92, 98
Adjustment, areas, 71
Advancement, 94
After life:
  discussion, 175
  levels, 102
  life and, 83–108
A.M.A., 39
Ancestors, 71
An Explosion of Being, title, 87, 156, 163–164, 165, 166, 167
Animal inheritance, 75
Apparitions, 42, 155
Aptitudes, 105, 183
Areas of adjustment, 71
Art, children's, 127–128
Asthma, cause, 173
Astral projections, 55
Atlantis, 74, 75
Aura (haze), 18, 32, 51, 144, 202
Author (in spiritual realm), 99
Automatic Writing, 34, 35, 42, 43, 45, 46, 53, 86, 208
Awareness:
  expand reality comprehended, 50
  only of earthly existence, 50
  psychic, 91, 107, 109–131
  shallow, 50

B

Belief in yourself, 188–189
Beliefs, 70–71, 91, 93, 95, 101, 142, 180, 190, 196–197, 198

Beyond the Body, 62
Birth, 92, 101, 180, 184, 185, 188, 189, 207
Body:
  anger as method to control, 123
  death, 67
  physical, 70, 105
  spirit, 56
  tired, 91
Books:
  author in spiritual realm, 99
  children's, 57, 126–127, 158
  educational benefits, 102
  pliable force in life, 108
  psychic, 57, 197
  publisher, 103, 105
  recited to minds' eyes, 101
  spiritual, 197
Bunn, Thomas, 36
Business venture, 86, 97, 106, 175
Butts, Robert, 46

C

Callousness, 81
Calm, 43, 50, 99, 100, 101, 104, 105, 158, 161, 187, 189
Career, 86, 96
Cassadaga, 11, 23
Catastrophe, 84
Caution, 107, 206
Character, 102
Children:
  art by, 127–128
  books for, 57, 126–127, 158
  colleagues in awareness, 109–131
  communications, 115, 116, 119–120, 121–122, 123

217

Children (cont'd.)
  decision to share findings with, 26
  dreams, 111, 115, 116, 125, 126, 127, 130
  grandfather's death, 20, 21
  illness, 13, 109, 113, 114
  karmic obligations of soul, 63
  learning from, 110, 112, 115, 130
  nonverbal rapport, 112–113
  openness with, 112, 118
  Ouija Board, 110
  out-of-body experiences, 110, 113, 114, 116
  past lives, 121–122, 127, 130
  points for starting, 210
  psychic abilities, 109
  psychic discussions, 116–118, 124, 125
  readiness, 115, 116, 117, 125
  self-development, 127–130
  teaching, 110, 112, 115–121, 130
  teenagers, 114, 117, 123, 124–125
  trance messages, 119–120, 121–122, 125
  visions, 111, 117, 125, 129
Children and death, 24, 126, 127
Children and ghosts, 128–129
Children and super heroes, 130–131
Children and visions, 117, 125, 128–129
Choice, 162, 179, 180, 181, 182, 183, 186, 192, 197
Christ, 17, 51–52, 71
Church, 17, 153–154
Circular vision, 69
Coincidences, 168, 174–175, 198, 201
Collective consciousness, 88
Color:
  around Barb, 58
  future, 103
  people and objects, 202
  radiates from you, 50
  spiritual existence of life, 50
  waking dreams, 157, 158, 159
Communication:
  better, 92
  children, 115, 116, 119–120, 121–122, 123
  direct, 93, 203–206 (see also Contact)
  instrument, 92
  levels, 161
  open the channel or lines, 44
  skills, development, 125
  spirit, 11
Compassion, 80, 81, 151
Conference, 96
Connections, purposeful, 174, 175

Consciousness, 35, 42, 44, 46, 55, 87, 88, 97, 113, 128, 139, 162, 163, 174, 177, 193, 202
Consciousness, stream, 156, 208
Contact:
  direct, 203–206
    before starting, 203–205
    evaluation, 205–206
    initial, 203, 205
  establishing, 120
  levels, 209
  preparation, boys, 119–120
Coords, Nana Bird, 139–155, 164
Courses, 197–198
Creativity, 79
Crystalline soul structure, 149, 168, 169, 170
Crystals, cut, 149–150, 168–169, 204
Cults, religious, 92

D

Daily existence/events, 190, 201, 202
Daily routines, 47
Daydreams, 200–201
Death:
  after, 148, 154, 155
  communications predicting, 134
  fear, 138, 141, 142–143, 145, 151
  felt comfortable with, 43
  helping others after, 148, 149, 151
  memories, 22
  no aura, 144
  preparation, 20
  reaction of child, 24, 126–127
  realization, 18
  relax with, 37
  story eases sadness, 126–127
  transition to next reality, 126, 145, 148
  way of life, 84
  what happens, 67–69
  your concept, 69
Death-watch, 143
Demons, 121
Destructive nature, 128
Development, psychic, 184–186, 195–210
Devil, 71
Dillon, Barbara, 15, 19
Dillon, Doug, 12, 13
Dillon, Fred, 20, 21
Dillon, Greg, 20, 21
Dillon, Muriel, 11
Dillon, Nicole, 26, 52, 54, 55, 59, 60

Index

Dillon, Walter, 16, 18, 24, 29, 32
Dillon, Walter Jr. (Wally), 135–138, 154
Disasters, 80–81, 84, 85
Discovery, 72, 99
Disease, 77–78
Doubt, 61, 65
DREAMING POOL, 126, 127
"Dream Man," 59
Dreams:
  conclusion in real world, 176–177
  discussions with children, 115–118, 125, 130, 152
  explosion, 162–163
  giving voice to own inner beings, 62
  molecular structures, 157, 158, 159, 164, 165, 166–167
  Mom saw Dad, 19, 21
  nightmares, 111, 127, 176–177
  past lives, 72, 170–173
  patterns of relief, 91–92
  precognitive, 58–60
  recording, 30, 32, 156, 199–200, 204
  recurring, 170–172
  "soap opera," 30
  waking, 156–167

E

"Earthly reality," 87
Earthquakes, 80
Ego, 36, 37, 160, 191
Electrical power, 113–114
Elite, 36, 37
Emotion, vision, 202
Energy, 52, 78, 90, 96, 160
Entities, 66, 67, 68, 74, 96, 102, 106, 128, 169, 180, 181, 183, 202
Environment, 96
ESP, 90
Evaluation of contact, 205–206 (see also Contact)
Evil spirits, 31
Evolution, 74
Evolutionary process, 47
Existence, 33, 41, 43, 44, 46, 62, 72, 73, 80, 82, 84, 92, 109, 121–122, 133, 167, 169, 187, 188, 206
Existentialism, 46
Exorcism, 175, 176
Experience, 87
Explorations, psychic, 117
Explosion, 162, 163

Explosion of Being, title, 87, 156, 163–164, 165, 166, 167
"Explosive interaction," 163

F

Facets, 49, 149, 169, 171
"Factory of ideas," 89
Factory (school system), 96
Faith, 73, 104, 129, 130
Family:
  children, awareness, 109–131 (see also Children)
  discussions, 116–118, 124, 125
  guidance, 185
  relationships, 47
  treasury of experiences, 198
Family night, 118, 168
Fate, 85, 107
Fear, 61, 68, 73, 76, 78, 80, 81, 123, 130, 138, 141, 142–143, 145, 151, 177, 180, 182
Financial destruction, 107
Fish tank, 120, 146, 148, 150, 164
Form, 68, 92, 94, 96, 107
Fraudulent practices, 14
Friends, information, 198
Friendships, 95
FROG FINGERS, 126, 127, 148
Funerals, 19, 21, 147, 153–154
Future, 58–60, 69, 72, 92, 94, 169, 201

G

Ghosts, 58, 73–74, 118, 128–129, 175–176, 202
Gibson, Sandy, 62–63
God, 17, 18, 44, 51, 70–71, 90
Gordon, Thomas, 210
Grandfather Hill, 13, 27, 38–41, 43
Grief, 19, 81, 86, 133, 149
Growth, 73, 74, 85, 93, 110, 128, 184, 187, 190, 191, 192
Guidance, 70, 73, 87, 92, 124, 160, 182, 185, 198
Guides, spirit, 46, 52, 53, 56, 78, 94, 101, 166, 175, 183

H

Hardships, 79
Heaven, 36, 71–72

Hell, 71–72
Helping others, 91, 92, 93, 102
Hill, Grandfather, 13, 27, 38–41, 43
Hill, Lettie, 13
Historical aspects of writings, 37
Hope, 92
Hospitals, 12, 15, 16, 24
Hyatt Regency Hotel, 80

I

Ideals, 92
Illness, 13, 16, 24, 61–62, 77, 99, 109, 113, 114, 135, 141, 202
Images, 58, 73, 74, 92, 102, 128, 164, 167, 175, 186, 187, 191, 202
Imagination, 119, 131, 200–201, 202, 203, 204
Immortality, 93, 137
Incarnations, 170, 171, 173
Inner knowledge, 81
"Insights," 197, 206
Intellect, 33
Intermediaries, 198
Interpretation, 47
Intuition, 112, 115
Isabella, 37, 44
Isolation, 182, 191, 197

J

Jamestown, Va., 26
Jesus Christ, 17, 51–52, 71
Journal or record of dreams, 156

K

Karma, 63, 79
Knowledge, 63, 75, 81, 93, 94, 96, 100, 108, 191
Kruger, Sally, 32

L

Leah, 154
Learning, 85, 86, 92, 93, 94, 102, 103, 106, 108, 110, 112, 115, 130, 160, 185, 186, 191
Learning capacities, 49
Learning processes, 61
Learning sequences, 87
Lessons, 63, 72, 74, 76, 77, 94, 106, 166, 185
Levels:
  afterlife, 102
  communication, 161
  spiritual, 166
Life:
  on other planets, 75
  poverty and wealth, 79
Life after death, 173
Life After Life, 28
Life pattern analysis, 201
Lifetimes, 63, 127
Life value systems, 71
Lights, 58, 92, 111, 120, 158, 190, 202, 204
Listening, 210
Literature, psychic and spiritual, 197
Love, 20, 29, 36, 48, 49, 100, 105, 159, 185, 206
Low level spirits, 31, 207

M

Magical powers, 52
Man, origins, 74–75
Manifestation, physical, 54
Masters, 91, 95, 104
Materialism, 79
Materialization, 73
Media, new, 103
Meditation, 119, 200, 204
Mediums, fake, 14
Memory, 98, 99
"Mental trigger," 204
Messages, 86, 88, 89, 97, 103, 105, 111, 118, 119, 124, 125, 159, 176, 180, 187, 205–206, 207, 208
Millie (*see* Stephens, Millie)
Mind, 69, 99, 114, 174
Misty images, 202
Molecular dream structures, 157, 158, 159, 164, 165, 166–167
Multidimensionality, 78, 121, 126, 170, 174, 193, 194, 200, 202, 203

N

Names, showing importance, 102
Nana Bird Coords, 139–155, 164

Index

Needs and thoughts of others, sensing, 201–202
Negative existence, 55
Negative reality, 80
Negatives, transform, 92
Negativity, 62, 65, 97, 107, 185, 188, 191, 192, 200, 203, 205
Nightmares, 127
"Nikki's Place," 127
Notebook, psychic, 195–196, 202, 203, 205, 207

O

Objectivity, 134
Old souls, 56
Ollie, 47, 52, 54, 56, 57, 88, 96, 110, 117
Ouija Board, 29, 31, 34, 35, 36, 37, 46, 110, 156, 207
Out-of-body experiences, 55, 56, 110, 113, 114, 116, 126, 165, 173, 174, 202–203

P

Pain, 77–78, 84, 85, 108, 114, 177
"Parallel development," 87
Paralysis, 203
Parent Effectiveness Training, 210
Partner, 209
Past, 68, 69, 72, 78, 94, 105, 121–122, 169–172, 198
Past life recall, 116, 127, 130
Past lives, 121–122, 127, 130, 140, 159, 166, 167
Patience, 93, 95, 185
Pattern analysis, life, 201
Patterns, 75, 88, 90, 91, 92, 98, 100, 101, 102, 104, 112, 141, 167, 169, 180, 181, 184, 185, 187, 190, 191, 201, 202
"Patterns of Existence," 49, 50–51, 112
Peace, 84, 107, 180, 181
Perception, 77, 160, 161, 163, 166, 179
Personalities:
    evolving at will, 49
    traits, 121
    trance, 30
Personality restructuring, 128
Perspective, 97
Photographs, 39, 40
Physical being/existence, 150, 169, 170, 171, 177, 183, 185, 186, 188, 202

Physical manifestation, 54
Planets, life on other, 75
Possessions, 44, 160
Poverty, 79–80
Power, source, 51, 52, 55
Power communication, 52
Prayer, 17, 24, 200, 204
Pre-birth decisions, 90
Precognition, 58–60, 116
Predestination, 69, 70
Predictions:
    caution, 206–207
    distortions, 207
    Mae Ward, 13
    source, 13–14
    symbolisms, 207
    time frames, 207
Present, aptitudes create, 105
Privacy, 80
Psychic, 29, 43, 55
Psychic abilities, 90, 107, 109, 128
Psychic awareness, 91, 107, 109–131
Psychic development, 184–186, 195–210
Psychic energy, 52, 78
Psychic explorations, 117
Psychic house, 120, 141, 145, 146, 164, 204
Psychic literature, 197
Psychic notebook, 195–196, 202, 203, 205, 207
"Psychic phenomena," 177
Psychic verification, 53
Publisher, 103, 105
Purpose, 41, 48, 67, 68, 69, 70, 72, 74, 75, 78, 79, 80, 81, 84, 85, 87, 90, 93, 97, 106, 128, 133, 142, 143, 160, 169, 180, 181, 182, 186, 201, 205, 206

Q

Questions, 65–82

R

RAINING TIME, 126, 127
Reader, connections with authors, 186
Readiness:
    adult, 161, 162
    children, 115, 116, 117, 125
Reality:
    created within own mind, 31, 82
    dreams, 170

Reality (cont'd.)
  earthly, 87
  ever changeable, 71
  expand area you comprehend, 50
  future, 100
  imagination, 200, 204
  in which soul exists, 169
  in which you exist now, 181
  multi-faceted aspects, 172
  negative, 80
  out-of-body experiences, 173
  overflow between realities, 73
  physical change, 80
  present, 70
  see the nature as it is, 50
  self development, 74
  soul's decisive points, 70
  spiritual, "rebirth" into, 173
  subconscious link with other level, 66
Rebirth, 173, 181, 184
Recognition, 99
Recurring dreams, 170-172
Reincarnation, 43, 69, 70, 72-73, 101, 120, 127, 137, 159, 166, 167, 169-172, 194
Reincarnational dreams, 159, 166, 167
Relationships, family, 47
Relaxation, vision, 202
Religion, 17, 25, 190
Religious cults, 92
Remembrance toward past, 99, 129, 130, 183
Response, level, 97
Retardation, 16, 48-49, 135, 154
Riches, 79-80
Rigidity of body, 203
Roberts, Jane, 30, 46
Routines, daily, 47

S

School system (factory), 89, 96
Scott, Willard, 132
Seance, 33
Searching, 98, 103, 107, 180, 187
Self, 36, 95, 160
Self development, 74
Seminars, 182, 197-198
Senility, 78
Senses, 183
Seth books, 30, 46, 82, 140
Seth Speaks, 30
Shelly, 52, 53, 58
Sickness, 13, 16, 24, 61-62, 77, 99, 109, 113, 114, 135, 141, 202

Sleep, 18, 30, 91, 116, 129, 170, 173, 184, 199
Sleepiness, vision, 202
"Soap opera dreams," 30
Solitude, 191
Son of God, 51-52
Soul, 46, 48, 49, 50, 52, 55, 63, 67-70, 72-73, 90, 94, 99, 105, 107, 110, 149, 184
Soul catcher, 121
Soul facets, 49, 149, 169, 171
Soul mates, 56
Soul's crystalline structure, 149, 168, 169, 170
Sounds, 20, 22
Source:
  choice, 209
  instilled in you, 90
Southbury Training School, 136, 154
Spirit bodies, 56, 58
Spirit communication, 11
Spirit guides, 46, 52, 53, 56, 78, 94, 101
Spiritual contact, 34, 42, 124
Spiritualism, level, 89
Spiritualists, 12
Spiritual levels, 166, 182, 183, 184
Spiritual literature, 197
Stephens, Millie, 52-58, 110, 124, 125, 126
"Still life," 51, 52, 89
Stream of consciousness writing, 156, 208
Subconscious, 14, 30, 35, 37, 46, 53, 66, 116, 130, 173, 203, 204, 205, 206, 207, 208
Suicide, 123
Sunshine Skyway Bridge, 83, 85
Super heroes, 130-131
Supernatural, 28
Support system, 197

T

"Talking board," 29 (*see also* Ouija board)
Teacher, Son of God, 51
Teaching, 93, 94, 96, 106, 110, 112, 118, 130
Teaching career, leaving, 86, 96
Technology, 75
Teenagers, 17, 114, 117, 123, 124-125
Telepathy, 14, 113, 114, 116, 117
Time, 33, 37, 41, 50, 51, 55, 59, 62, 76, 93, 97, 110, 166, 169, 207
"Time of troubles," 86
Today Show, 132
Tragedies, 80-81
Trance, 30, 48, 63, 67, 84, 85, 116, 119, 124, 127, 134, 141, 176, 177, 209 (*see also* Contact)

Index

Trance, preparation, 119–120
Trance personalities, 30
Transition to next reality, 145, 148
Truth, 44, 64, 80
Twin spirits, 49, 95, 170

U

U.F.O.s, 18, 76–77

V

Validity, 52, 65, 66, 90, 169, 205
Values, 68, 71, 98, 105, 106, 160
Verbalizing messages, 208–209
Vibrations, 61, 77, 84, 97, 158, 166, 182
Violence, 176–177
Visions, 18, 21, 42, 58, 73, 74, 111, 117, 125, 128–129, 141, 142, 144, 155, 158, 159, 160, 163, 168, 198, 202, 205

W

Waking dreams, 156–167
Wally (Walter Dillon, Jr.), 135–138, 154
War, 170, 171–172
Ward, Mae, 11, 13
Weakness, 99
Wealth, 44, 67, 79, 187, 207
West Point, N.Y., 16, 20–21
Williamsburg, Va., 23, 24, 27, 28
Wisdom, 73, 77, 100, 101, 103, 104, 121, 130, 160, 166, 180, 185, 187, 194, 203, 205
Writing:
   automatic, 34, 35, 42, 43, 45, 46, 53, 86, 208
   books, 57, 85, 87, 99
   stream of consciousness, 156, 208
Writings, The, 43, 47, 56, 57, 60, 61, 62, 65, 66, 82, 85, 86, 87, 93, 110, 111, 112, 116, 121, 122, 127, 129, 133, 134, 135, 141, 150, 155, 165
Writing sessions, 43, 61, 66, 117, 118, 122, 123, 128, 140, 145, 150, 159, 175

www.ingramcontent.com/pod-product-compliance
Lightning Source LLC
Chambersburg PA
CBHW031345040426
42444CB00005B/199